Alasdair MacIntyre, George Lindbeck, and the Nature of Tradition

Alasdair MacIntyre, George Lindbeck, and the Nature of Tradition

DAVID TRENERY

Foreword by Karen Kilby

⁌PICKWICK *Publications* · Eugene, Oregon

ALASDAIR MACINTYRE, GEORGE LINDBECK, AND THE NATURE OF TRADITION

Copyright © 2014 David Trenery. All rights reserved. Except for brief quotations in critical publications or reviews, no part of this book may be reproduced in any manner without prior written permission from the publisher. Write: Permissions. Wipf and Stock Publishers, 199 W. 8th Ave., Suite 3, Eugene, OR 97401.

Pickwick Publications
An Imprint of Wipf and Stock Publishers
199 W. 8th Ave., Suite 3
Eugene, OR 97401

www.wipfandstock.com

ISBN 13: 978-1-62564-705-4

Cataloguing-in-Publication Data

Trenery, David.

    Alasdair MacIntyre, George Lindbeck, and the nature of tradition / by David Trenery ; foreword by Karen Kilby.

    xvi + 272 p. ; 23 cm. Includes bibliographical references and index.

    ISBN 13: 978-1-62564-705-4

    1. MacIntyre, Alasdair C. 2. Lindbeck, George A. 3. Religion—Philosophy. I. Kilby, Karen. II. Title.

B1647.M124 T79 2014

Manufactured in the U.S.A.   11/05/2014

This book is dedicated to the memory of four people. Firstly, to the memory of my parents, John and Evelyn Trenery, who did not have the opportunity to pursue higher education for themselves, but made sure that their four children all benefitted from going to University. They ignited a desire for learning that has never left me.

Secondly, this book is dedicated to my late brother Leslie who would have been proud of my efforts, and delighted to celebrate my successes, and sympathize with my setbacks.

Thirdly, it is dedicated to the late Doctor James Logue, Fellow of Somerville College Oxford, with whom I shared many hours of philosophical debate, first when we were undergraduates, and later as he established his own philosophical reputation and career.

They are all sorely missed.

CONTENTS

Foreword by Karen Kilby ix
Preface xi
Acknowledgments xiii
Abbreviations xiv

1 The Roots of *After Virtue* 1

2 MacIntyre's Mature Position 60

3 Lindbeck and the Identity of the Christian Tradition 140

4 Lindbeck and MacIntyre as Complementary Thinkers 171

Bibliography 249
Index 265

FOREWORD

In a time of academic specialization, Alasdair MacIntyre is one of the few thinkers—fewer still in the English speaking world—whose work is influential across a range of disciplines. MacIntyre's thought is rich and provocative, and it offers, or seems to offer, an enticing framework within which one can wrestle with such things as truth and tradition, rationality and the nature of intellectual enquiry. But at the same time his oeuvre can be frustratingly confusing and elusive: the harder one looks, the harder it seems to become to get to grips with.

In this volume Dave Trenery offers us something which is helpful on at least three levels. First of all, one can find here a lucid, fluent, readable exposition of the broad lines of MacIntyre's thought. This alone would be enough to justify the purchase of the book. Second, one finds a sustained and persuasive exploration of what is I think *the* key question in relation to MacIntyre's position, a question which comes up again and again in various forms in the secondary literature—the question of whether MacIntyre in the end manages to escape the charge of relativism. And finally one finds here, through an engagement with George Lindbeck's *The Nature of Doctrine*, a careful exploration of the "fit" of MacIntyre's thought with Christian theology, and the way in which the positions of MacIntyre and Lindbeck can each be used to strengthen the other.

This is a book, then, which should prove valuable to scholars of any field who are wrestling with MacIntyre's thought, and particularly important for theologians wanting to deepen their understanding of MacIntyre's signficance for theology and their grasp of the work of Lindbeck.

As a former student of George Lindbeck, I found it a pleasure to supervise Dave Trenery's doctoral work at Nottingham University, and it is particularly gratifying to see his excellent study now appear in print.

Karen Kilby
Bede Professor of Catholic Theology, Centre for Catholic Studies, Department of Theology and Religion, University of Durham

PREFACE

This book is based on my doctoral dissertation, which was submitted to the University of Nottingham, United Kingdom, in 2013. It focuses on the question of the justification of belief in a comprehensive metaphysical system, which I define in the text as a philosophy or faith that provides an account of ontology and human nature and a basis for practical reasoning and action.

I first became interested in this question when I was a young postgraduate student at the University of Stirling in the 1970s. Marriage and the pressing need to earn a living intervened and I deferred my philosophical research until time allowed. I became a social worker, and then a social work manager, as well as a husband and father. Thirty years later I found myself changing career when I became a part-time manager and social work lecturer with the Open University in the United Kingdom. I decided at that point that the time was right to resume my studies, and, after seven years of part-time research, I completed my PhD.

This book is, therefore, the product of a scholar of mature years (to employ a euphemism). In 2009 Alasdair MacIntyre, the philosopher whose work is the focus of this book, gave the keynote address to a conference at University College Dublin held to celebrate his 80th birthday. In that speech he suggested that doctoral studies would be more valuable if research students were drawn from those individuals who have greater life experience than can be acquired through University study alone. Whether or not MacIntyre's dictum is generally true, I certainly believe that my own life experience has been an advantage in writing the present book, and that its defects would have been more numerous if it had been written forty years ago when I first began to reflect on these issues, while its strengths would have been far fewer.

ACKNOWLEDGMENTS

My debts are too numerous to list in full, but I have to pay tribute to the support and dedication of my wife, Alison, and my son Sam, who have spent several years patiently waiting for me to complete this book. Without Alison's eagle eyes the errors in the text would have been far more numerous.

This book is based on my doctoral thesis, and I am greatly indebted to Professor Karen Kilby, who was my supervisor at Nottingham University, for her excellent academic support and guidance. I am also grateful to the rest of the Faculty and to the students of the Theology and Religious Studies Department at Nottingham University for the opportunities for discussion and learning they have provided over the years.

I am also indebted to the perceptive comments of my most long-standing friend, Bob Waring, who has continued the tradition of constructive criticism of my work that he first initiated when we met in primary school.

ABBREVIATIONS

ASI	Alasdair MacIntyre, *Against the Self-Images of the Age: Essays on Ideology and Philosophy.*
AV	Alasdair MacIntyre, *After Virtue: A Study in Moral Theory.*
CL	Cultural-Linguistic
DCB	Alasdair MacIntyre, *Difficulties in Christian Belief.*
DRA	Alasdair MacIntyre, *Dependent Rational Animals Why Human Beings Need the Virtues.*
EC	Epistemological crisis
ECS	Alasdair MacIntyre, "Epistemological Crisis, Dramatic Narrative and the Philosophy of Science."
GB	Alasdair MacIntyre: "An Interview with Giovanna Borradori."
HF	Hermeneutic framework
LS	Alasdair MacIntyre: "The Logical Status of Religious Belief." In Alasdair MacIntyre, ed., *Metaphysical Beliefs.*
MC	Alasdair MacIntyre, *Marxism and Christianity.*
M	Alasdair MacIntyre, *Marxism: An Interpretation.*
ND	George A. Lindbeck, *The Nature of Doctrine: Religion and Theology in a Postliberal Age.*
NE	Aristotle, *The Nichomachean Ethics.*

Abbreviations

NMW	Alasdair MacIntyre, "Notes from the Moral Wilderness 1 and 2." Reprinted in Kelvin Knight, ed., *The MacIntyre Reader*.
PEO	Principle of epistemological openness
RSA	Alasdair MacIntyre and Paul Ricoeur, *The Religious Significance of Atheism*.
SHE	Alasdair MacIntyre, *A Short History of Ethics*.
SMC	Alasdair MacIntyre, *Secularization and Moral Change*.
TRV	Alasdair MacIntyre, *Three Rival Versions of Moral Enquiry*.
WJWR	Alasdair MacIntyre, *Whose Justice? Which Rationality?*

1

THE ROOTS OF *AFTER VIRTUE*

1.1 Overview

This book considers how one might justify belief in a comprehensive metaphysical system, through an exposition and evaluation of the philosophy of Alasdair MacIntyre. What is meant by the phrase "a comprehensive metaphysical system" will become clearer as the book unfolds, but I will define it initially as a set of ontological and ethical presuppositions which are taken to encompass and explain the nature of the universe of which our species is a part, and which also provide a framework for human practical reasoning and action. On the basis of this definition secular philosophies such as Marxism and religions such as Christianity are comprehensive metaphysical systems. A comprehensive "theory of everything," such as modern physics has tried to develop, would not be such a metaphysical system, unless it sought to encompass ethics and an understanding of humanity within its framework, as well as providing an account of ontology.

I need to qualify my description of Christianity and Marxism as metaphysical systems. This is not an attempt to characterize all aspects of their identity in a reductive fashion. It is, however, a way of pointing to some common features of these belief systems, which constitute them as "hermeneutic frameworks": that is, all-encompassing ways of understanding the universe, humanity, and human action (see section 4.3). A comprehensive metaphysical system as defined above is, I shall argue, primarily a way of *interpreting* the world and our place within it, rather than a speculative theory. Whether it is legitimate to speak of the justification of such a hermeneutic framework remains part of the question I am exploring. The decline of Enlightenment epistemological foundationalism undermined notions of universal standards of argument and legitimacy, and emphasized the importance of the role of authority and faith in underpinning commitment to such comprehensive metaphysical systems. My exploration of MacIntyre's philosophy, and my use of the work of the theologian George Lindbeck in the latter part of this book, is intended to deepen the understanding of the issues associated with the question of justification and commitment in a postmodern philosophical and theological context.[1]

My reasons for exploring these issues are personal as well as intellectual. Like MacIntyre I am a child of the intellectual and moral culture of the mid-twentieth century. My education emphasized the importance of intellectual rigor and objective justification as a pre-condition of belief, and rejected tradition as a foundation for rational investigation and knowledge. This education emphasized that the foundations of morality are indeterminable and encouraged tolerance of diversity and (less happily) moral relativism. It left me agnostic with respect to religion and the foundations of ethics, but it also left me with no choice but to *act* at a personal, community and political level, even though the principles that guided my actions appeared to be arbitrarily adopted. My education and upbringing therefore created a disconnection between my theoretical beliefs on the one hand, and the principles that underpinned my practical reasoning on the other. MacIntyre's philosophy has sought to address such disconnection by developing an account of rationality as constructed and tested within a tradition of enquiry. The beliefs and principles that form the basis of such traditions are not demonstrable, but their adequacy can be evaluated as enquiry unfolds. It therefore provides an alternative to the Enlightenment perspective on the questions "what should I believe?" and "why should I believe it?"—questions to which I will return at the very end of this book.

---

1. MacIntyre maps the challenges to such Enlightenment epistemological assumptions, and his account is discussed in section 2.2. MacIntyre's philosophy is based on the postmodern view that Enlightenment ideals of knowledge are unachievable, but this assessment is contested. John Searle, for example, dismisses the claim that the Enlightenment vision of universal knowledge is unachievable (Searle, *Mind, Language and Society*, 4–6). However, my book explores the nature of justification on the basis of the conditional question: "*If* MacIntyre is correct in his assessment of our inability to demonstrate the truth of our presuppositions, is it still possible to create a robust account of the justification of belief?" As a result, I do not need to resolve the fundamental question of the (il)legitimacy of Enlightenment epistemological assumptions for my argument to proceed.

This book, does not, of course, resolve the major and fundamental questions about the nature of knowledge and the meaning and legitimacy of the concept of justification. However, it makes a contribution to knowledge in four areas that are relevant to this debate. Firstly, it provides a contribution to MacIntyre studies by plotting the relationship between his early philosophy, and his mature position. It also argues that the later development of his position in *Dependent Rational Animals*[2] (henceforth DRA) should be given a more central role in the interpretation of his philosophy than has been granted by some other commentators[3] (chapter 2). The concepts of tradition and tradition-constituted rationality are central to MacIntyre's mature philosophy, and the second contribution of the book is to provide a more precise definition of the concept of tradition, by interpreting the "fundamental agreements" that constitute the identity of a tradition in terms of Lindbeck's regulative account of doctrine, as set out in his book *The Nature of Doctrine* (henceforth ND).[4] This contribution provides greater clarity to the concepts of incommensurability, tradition-constituted rationality and epistemological crisis, which are central to MacIntyre's account of the superiority of one tradition to another. It therefore strengthens MacIntyre's overall position.

The notion of superiority that emerges from MacIntyre's work provides a retrospective measure of the extent to which one tradition can be held to be (provisionally) justified or (absolutely) unjustified as a comprehensive metaphysical system. This notion of superiority therefore provides a means of reframing the question of justification in pragmatic and empirical terms. Lindbeck also seeks to provide an account of the superiority of one set of beliefs to another, and the third contribution of the book is an evaluation of Lindbeck's account of superiority in ND. Lindbeck is concerned not only with the question of how one might conceptualize the superiority of different religions to each other, but also with the question of how one position may be judged to be superior within the same religion. I argue that neither of Lindbeck's accounts of superiority can be applied in practice, but that his position can be strengthened by incorporating MacIntyre's notion of tradition-constituted rationality into his perspective (section 4.7).

---

2. MacIntyre, *Dependent Rational Animals*; henceforth DRA.

3. See, for example, Lutz, *Tradition in the Ethics of Alasdair MacIntyre*. Lutz does not mention DRA in the body of his text, and dismisses the importance of DRA in his preface to the paperback edition (2009): xi–xv; xiii–xiv. See section 2.4 below for my counterarguments to Lutz's assessment.

4. Lindbeck, *The Nature of Doctrine*; henceforth ND. All references are to the first edition unless otherwise indicated.

Without a persuasive account of the superiority of one comprehensive metaphysical perspective to another, any philosophical position appears to be open to the challenge of relativism or perspectivism. Both challenges are based on the assumption that a failure to establish some indubitable tradition-transcendent foundation for knowledge means that there can be no good reasons for preferring the claims of one tradition to another. The relativist makes this claim on the grounds that, if rational standards of justification only apply within each tradition, there can be no compelling basis for choosing between the competing claims to truth made by different traditions.[5] The perspectivist agrees with this assertion but argues further that the incommensurability of rival traditions subverts the very notion of truth itself, and claims that different traditions should be understood as offering "very different, complementary perspectives for envisaging"[6] the world in which we live.

The question of whether one can construct a non-foundationalist defense against relativism is an integrative theme throughout this book. The final section of the book addresses this question directly and concludes that MacIntyre's position provides an effective response to the challenge of relativism, but that Lindbeck's account of the nature of religion is vulnerable to the charge of relativism without the incorporation of a notion of tradition-constituted rationality derived from MacIntyre. This is the fourth contribution of the book (section 4.8). The first step in the development of my argument is to review MacIntyre's philosophical development, and this is the focus of the rest of this chapter.

1.2 MacIntyre's Early Philosophical Development

Context

This chapter explores MacIntyre's early philosophical, religious and political writings in order to identify the problems that led MacIntyre to write his most famous work, *After Virtue* (AV),[7] and its sequels. It undertakes this task in order to show how MacIntyre's earlier concerns have shaped the development of the notions of tradition and tradition-constituted rationality in his later philosophy. It argues that the stimulus for the construction of his mature position was his recognition that his early work exposed problems

---

5. MacIntyre, *Whose Justice? Which Rationality?* (henceforth WJWR), 351–53.
6. WJWR, 352.
7. MacIntyre, *After Virtue* (henceforth AV). References are to the second edition (1985) unless otherwise indicated.

that he could not resolve without the construction of an alternative approach to philosophy and ethics.

The secondary literature has recognized that there is a significant continuity between MacIntyre's early work and his mature position, but it has not fully articulated the logical connections between the problems that emerged in MacIntyre's initial attempts to justify his religious, moral, and political beliefs, and the solutions to those problems that are set out in his mature work. For example, while Kelvin Knight acknowledges the connection between MacIntyre's early works and the themes of AV in his introduction to *The MacIntyre Reader*,[8] his otherwise excellent compilation of MacIntyre's work includes only "Notes from the Moral Wilderness 1 and 2" (henceforth NMW) from his publications prior to 1979.[9] It does not, therefore, provide an overall map of MacIntyre's development. Thomas D'Andrea's exhaustive review of MacIntyre's work describes every tree in the wood—but as a result, makes it difficult to discern the overall shape of the forest.[10] Peter McMylor has provided a helpful analysis of the relationship between MacIntyre's Marxism and his Christianity, and his later adoption of an Aristotelian position in AV, and I will draw on some of his points in my discussion. However, McMylor's main focus is on the application of MacIntyre's mature thought to the social sciences rather than on the issues of rational justification that are my own focus.[11] As a result MacIntyre's later work in WJWR and *Three Rival Versions of Moral Enquiry* hardly figures in his account.[12]

Christopher Lutz's exposition of MacIntyre's development provides an illuminating map of the relationship between MacIntyre's early work and his mature position, and his account of that development overlaps with mine to some extent.[13] Lutz emphasizes the difficulties MacIntyre faced in addressing the question of the justification of his Marxist and religious beliefs.[14] He also notes that MacIntyre's adoption and subsequent repudiation of a form of fideism resulted in MacIntyre experiencing a long-standing epistemological crisis, which was only resolved through the construction of

---

8. Knight, "Introduction" to Knight, ed., *The MacIntyre Reader*, 3.

9. MacIntyre, "Notes from the Moral Wilderness 1 and 2," in Knight, ed., *The MacIntyre Reader*; henceforth NMW.

10. D'Andrea, *Tradition, Rationality and Virtue*.

11. McMylor, *Alasdair MacIntyre: Critic of Modernity*. See also McMylor, "Marxism and Christianity: Dependencies and differences in Alasdair MacIntyre's critical social thought."

12. MacIntyre, *Three Rival Versions of Moral Enquiry*; henceforth TRV.

13. Lutz, *Tradition in the Ethics of Alasdair MacIntyre*, chapter 1.

14. Ibid., 16–17.

the position set out in AV.[15] These observations are consistent with my own interpretation, as we shall see below. However, my account provides a more detailed analysis of the factors that underlay the failure of MacIntyre's initial attempts to address the question of the justification of belief in a comprehensive metaphysical position, and helps to identify the logical and other requirements that had to be met if he was to be successful in addressing these problems. It therefore provides a more comprehensive perspective on the genesis of MacIntyre's mature position.

Stages of Development

In an interview with *Cogito*, Macintyre divided his philosophical development into three main periods:

> The 22 years from 1949 . . . until 1971 were a period . . . of heterogeneous, badly organised, sometimes fragmented and often frustrating and messy enquiries, from which nonetheless in the end I learned a lot. From 1971 . . . until 1977 was an interim period of sometimes painfully self-critical reflection . . . From 1977 onwards I have been engaged in a single project to which *After Virtue, Whose Justice? Which Rationality?* and *Three Rival Versions of Moral Enquiry* are central, a project described by one of my colleagues as that of writing *An Interminably Long History of Ethics*.[16]

Despite MacIntyre's comment about the fragmented nature of his studies during his early years, an examination of his published work reveals greater coherence and focus than this description would suggest. His work during this period was characterized by his engagement with Marxist theory; with Christian apologetics; with the philosophy and sociology of religion; with the nature and foundations of ethics; and with the relationship between philosophy and social theory. He condemned the way in which liberal culture had fragmented human life into a set of discrete and independent arenas, compartmentalizing religion and secular life,[17] and his engagement with Marxism reflected his critique of Western society and his commitment to social improvement. He sought to defend Marxism as the most coherent basis for political analysis and action,[18] and attempted to clarify the rela-

---

15. Ibid., 20–21.
16. MacIntyre, "An Interview for *Cogito*," 268–69.
17. See MacIntyre, *Marxism: An Interpretation*, 9–10.
18. See Blackledge and Davidson, eds., *Alasdair MacIntyre's Engagement with*

tionship of that philosophy to Christian belief. MacIntyre's religious commitment led him to contribute to Christian apologetics and philosophical theology,[19] and he also explored the impact of social change on contemporary trends in religious belief.[20]

His concern with society and social improvement also underpinned his work in ethics and moral theory.[21] For MacIntyre, every ethical perspective implies a particular form of social and political organization which enables the expression of its moral possibilities, and there is, therefore, an inter-relationship between his political, ethical, and religious concerns, which is manifested in his critique of contemporary Western society. A fourth strand in his early philosophical contribution is the critical evaluation of some contemporary theories in social science,[22] and one important focus of this work is the repudiation of deterministic accounts of human action.[23] His rejection of determinism led him to focus on the explanation of human action in terms of purpose, and this led in turn to attempts to elucidate some telos that gives coherence and intelligibility to human existence. MacIntyre's philosophical output during this period reflects the recognition that Christianity, Marxism (and other political philosophies), ethical theory, and social theory all provide differentiated and potentially competing perspectives on the question of what it is to be human and what it is to live a good life. His early work represents an ambitious attempt to reconcile these conflicting strands of thought, and through this to construct a comprehensive and coherent account of human nature that combines both religious and political perspectives within a radical programme for social improvement.

Marxism for a comprehensive selection of MacIntyre's Marxist writing from this period.

19. Flew and MacIntyre, eds., *New Essays in Philosophical Theology*; MacIntyre, *Difficulties in Christian Belief* (henceforth DCB).

20. MacIntyre, *Secularization and Moral Change*; henceforth SMC; MacIntyre and Ricoeur, *The Religious Significance of Atheism*: henceforth RSA.

21. See for example NMW and MacIntyre, *A Short History of Ethics*: henceforth SHE.

22. MacIntyre, *The Unconscious*; see also MacIntyre, "Psychoanalysis" (in MacIntyre, *Against the Self-Images of the Age*; henceforth ASI) and MacIntyre, *Marcuse*.

23. See, for example, MacIntyre, *The Unconscious*, in which MacIntyre's analysis of Freud's concept of the unconscious provides a critique of the underlying mechanistic model of causation and human behavior. See also MacIntyre, "Determinism"; MacIntyre, "Purpose and Intelligent Action," 95; and MacIntyre, "The Antecedents of Action."

The Search for Intellectual Coherence

A commitment to either Marxism or Christianity (or both) raises some fundamental questions about the extent to which the beliefs to which one is committed can be held to be rational, intelligible and true, and the degree to which they can provide a coherent basis for moral evaluation and ethical action. MacIntyre was conscious of the inconsistency and lack of justification of his beliefs at an early stage. He recalled in an interview with Giovanna Borradori that "The reading that first my undergraduate and then my graduate studies required of me only accentuated the incoherence of my beliefs . . . I found it increasingly difficult to discover adequate rational grounds for the belief in Christianity that I thought I had and that faith came to look like arbitrariness."[24]

The need to reconcile conflicting strands in his belief system can be seen as originating in MacIntyre's upbringing and education. In the same interview he commented that his early life

> educated me in two antagonistic systems of belief and attitude. . . my early imagination was engrossed by a Gaelic oral culture of farmers and fishermen, poets and story tellers . . . [In contrast] the modern world was a culture of theories rather than stories . . . Its claims upon us were allegedly not those of some particular social group, but those of universal rational humanity. So part of my mind was occupied by stories about Saint Columba, Brian Boru, and Iain Lom, and part from inchoate theoretical ideas which I did not as yet know derived from the liberalism of Kant and Mill.[25]

The inconsistencies in MacIntyre's noetic structure created by his exposure to Gaelic myth and liberal philosophies were mirrored in the tensions created by his commitment to both Marxism and Christianity. MacIntyre had become a Marxist at the age of seventeen,[26] and during the late 1940s was both a member of the Communist Party of Great Britain and a communicant in the Church of England.[27] These commitments drove his earliest intellectual concerns, and his first published work was an attempt to integrate Christianity and Marxism into a single comprehensive framework for

---

24. MacIntyre, "An Interview with Giovanna Borradori," in Knight, ed., *The MacIntyre Reader*, 257; henceforth GB.

25. GB, 255.

26. Lutz, *Tradition in the Ethics of Alasdair MacIntyre*, 14.

27. Blackledge and Davidson, "Introduction" in Blackledge and Davidson, eds., *Alasdair MacIntyre's Engagement with Marxism*, xxi.

social and political action.[28] However, his Christian commitment proved to be problematic and he was no longer a believer by the end of the 1950s. In 1961 MacIntyre described his religious and political position in the following trenchant terms. "I was a Christian. Am not. It is less misleading when asked if I'm a Marxist to say 'yes' rather than 'no.' But other Marxists have been known to say 'no.'"[29]

His commitment to Marxism was sustained over a longer period than his initial commitment to Christianity, but the breach was more final when it came. In the 1950s MacIntyre had become a leading figure in "The New Left," a loose agglomeration of leftist thinkers which had developed in response to the repression of the Hungarian uprising in 1956, and the resultant rejection of Soviet style communism.[30] In 1959, MacIntyre had joined a Trotskyist organization, the Socialist Labour League, but he left this organization in 1960 because of differences with the leadership, and became a member of another Trotskyist grouping centered on the journal *International Socialism*.[31] Over the next few years MacIntyre played a leading role within this organization, but ceased active participation around 1965, and formally resigned from the editorial board of *International Socialism* in 1968.[32] His withdrawal reflected his growing disillusionment with left wing politics.

By the end of the 1960s, therefore, MacIntyre had abandoned his commitment to both Christianity and Marxism. His disillusionment ended his initial attempts to integrate these belief systems into a coherent alternative to liberalism, an alternative that he had hoped would provide the basis for a new form of community that would embody the religious, social, and political relationships required to realize human potential and freedom. My argument in this chapter is that MacIntyre's rejection of Christianity and Marxism reflected his inability to provide a robust account of the justification of these comprehensive metaphysical systems. His mature philosophy represents his ultimate response to this question of justification in an intellectual context in which foundationalist accounts of knowledge are no longer considered viable.

---

28. MI. See section 1.3 below.

29. This quotation is taken from the editor's preface to MacIntyre, "Marxists and Christians." This introduced the paper on its original publication in Twentieth Century in 1961. The preface and the paper are reprinted in Blackledge and Davidson. See footnote 1, page 179 for the quotation.

30. Blackledge and Davidson "Introduction," xxii–xxvi.

31. Ibid., xxvii–xxviii.

32. Ibid., xlii.

A Map of This Chapter

In the next section I will describe MacIntyre's analysis of Marxism and Christianity in his first book, *Marxism: An Interpretation*, in order to identify some of the general issues which arise when considering the justification of such comprehensive metaphysical perspectives. Both Christianity and Marxism embody presuppositions about the nature of the world, the nature of explanation, and the nature of humanity, which give them the capacity to create a comprehensive interpretative medium (in George Lindbeck's phrase[33]) that can be applied to all aspects of human existence. In MI MacIntyre characterizes the narrative framework which generates this interpretive capacity as a "rational myth." However, neither Marxism nor Christianity conceptualizes itself as simply aesthetically pleasing or ethically effective ways of viewing the world: they claim to be true, and this claim requires an exploration of the nature and justification of such claims. MacIntyre addressed this question of justification in a number of works addressing the grounds of religious belief that were published in the 1950s, and these are discussed in section 1.4.

Marxism and Christianity are not simply speculative theories. They both seek to answer the moral question "what ought to be done?," and their answers to these questions are linked to the beliefs they express about human nature, human potential and its relationship to ultimate reality. To reject these ontological beliefs is to undermine the foundations of the moral frameworks they provide. The nature of the relationship between a commitment to a set of theoretical beliefs and the ability to justify a moral perspective was explored in two articles MacIntyre published at the end of the 1950's, "Notes from the moral wilderness 1 and 2," and these articles form the focus of section 1.5. In these papers MacIntyre had set out what he considered to be the preconditions of a coherent ethical framework. He argues that such a framework has to be rooted in the achievement of human desire, albeit desires that are moderated and mediated through participation in a community.

This understanding of human desire, need and potentiality is ultimately dependent on beliefs about human nature that will be shaped by the conceptual resources available to a community at a particular point in time. This understanding will therefore vary as the historical context varies. Section 1.6 reviews MacIntyre's analysis of social change in post-Enlightenment culture, which he set out in *The Religious Significance of Atheism*

---

33. See Lindbeck, *The Nature of Doctrine*, 80. Lindbeck's account of religion as an interpretative medium is the focus of chapter 3, and chapter 4 discusses the relationship between this concept and MacIntyre's notion of a tradition of enquiry.

(henceforth RSA) and *Secularisation and Moral Change* (henceforth SMC). In these publications he argued that the dilemma for contemporary Western culture is that the social changes associated with urbanization had eroded the coherence of the conceptual resources required to formulate a substantive ethical viewpoint. This analysis illustrates the interdependency between ontological presuppositions and moral principles, and further illustrates the necessity of adopting such presuppositions as a precondition of rendering human life intelligible and constructing a substantive moral position.

The dilemma for MacIntyre is that different conceptual schemes offer different images of human nature, different accounts of the moral life, and imply the construction of different forms of community if one is to be able to live such a life. Are such views all on the same footing, or is there some basis for judging that one is superior to another? Section 1.7 provides a brief exposition of MacIntyre's position in *A Short History of Ethics* (henceforth SHE). In this book he appears to espouse an account of ethics in which it is not possible to demonstrate the superiority of the claims of any particular moral perspective, at least to the external critic who does not accept any of the presuppositions of such a perspective.[34] It was his failure to provide an account of such superiority which led others to accuse him of a form of relativism or incoherence in ethics.[35]

The overall conclusion of this chapter is that a substantive ethical position requires a set of ontological presuppositions about human nature, human purpose and human potentiality However, unless these presuppositions can be held to be justified in some way—or at least held to be superior to other rival notions—the associated ethical position and its underlying interpretive framework will appear to be arbitrary. MacIntyre's failure to provide a robust account of justification in relation to either the ontological presuppositions of Marxism, Christianity or the beliefs that underpin an Aristotelian ethic, or indeed with respect to any of the alternatives, led to the period of re-evaluation he identified in his analysis of his philosophical development, and ultimately to the construction of the position set out in AV, TRV, WJWR, and DRA.

1.3 Marxism: An Interpretation

MacIntyre's first book *Marxism: An Interpretation* (MI) was published in 1953, although it had been written a year earlier when MacIntyre was just twenty-three years old. Its purpose was to radicalize a Christian readership

---

34. SHE, 266–68.
35. Preface to the 2nd Edition of SHE, xv.

by showing how it was possible to integrate Marxism with a Christian faith.[36] This process of integration would involve the radicalization of religion[37] and the creation of "a form of community"[38] which could exemplify a Christian pattern of life and "serve in the renewal of the whole church."[39] This integration of politics and religion would also overcome the unquestioned, but (to MacIntyre) pernicious, separation of the sacred and the secular in contemporary Western society, and ensure that all aspects of life were governed by religious faith:

> The division of human life into the sacred and the secular . . . witnesses to the death of a properly religious culture. For when the sacred and the secular are divided, then religion becomes one more department of human life, one activity among others . . . Likewise if our religion is fundamentally irrelevant to our politics, then we are recognizing the political as a realm outside the reign of God. To divide the sacred from the secular is to recognise God's action only within the narrowest limits. A religion which recognises such a division, as does our own, is one on the point of dying.[40]

MacIntyre's analysis in MI led him to make social and political proposals that are analogous to the programme he advocated in AV, in which he saw the practical task arising from his philosophy as the construction of "local forms of community" which would enable a society of the virtues to survive the "new dark ages" that he believed were already evident in Western culture.[41] AV's image of a cultural dark age is presaged In MI by the image of a society fragmented by secularization.[42] Without a renewal of Christian faith and institutions within local communities, the early MacIntyre feared that secularization in Western Liberal societies would continue to partition

---

36. See MI, 120; MacIntyre was not alone in seeking to find common ground between Marxism and Christianity, despite the apparent opposition between a materialist philosophy and a spiritual religion. See Blackledge and Davidson, xxi. The SCM Press which published MacIntyre's book advertised other works on Christianity and Marxism on the dust jacket of MI, including John C. Bennett, *Christianity and Communism* (1948); J. M. Cameron, *Scrutiny of Marxism* (1948); and A. Miller, *The Christian Significance of Karl Marx* (1946).

37. MI, 120.

38. MI, 121.

39. MI, 122.

40. MI, 9–10; also quoted by McMylor, *Alasdair MacIntyre*, 3–4 who makes a similar point.

41. AV, 263.

42. The nature of secularization is discussed further in section 1.6.

the relationship between the individual and society into a set of ethically independent spheres of operation. In such a secularized society morality and religion are relegated to the realms of private conviction and the governance of personal behavior, and do not have a wider function in terms of integrating social life. Contemporary Western society does not, therefore, provide a basis for the type of community that MacIntyre saw as being essential to the realization of human potentiality.

The Alternative to Western Liberalism

For MacIntyre a community that is capable of realizing human potentiality will be characterized by three elements. Firstly, it will possess an account of human nature and its potential that is accepted by all members of the community; secondly, the realization of that potentiality will form the overall aim of the community; and thirdly, the community will share an overall critique of the extent to which existing social arrangements enable the realization of that potential, which provides a basis for communal action towards social improvement. MacIntyre argues in MI that Marx in his early writings and Christianity in its original form[43] could act as the basis for such a critique of social arrangements. They could also provide the ethical and spiritual basis for the construction of communities that could realize human potential, because both belief systems share a common schema of human corruption, redemption and renewal which Marxism had derived from Christianity.[44]

He argues that the religious impetus behind Marxism can be seen in the early Marx's moral commitment to the poor, a commitment most strongly expressed in an 1844 manuscript entitled *National Economy and Philosophy*.[45] MacIntyre comments that "This essay is a watershed for Marx's thought. It is at this point that he gives the fullest meaning to the Christian patterns he inherits from Hegel. He is far more Biblical than Hegel both in his concreteness and in his seeing the proletariat, the poor, 'the least of these' in the parable of the sheep and the goats, as those who bear the marks of redemption."[46] MacIntyre asserts that the account of humanity's alienation in Marx's early work is, like Hegel's account of alienation, a re-creation

---

43. MI, 83.

44. MacIntyre traces this correspondence between Christian and Marxist thought to the influence of Hegel and Feuerbach on Marx's early work. See MI chapters ii–v for his account of this development.

45. MI, 48.

46. MI, 57.

of the Christian image of the human being estranged from God and her true self through the consequences of original sin.[47] In Marxism the Christian image of the fall is replaced by the image of humanity deformed by economic and social relationships. MacIntyre comments that for Marx "the evil in the world goes deeper than merely an accidental perversion of the will."[48] Both the exploited and the exploiters are corrupted in capitalist society, for both the proletariat and the bourgeoisie are dehumanized by the economic system. Marxism and Christianity therefore share a notion of an essential human nature which might be fully realized through a form of redemption. But Marx rejected a Christian vision of such redemption and envisaged the full realization of human nature as being achievable through processes of historical development driven by class conflict.

The Corruption of Church and Party

Despite the shared image of redemption and renewal that lies at the heart of Christianity and Marxism, MacIntyre holds that neither belief system is capable of providing the basis for a coherent ethical and political life in the contemporary world, because both have been corrupted in ways that reflect their historical and social origins: "Roman Catholicism in its worst aspects is the corrupted religion of a subsistence economy; Communism, the corrupted religion of modern industrial society."[49] The church has been discredited "by the way in which it has continually sanctified the political and social *status quo*."[50] By assuming that the abolition of social and all other evils depends on the establishment of the Kingdom of God at the end of history, and embodying within its structure the inequalities of the host society, Christianity risks being unable to challenge exploitation or offer political guidance in the present. As a result, the church has disengaged from the social and political life of the community,[51] and come to identify the good with the religiously orthodox:

> the identification of outward religion with inward righteousness is just the source of that self-righteousness of religious believers that leads them to withdraw from the world for which Jesus died and to see the Church not as a community that redeems the world but as a fixed community of the redeemed. To escape

---

47. MI, 57–58.
48. MI, 88.
49. MI, 108.
50. MI, 120.
51. MI, 20–21. See also 121.

this error we must look for ultimate significance in the secular world itself.[52]

Marxism's rejection of religion as superstition and its adoption of a materialist ontology had indeed shifted the center of significance to the secular world, and MacIntyre argues that Marxism's unconscious assimilation of the central concepts of Christian belief had enabled it to assume the revolutionary mantle which was originally worn by the early Christian religion in a form relevant to a secular culture.[53] It therefore represents the only belief system which incorporates Christian beliefs in a form that can challenge the complacency of the Western elites

> in a way in which the Christianity of the average parish will never do. For Christianity is a stranger in the modern world. The church has never come to terms with the world of science . . . Communism is in fact the form under which such strains in Christian thinking as were relevant had to enter the modern world: and because communism was religion it was open to the corruptions which always beset political religions.[54]

As a result of this openness to corruption, the distortion of Christianity in the institutions of the Church is mirrored by the distortion of Marx's vision of redemption through the emergence of a Communist party that demands doctrinal purity and unquestioning obedience from its adherents—no matter how morally bankrupt its demands.[55] This corruption has vitiated the capacity of Christian institutions and Communism to address social ills, and they therefore need to be cleansed of the worst elements of their corruption if they are to realize their revolutionary potential.

The church has remained ambivalent as to whether the establishment of the Kingdom of God ought to be pursued through human action, or should be left to God's grace, and has rendered itself irrelevant to the modern world, not only because of this political uncertainty but also because it has failed to accommodate itself to the modern intellectual context that is defined by science. In contrast, Marxism's adoption of a materialistic ontology and a quasi-scientific methodology has enabled it to translate a version of Christian eschatology into a political agenda which is relevant to the modern world. MacIntyre argues that Christianity must also identify and pursue political ends, if it is to become equally relevant to the contemporary

---

52. MI, 21.
53. See MI, 15 and passim
54. MI, 106–7.
55. MI, chapter 8, 107–8.

world, despite the consequent need for it to deal with the "half-truths of political morality"[56] and Marxism can provide it with the necessary political framework:

> If the Christian hope is to be realised in history, it must assume the form of a political hope . . . In other words, the religious content must be realised in political terms. But this is exactly what the young Marx did in his criticism of religion. Marxism is in essence a complete realisation of Christian eschatology.[57]

In principle, therefore, Marxism and Christianity provide complementary frameworks for the creation of communities which can realize human potential. However, while Christianity has abandoned a coherent political role, Marxism has abandoned the religious beliefs that underpin Christian ethics because it has assimilated a Christian ontology of human nature and a Christian eschatology into a deterministic and materialist conceptual scheme. MacIntyre's reintegration of Marxism and Christianity in MI requires the replacement of these elements with Christian beliefs, so that Marxism can be reconnected to its moral and spiritual compass. If this is done, Marxism will become available to Christians as a political and social programme that can reinvigorate the political relevance of a Church that has surrendered itself unto Caesar. But this process of reintegration makes the coherence and legitimacy of Marxism dependent on the coherence of the beliefs and presuppositions of Christianity. While Marxism and Christianity share a moral outrage at the fate of the poor and exploited, they embody incompatible beliefs about ontology and explanation. Marxism is a materialist philosophy and "since matter is the primary reality [it excludes] the possibility of the existence of a god or gods"[58] and dismisses religion as superstition. Christianity, on the other hand, is a theistic system of belief. How could such a fundamental incompatibility be resolved?

Marxism and the Rationality of Belief

Marxism rejects religious belief on the basis that it is an irrational superstition which serves only to reconcile the exploited to their hardships. But, MacIntyre argues, this judgment is based on some unevaluated assumptions about the nature of rationality. In MI MacIntyre suggests that different forms of human activity set their own standards of rationality, because these

56. MI, 120.
57. MI, 120.
58. MI, 81.

standards are constructed within each particular form of life or practice. There are no general *a priori* standards of rationality which can be used to evaluate these practice-specific standards.

> Marx assumes that there are standards of rationality and intelligibility to which human relations should conform . . . It must be said . . . that the formulation of *a priori* canons of rationality, of significance, is a highly suspect procedure. For how can we determine *a priori* what are significant forms of discourse and what are not? We must rather patiently work out *a posteriori* the different logics which govern different forms of speech. The ultimate justification of religious language is that it is the only language in which man can understand himself as man-who-prays. It is open to argument whether and in what ways prayer is a significant activity. But one cannot *a priori* lay it down that it is rational for man to eat, to love and to think, but not to pray.[59]

There are echoes of Wittgenstein in this passage, implicit in the view that practices such as prayer determine their own standards of coherence and intelligibility, and cannot be evaluated from a universal and practice-independent perspective.[60] For MacIntyre, prayer has to be understood in terms of the logic of a personal communicative relationship rather than justified through a demonstration of the rationality of some theoretical beliefs about God: "When a man prays, he speaks not about God, but to God. He envisages himself in a dramatic, rather than a speculative relationship to God. The drama which he envisages takes the form of religious myth."[61]

The practice of prayer is intelligible because it is embedded in a myth that gives coherence to this communicative activity. While MacIntyre accepts that Marxism's criticism of religion acts as a necessary prophylactic against "magic and superstition,"[62] he argues that religion as a whole should not be identified with such superstitions. Marxism's assimilation of religion

---

59. MI, 85–86.

60. Wittgenstein arguably takes the view that what counts as justification depends on the nature of the practice within which the question of justification is being raised. This has two implications. Firstly there is no universal standard of justification that can be used as a test of the legitimacy of any set of truth-claims (for example) because such claims can only be justified in the context of the particular practice in which they have been formulated. As a consequence of this there will be no general test of whether particular practice based forms of justification are themselves justified: the process of justification has to come to an end which is embodied in our day to day justificatory practices. See Wittgenstein, *Philosophical Investigations*, paragraphs 217, 325 and 483–5; and also Wittgenstein, *On Certainty*, paragraphs 192 and 212.

61. MI, 86.

62. MI, 13.

to the irrational is due to its failure to understand the distinction between mythical and scientific thought.[63]

> First, myth pictures the world as a whole. But to picture the world as a whole from the limited viewpoint of the myth maker who is himself part of the world means a stretching of ordinary language, so that extended metaphor is essential to the insight of myth. Secondly, scientific thinking must eliminate the emotive elements, must distinguish sharply between the emotive and the cognitive . . . but some uses of language, among them those of myth, are both descriptive and evaluative. For while myth and science both select certain facts as significant: they differ in their criterion of significance. A metaphysics is a rational myth. A superstition is a myth without the control and criticism of reasoning. A religion is a myth which claims both a foundation in history and to point beyond itself to God.[64]

MacIntyre's observations about myth are not fully developed in MI.[65] However, the points he make in the passage above suggest that a myth has five characteristics.

1. It enables the individual who has been educated in the myth to interpret the whole universe, including herself.
2. There is, therefore, no external perspective from which that individual can construct an "objective" description of reality.
3. Where science seeks to construct value neutral descriptions of reality, myth attempts to describe reality from a perspective which is shaped by a set of values that form part of its interpretative framework.
4. A myth can be distilled into a "rational metaphysics" if it is subject to critical scrutiny and challenge.
5. A religion (or perhaps it should have been "the Christian religion") is a myth that has a foundation in historical events and points towards the nature of God.

If one adds an additional point about the myth shaping the individual's assessment of right action to the list above, MacIntyre's account of a rational myth is equivalent to what I described as a comprehensive metaphysical

---

63. MI, 13.

64. MI, 13–14. MacIntyre's image of myth as world-encompassing resonates with Lindbeck's notion of religion as an interpretative medium capable of absorbing the universe (see ND, 117 for example).

65. MacIntyre's position is developed further in his paper "The Logical Status of Religious Belief" (henceforth LS): see section 1.4 below.

position in section 1.1 above. My addition is legitimate because worldviews such as Marxism and Christianity are forms of praxis, as McMylor points out,[66] and underpin practical reasoning and decision making.[67] What this passage also makes clear is that some elements of MacIntyre's description are analogous to his account of a tradition of enquiry in his later philosophy. For the later MacIntyre, traditions of enquiry begin in myth, and become transformed into a rational metaphysics through processes of criticism and evaluation which lead to the formulation of standards of coherence and rationality that are internal to the world of that tradition, as we will see in chapter 2. MacIntyre makes a similar claim In MI when he argues that Christian beliefs should not be rejected as superstitions, because their rationality has been secured by a "vigorous negative theology" and through "the strictest criticism of [their] foundations in the gospel documents and in the life of the Church."[68] It is their consistency with these internally generated criteria of coherence and adequacy that demonstrates their justification—provided one accepts the presuppositions that define the overall belief system.

MacIntyre's position in MI suggests that in so far as religions generate a "rational metaphysics," they also define their own standards of adequacy. Marxist criticism of religion therefore reflects a failure to appreciate the logic that governs the rationality of myth, and also embodies a misunderstanding of its own status as a form of knowledge. Although Marxism had come to conceptualize itself as a theory constructed within the natural science framework of the nineteenth century, MacIntyre argues that the essence of Marx's initial philosophy lay in his espousal of a Christian ethical perspective. "Marx's vision of estrangement would have been impossible without his vision of what man ought to be. Marx's doctrine here is a moral doctrine. His view of labour derives not at root from economic theory but from moral insight . . . He moves between the poles of man fallen, man redeemed."[69]

Marxism (like Christianity) is, therefore, a form of myth and, in its early stages at least, provided a *prophetic* vision of life as it would be when human beings have been healed of their corruption by the advent of a socialist society: "Side by side with [Marx's depiction of estrangement] . . . is a picture of what human life no longer estranged should be. Marx's activity here is prophetic, discerning the signs of the times."[70]

---

66. McMylor, *Alasdair MacIntyre*, 10.
67. MI, 111.
68. MI, 14.
69. MI, 57–58.
70. MI, 68–69.

However, as Marx's thought developed he abandoned this original moral and prophetic condemnation of humanity's self-estrangement, and came to argue that his account of the outcome of class struggle in socialism represented a *prediction* based on a scientific analysis of history. But Marxism's judgment on itself is based on an erroneous perception of itself as engaged in a process of scientific extrapolation, when in fact it is engaged in a process of moral evaluation and prophecy. While prophecy and prediction both seek to identify and explain patterns in history, prophecy provides a general framework for the interpretation and evaluation of future events within the world view defined by a myth, and a particular prophecy may be taken to be confirmed by quite different outcomes—unlike scientific prediction. Marxist predictions have not been borne out in practice and the fact that Marxism has not been abandoned despite the failure of these predictions undermines its claim to be a scientific theory. For MacIntyre, the reluctance of Marxists to accept that there is a mixture of error as well as truth in Marx indicates that "Marxism is not simply an economic doctrine: it is a doctrine about the universe, and such doctrines are held with religious rather than scientific attitudes."[71]

One consequence of the flexibility of interpretation associated with religious attitudes is that such doctrines cannot be falsified in the way that the failure of prediction may falsify a scientific hypothesis. Nevertheless, despite their resistance to falsification comprehensive metaphysical positions such as Marxism and Christianity claim to be true.[72] MacIntyre seeks to maintain a connection between these claims to truth and confirmation through historical events:

> Both Christianity and Marxism . . . claim truth as metaphysical systems rather than utility; and both vindicate that claim by laying themselves open to falsification on questions of fact. The Marxist asserts materialism in metaphysics because it is only the insights of materialism that will enable him to change the world effectively. Consequently the claims of Marxist materialism are vindicated, if, and only if, the predictions of Marxist social theory are verified. The achievements of Communist revolution are the test of Marxist metaphysics . . . the Christian claim rests on the fact of the Resurrection of Jesus . . . both Christianity and Marxism assert patterns in history by pointing to vindicating events.[73]

71. MI, 101.
72. MI, 117.
73. MI, 117–8.

At one level it is clearly true to argue that if one becomes a Marxist, for example, one accepts its vision of the achievement of a socialist end-state as a basis for action and that the realization of that end-state will vindicate the metaphysical system.[74] But the claim that both Marxism and Christianity can be vindicated by particular historical events ignores their power to shape the interpretation of such events. It is as if MacIntyre, faced with the problem of defining the nature of truth of such metaphysical positions, has fallen back on a vestigial falsificationism. But if a myth can interpret a range of different outcomes in ways that are consistent with its presuppositions, it will be able to deflect the challenge of events that are apparently inconsistent with its predictions.[75] MacIntyre therefore fails to specify a basis on which one such rational metaphysics might demonstrate its superiority to another. As a result MI leaves unresolved the questions which are the main focus of this book: under what circumstances is it legitimate to hold that belief in a comprehensive metaphysical position is justified, and indeed, is the notion of justification applicable to such beliefs?

Anticipations of AV

MacIntyre did not set out to provide an explicit account of the justification of a belief in a comprehensive metaphysical position in MI. But his exploration of the relationship between Christianity and Marxism begins to expose some of the important questions around such justification, and part of my argument is that the consideration of these questions plays a central role in the evolution of MacIntyre's mature philosophy. The continuity between MacIntyre's early and his later work is illustrated by the fact that MI embodies some important anticipations of that mature perspective. Both MI and AV are responses to the perceived failings of liberal Western culture, and in both books MacIntyre advocates a similar solution: the establishment of small communities which can provide an alternative to the mainstream culture. As we will see, MacIntyre's advocacy of Marxism also led him to advocate a quasi-Aristotelian moral framework as an essential precondition

---

74. This point is central to his argument in NMW as we shall see in section 1.4 below.

75. See MI, 98–100 for MacIntyre's description of the way in which Marxists have adopted such a strategy.

of the overall coherence of such a philosophy,[76] although he did not fully adopt an Aristotelian perspective until the 1970s.[77]

However, the connection between MI and AV lies not only in the anticipation of themes that are more fully and more effectively explored in his later work, but also in the fact that MI raises a central problem that is only adequately addressed in MacIntyre's mature work. That problem is the basis on which one might hold a philosophical perspective to be justified. MI was significantly revised and republished as *Marxism and Christianity* (henceforth MC) in 1968, and this version entered a second edition in 1995. When MacIntyre came to write an introduction to this third incarnation of MI he was able to look back on its first publication in 1953 and recognize that in MI he had identified but had been unable to adequately formulate or resolve a "fundamental problem." MacIntyre asserts that MI "embodies a conception of philosophy as a form of social practice embedded in and reflective upon other forms of social practice."[78]

Such a conception of philosophy has four main characteristics according to MacIntyre. Firstly, philosophy should be concerned with understanding the rules and standards of justification that are embodied in the social practices under consideration—Marxism and Christianity in the case of MI. Secondly, it should be concerned with articulating the way in which participants in these practices understand or misunderstand these rules and standards. To take Marxism as an example, its adherents have systematically misinterpreted its nature by conceptualizing it as a science, when in fact it more closely embodies the characteristics of a religion. Such misinterpretations may lead members of the community to make erroneous judgments about their own perspective and the truth and justification of their beliefs. Therefore the third characteristic of such an understanding of philosophy is that it is concerned with evaluating the extent to which the distorted interpretations of participants in these practices has led to a systematic misunderstanding of the nature of those practices, and of the goods that are being pursued through these practices.[79] Philosophy therefore reveals the truth through the exposure of systematic error. But the views of the philosophical critic are not themselves immune to distortions caused by their own social and intellectual context, and the fourth requirement is that the philosopher

---

76. See the discussion of NMW 1 and 2 in section 1.5 below. MacIntyre's attempt to combine a quasi-Aristotelian moral framework with Marxism is consistent with MacIntyre's view that Marx himself was significantly influenced by his study of Aristotle and post Aristotelian Greek philosophy. See MI, 38–40.

77. Introduction to MC, xxvi–xxvii.

78. Introduction to second edition of MC, xvi.

79. Ibid., xvi–xvii.

should be able to demonstrate that their account has in fact "transcended whatever limitations have been imposed by her or his historical and social circumstances, at least to a sufficient extent to represent truly the first three [tasks] and to show not just how things appear to be from this or that historical and social point of view, but how things are."[80]

But how could the philosopher demonstrate that their own position is (happily) immune to the type of distortions that arise within other practices? If she is unable to demonstrate this, the critic would appear to have no clear grounds on which to claim to have exposed the truth, or on which she can show that her account is demonstrably superior to those of others. As MacIntyre puts it "How is it possible to identify in the case of other and rival theses and arguments a variety of distortions and limitations deriving from their author's historical and social context, while at the same time being able to exhibit one's own theses and arguments . . . as exempt from such distortion and limitation?"[81]

In raising this question MacIntyre has rediscovered a version of Cartesian doubt, in which the fear that one's beliefs may be delusions fostered by an evil demon is replaced by the fear that one may be equally deluded in one's beliefs because of the distortions created by the historical and intellectual context within which each of us is embedded.

When MacIntyre published a revised version of MI as the first edition of *Marxism and Christianity* in 1968 he had no answer to these questions. As a consequence he found himself unable to make any commitments to a comprehensive metaphysical perspective.

> Because I did not as yet know how to formulate this question adequately enough even to know where to look for an answer to it, I found myself distanced from identification with any substantive point of view. Whereas in 1953 I had . . . supposed it possible to be in some significant way both a Christian and a Marxist, I was by 1968 able to be neither, while acknowledging in both standpoints a set of truths with which I did not know how to come to terms.[82]

This inability to identify with any substantive point of view precipitated the longstanding epistemological crisis[83] that characterized MacIntyre's middle period, a crisis which he was only able to resolve in his mature work. This

---

80. Ibid., xvii.
81. Ibid., xix.
82. Ibid.
83. See sections 2.5, 4.4 and 4.7 below for a fuller discussion of the concept of epistemological crisis.

crisis reflected the impact of three unresolved questions about the nature of justification that had first begun to emerge in MI. Firstly, there is the overall question of specifying the circumstances in which it is legitimate to believe in the ontological and other presuppositions of a comprehensive metaphysical system. Secondly, this question will also arise with respect to the justification of our moral beliefs, if such beliefs are logically related to our (unsubstantiated) ontological presuppositions. Thirdly, our social and cultural environment will tend to shape our views as to which beliefs can be legitimately held. But these cultural factors may change over time. As a result, beliefs that are held to be fully justified at one time may no longer be plausible, or even coherent, at a later time. In the next three sections I am going to describe MacIntyre's early attempts to address these questions, beginning with his initial account of the justification of religious belief.

1.4 Myth and Justification: The Logical Status of Religious Belief

As we have seen, MacIntyre's attempt to integrate Marxism and Christianity in MI raised questions about the grounds for accepting the truth of a comprehensive metaphysical system. One example of such a system is the set of beliefs associated with the Christian faith,[84] and in the 1950's MacIntyre published several works that are particularly relevant to the question of the grounds of such beliefs. In 1955 MacIntyre jointly edited a collection of papers with Antony Flew (*New Essays in Philosophical Theology*),[85] and published a paper on "Visions" in that book.[86] He contributed an article to a second collection, *Metaphysical Beliefs* (1957), called "The logical status of religious belief" (henceforth LS).[87] These two collections of papers were particularly influential in resurrecting general interest in metaphysical questions about the nature and justification of religious belief, and have proved to be of enduring interest.[88] In 1959 he published a book which addressed

---

84. I do not mean to imply that Christian belief means that all adherents accept a single set of beliefs, but rather that Christian faith typically involves accepting *some* set of beliefs about God, the creation and human nature and destiny.

85. Flew and Macintyre, eds., *New Essays in Philosophical Theology;* henceforth *New Essays*.

86. MacIntyre, "Visions," in *New Essays*.

87. MacIntyre, "The Logical Status of Religious Belief" in MacIntyre, ed., *Metaphysical Beliefs*, henceforth LS; references are to the 1957 edition unless otherwise indicated.

88. Both collections were intended to resurrect philosophical interest in large scale metaphysical questions (see Flew and MacIntyre "Preface to *New Essays*," ix; and MacIntyre "Preface to the 1970 Edition" in Metaphysical *Beliefs*, 2nd Edition, vii–viii. Their

Difficulties in Christian Belief (henceforth DCB).[89] I will consider each of these publications in turn.

Visions

"Visions" is a brief and trenchant dismissal of the claim that religious experience can justify religious belief. MacIntyre's argument is as follows. Visions are the best candidate for experiences that might justify religious beliefs. Therefore, if visions can be shown to fail in this role, one can demonstrate that no experiential justification for religious belief is possible, as any other experience that might be cited will provide weaker evidence. He argues that visions cannot provide evidence for the existence of "invisible and supernatural beings"[90] for three reasons:

1. There can be no criterion that can be used to distinguish a veridical from a non-veridical experience of "seeing an angel" (for example), as there are criteria that enable us to distinguish between having a hallucination of an elephant and the genuine experience of seeing an elephant in the zoo.[91] Without such a criterion, religious experience cannot be distinguished from hallucination.

2. There is no rule of inference that we can refer to in order to justify the claim that a vision is indicative of some higher reality. If we claim that the smell of smoke means that there is a fire, we can point to empirical evidence which justifies the maxim "there is no smoke without fire." This is not the case with attempts to use visions to justify general assertions about the supernatural and transcendent.[92]

3. The appearance of an angel in a vision would not act as a "warrant for accepting any distinctively religious utterance he might make"[93] as there are no grounds for accepting his veracity, so the fact that the Angel claims to speak the word of God provides no basis for one to trust such an assertion.

---

success in achieving this objective can be seen in the fact that *New Essays* has been in continued demand since its first publication, and a third edition of *Metaphysical Beliefs* was published in 2012.

89. MacIntyre, *Difficulties in Christian Belief*; henceforth DCB.
90. "Visions," 254.
91. Ibid., 255.
92. Ibid., 257.
93. Ibid., 258.

MacIntyre's fundamental point therefore is in essence a reiteration of the Kantian principle that sensuous experiences cannot lead us beyond the world of experience.[94] In particular MacIntyre points out that a religious experience is identified as such through the application of religious beliefs to experience and therefore cannot in itself act as a warrant for those beliefs.[95] Indeed, in this respect his general argument resonates with George Lindbeck's dismissal of experiential-expressive accounts of religion.[96]

The Logical Status of Religious Belief

MacIntyre's arguments against experiential justifications of religious belief are not conclusive, and other philosophers have put forward robust accounts of the role that experience may play in underpinning faith.[97] However, the grounds for his rejection of the role of experience do not depend on the power of his critical arguments alone. In LS MacIntyre rejects the notion that religious language gains its meaning through its relationship to distinctive religious experiences,[98] arguing that Wittgenstein's private language argument had demonstrated that pre-linguistic experience can never be the determinant of meaning.[99] Words do not get their meaning from labelling some private experience, but from their functions within the practices of particular cultural groups.[100] As a result the characterization of religious language as expressive misinterprets its functions. MacIntyre's intention in LS is to provide a more adequate account of those functions. This approach is consistent with the 1950's view of philosophy as a descriptive rather than prescriptive discipline, which should elucidate the way in which language is

---

94. See ibid., 258; MacIntyre puts forward a similar argument in DCB, chapter 7.

95. "Visions," 259.

96. Similarly Lindbeck argues that his cultural-linguistic model of religion "reverses the relation of the inner and the outer. Instead of deriving external features of religion from inner experience, it is the inner experiences which are viewed as derivative" (ND, 34), and see section 3.3 below.

97. See, for example, Alston, *Perceiving God*.

98. For example, MacIntyre criticizes Schleiermacher for seeking to illuminate the meaning of an expression such as "God created the world," in terms of an experience of absolute dependence. MacIntyre argues that Schleiermacher is proposing an entirely new and idiosyncratic interpretation of the doctrine, rather than elucidating its meaning; LS, 176–77.

99. LS, 176–78.

100. George Lindbeck adopts a similar position in ND. See section 3.3 below.

used, but which should not seek to rule on the legitimacy of such usage on the basis of "*a priori* standards of meaningfulness."[101]

Words which are used in religious discourse, such as "love" or "father" or "peace" or "redemption" all have a non-problematic application in family and social life.[102] For MacIntyre, religious language gains its meaning from the use of the same words in these familiar and non-problematic settings. However, the difference between religious and secular contexts of use indicates that such words cannot possess the same meaning when they are applied to God:

> What is said of God is . . . familiar enough. God calls. God hears, God provides. But these verbs appear to lack the application which is their justification in non-religious contexts . . . the name "God" is not used to refer to someone who can be seen and heard, as the name "Abraham" is, and when descriptive verbs are used to state that God's call is heard, it is not ordinary hearing that is meant . . . if talk about God is not to be construed at its face value, how is it to be construed?[103]

MacIntyre seeks to answer this question through a discussion of what he calls the "religious attitude" which consists of two main elements. Firstly, the theist is committed in some systematic way to the *practice* of worship, and secondly, although the believer holds that God is so great that "nothing adequate can be said about him" he also wishes to say "that God acts in the universe," and seeks to describe these actions.[104] The first element in this framework enables MacIntyre to argue that the tension between the apophaticism required by the limits of language and the need to speak of God's works is managed, if not resolved, in the practice of worship by the use of a language that is largely vocative and gerundive.[105] Worship is a practice which is largely addressed *to* God, and is aimed at encouraging certain *responses* to God, rather than aimed at constructing a set of true propositions about him. And this is a clue to the way in which philosophers have over-emphasized the propositional nature of belief, rather than its performative aspects. What is central to religious commitment is the process of learning how to worship, rather than the acquisition of certain beliefs about the object of worship:

101. LS, 171.
102. LS, 175–76.
103. LS, 179.
104. LS, 186.
105. LS, 188–89.

> In worship we do not talk about God, but to him. We are apt to envisage the relation between religious belief and worship in terms of an intellectualist conception of theory as prior to and directive of practice. Prof. Ryle has shown us how this conception is in general mistaken. Knowing how to perform particular operations does not depend on knowing that particular theoretical principles are to be applied. Similarly we are wrong to conceive of religious practice as the application of religious doctrine. It is not just that as a matter of historical fact the practice of worship precedes the explicit formulation of belief, but that we can worship without being able to say clearly what we believe ... "The Catholic faith is this, That we worship ..." not that we believe. In formulating doctrine we are trying to say what we do when we pray.[106]

What God has done or said is sometimes described during worship, but such descriptions do not occur in the form of isolated assertions, demanding a decision as to the truth or falsity of each proposition. They are presented as part of "a total narration, in which a wholeness of vision is presented."[107] MacIntyre characterizes these narrations as myths, and develops the account of religious myth that he had first put forward in MI. We understand myths, he suggests, in precisely the same way that we understand other narratives such as novels or dramas. But unlike a novel, one has to either accept or reject a myth,[108] because the function of myth is to guide us in our lives. The acceptance of a myth enables us to respond coherently to the central issues of human life because "any given myth incorporates an attitude to ... [the critical issues of birth, love, marriage, death and so on] and to accept a myth is to identify oneself with that attitude and so to make the myth directive of one's behaviour. To accept a sufficiently comprehensive myth is to accept a whole way of living."[109]

Acceptance of a myth establishes a framework for practice that is elucidated and supported by the stories it embodies. Such stories cannot be translated into an abstract set of ethical principles. Rather, myths provide

---

106. LS, 188.

107. LS, 189. MacIntyre's position in LS is analogous to Lindbeck's argument that what are required for spiritual and moral guidance in contemporary life are "habitable texts." Lindbeck suggests that: "what is needed is texts projecting imaginatively and practically habitable worlds ... Much contemporary intellectual life can be understood as a search for such texts. Marxists and Freudians, for example, now rarely seek to ground their favorite authors' writings scientifically or philosophically. They simply ask that they be followable." Lindbeck, "The Search for Habitable Texts," 155.

108. LS, 191.

109. LS, 191.

guidance precisely at those points in experience where moral rules and principles break down—at points of crisis (for example) such as bereavement or, indeed, in the face of our own impending death. In accepting or rejecting a myth we accept or reject the way of life which is exemplified in the form and content of the story. "Generations of non-conformists found the shape of the moral life . . . in *The Pilgrim's Progress* . . . in accepting or rejecting what Bunyan says . . . we accept or reject a whole way of living."[110]

As we shall see when I describe George Lindbeck's position in chapter 3, there is much in LS that anticipates the perspective of postliberal theology. Both MacIntyre (in LS) and Lindbeck emphasise that the narratives that constitute a religion provide an interpretative framework which shapes the individual's theoretical and practical engagement with the world. But are the stories that constitute religious myths true, and if so, what sense of truth is being applied? For MacIntyre, the believer accepts that the Christian narratives are to be accepted as true stories about a being that exists and acts in the world. MacIntyre suggests that this particular use of myth "stands, therefore, in need of justification."[111] He rejects at once the idea that religious beliefs are quasi-scientific hypotheses that can be demonstrated to be true or shown to be false,[112] discarding the vestigial falsificationism that he seemed to express in MI. Religious beliefs are not hypotheses competing with other theories of the origin of the universe.[113] Attempts to demonstrate the existence of God (for example) mistakenly interpret religion as a theory about the nature of reality, rather than a faith in which an initial act of trust is central. If God's existence were demonstrable we would be denied the opportunity of choosing to love him.[114] The assimilation of religion to hypothesis "is alien to the whole spirit of religious belief. Having made our decision, we adhere to belief unconditionally."[115]

Demonstration may be alien to religious faith, but this does not imply that a religious assertion will lack justification. The issue of justification is, however, internal to the religious system rather than a matter of external justification. Religions, MacIntyre argues, have their own procedures "for deciding whether a given belief or practice is or is not authentic. Each has a criterion by means of which orthodoxy is determined. And in this sense a belief is justified in a particular religion by referring to that rule by means of

110. LS, 192–93.
111. LS, 193.
112. LS, 195–96.
113. LS, 196.
114. LS, 197.
115. LS, 197.

which it is determined what is and what is not included in the religion."[116] The justification of religious practices and doctrines are therefore analogous to the justification of claims about the nature of law. To ask: "what is the justification of a claim that such and such is the law?" is to ask for elucidation in terms of the established processes through which a sovereign state enacts legislation. Such criteria are the ultimate court of appeal, and as such cannot have, and do not stand in need of, any further logical justification.[117] Such an ultimate criterion of authenticity also serves as the criterion of identity of a religion, in that what belongs to the religion is that which has been endorsed with reference to whatever constitutes the source of authority within the religion. "Every religion therefore is defined by reference to what it accepts as an authoritative criterion in religious matters. The acceptance or rejection of a religion is thus the acceptance or rejection of such an authority."[118]

What defines a system of thought as a religion is the existence of a set of internal rules for determining what is and what is not doctrinally authentic, and an associated set of narratives that provides guidance as to how to one should live. To accept a religion is to accept the authority of these internal criteria of authenticity and the associated narratives. This account provides MacIntyre with a general definition of a religion which is very similar to that put forward by George Lindbeck some thirty years later. Both authors identify religion with the acceptance of the authority of a framework of belief rather than in terms of a specific type of content. As MacIntyre puts it "... by saying that religion is to be ... formally defined without reference to its content we allow for both theism and polytheism, religions of one God like Islam and of no God like primitive Buddhism."[119]

Lindbeck also defines a religion in terms of its function in providing a framework for living rather than in terms of some specific type of propositional content, and this allows both authors to include forms of belief which are secular or non-theistic within their definitions.[120] But however satisfactory such an account may be as a definition of a religion, it does not act as a basis for distinguishing between the claims of one religion over another or, indeed, provide any rationally arguable basis for choosing one religion over none. For MacIntyre in LS one can accept a religion in its own terms or one can reject it.[121] A decision to submit to authority is central to the nature of

116. LS, 197. See also DCB, 85 and MI, 14 for similar points.
117. LS, 198–99.
118. LS, 199.
119. LS, 201.
120. See ND 1st Edition, 32–33 and "Afterword" ND 2nd Edition, 132, where Lindbeck provides an equally broad definition of religion.
121. LS, 202.

religious belief,[122] but to make such a commitment is a question of emotion rather than reason. MacIntyre suggests that "to believe in God resembles not so much believing that something is the case as being engrossed by a passion: Kierkegaard compares the believer to a madman; he might equally have compared him to a lover."[123]

Once one has embraced religion one can apply internal standards of justification, but the question of commitment appears to involve a criterionless choice. Each religion appears to act as a hermetically sealed self-justifying system. MacIntyre came to recognize this aspect of his position, and its defects. He rejected the view that the criteria for judging the factual basis of Christianity could be fundamentally different from the criteria that are used in other aspects of life[124] and came to see his position in LS as essentially empty:

> Christianity, as I defend it here, becomes a belief which is in practice irrefutable at the cost of becoming a belief that is practically vacuous. Where the criteria for the truth of a position are laid down, so to speak, from within that position . . . it becomes impossible to differentiate a position for which one claims truth (in the ordinary sense) and a position which one merely entertains because of its aesthetic power.[125]

MacIntyre concludes that his account of religion in this essay is inconsistent with Christian belief because the latter claims truth in this "ordinary sense." However, his negative conclusion should not disguise the fact that in LS he identifies many of the issues that he sought to resolve in creating his mature philosophy. In particular, the article identifies, but does not resolve, the question: "How is it possible to have a non-vacuous account of justification where the criteria for justification are internal to the position to be justified?" and it is precisely this question that is addressed by the notion of tradition-constituted rationality.

Difficulties in Christian Belief

MacIntyre returns to the question of the justification of belief in DCB. He asserts that religious belief cannot be compelled by deductive argument, because any deductive argument is valid solely in so far as its conclusion is

---

122. LS, 200.
123. LS, 204.
124. MacIntyre, "Preface to the 1970 edition," *Metaphysical Beliefs*, x–xi.
125. Ibid., xi.

already contained within its premises. Such an argument cannot, therefore, compel the acceptance of those premises.[126] As a result such arguments have no power to convince the sceptic. As he had argued in LS, attempts to justify belief in this way mistake the function of religious faith, which requires an act of trust that would be obviated if God's existence could be demonstrated.[127]

Some people undertake such an act of trust, other people do not. For the MacIntyre of DCB what determines whether such trust is forthcoming is the extent to which the adoption of such beliefs can render our experience of the world intelligible. However, MacIntyre suggests that we can understand this process of rendering our experience intelligible in at least two different ways. For some people, it may involve materialist scientific explanation; for others teleological explanation may be required. MacIntyre suggests that arguments such as the cosmological argument have force only for those people who are already committed to a religious perspective because they require a form of explanation that assumes that what the existence of this world "requires . . . to be in any way intelligible is a necessary being."[128]

In contrast, the critic of such teleological arguments is likely to construe explanation in terms of the subsumption of phenomena under causal laws. Such explanations proceed by relating one set of natural phenomena to others and do not need to invoke some final supernatural cause.[129] Ultimately, any train of argument has to come back to some first principles and assumptions about the nature of explanation which are accepted by an individual without being justified by further inferential arguments. The difference between the Christian and the sceptic is not that one is breaching well established rational standards and making illegitimate assumptions while the other is arguing from well-founded principles, but that they are operating from incompatible sets of adopted first principles. The initial act of commitment to the preferred mode of explanation and to the system cannot be given a rational justification.

MacIntyre's position in DCB suggests that belief in a materialist and determinist viewpoint or a religious teleological perspective is a question of the extent to which each succeeds in making one's experience of the world intelligible. But this appears to justify belief by an appeal to contingent psychological facts about the individual. In a diverse society each of us will migrate towards forms of life that reinforce and are reinforced by our personal

126. DCB, 78–79.
127. DCB, 84; see also LS, 197.
128. DCB, 80.
129. DCB, 80–81.

need for different forms of explanation. However, our acceptance of the viewpoints embodied in such forms of life will not be justifiable to those who do not share our predilection for one set of presuppositions rather than another. Ultimately, I will have to justify my higher level beliefs by reference to these presuppositions. These commitments form the foundations of our attempts to make sense of the world; they are not positions justifiable by further argument.[130] As Wittgenstein said in *Philosophical Investigations*, "If I have exhausted the justifications I have reached bedrock, and my spade is turned. Then I am inclined to say: 'This is simply what I do.'"[131] The problem with this Wittgensteinian position is that it would appear to lead to a form of relativism if one accepts that it is possible to have more than one conceptual scheme, each of which can be justified by reference to the form of life in which it is embodied.[132]

In DCB MacIntyre argues that that there are at least two responses to this type of criticism. Firstly, one might evaluate the legitimacy of first principles by examining the type of consequences that flow from their adoption. This, however, invites an accusation of circularity, as MacIntyre suggests: "are we not bound to judge and assess the consequences also by our first principles so that all our arguments will be logical boa-constrictors in which every attempt to escape leads only to being swallowed still further?"[133] MacIntyre suggests that this consequence can be avoided if we acknowledge that we have multiple sets of criteria by which we judge whether something is worthy of acceptance or not:

> We tend to have a number of groups of criteria which we match against each other. Our acceptance of the authority of Jesus Christ . . . is compounded of the way in which he meets the demands of our moral insight, the way in which he comes up to

---

130. It is of course possible to argue that theistic and other metaphysical beliefs can be held as what Plantinga calls "properly basic" beliefs. This would mean that such beliefs do not require further evidential justification (see Plantinga, "Reason and Belief in God," 72–77, and other works by Plantinga listed in the Bibliography. Such a justificatory strategy would have been open to MacIntyre. However, although Plantinga rejects classical Lockean foundationalism his reformed epistemology is firmly tied to a modified foundationalist concept of knowledge, and it is this foundationalist understanding of knowledge that MacIntyre ultimately rejected. See section 2.5 below for an account of MacIntyre's mature position.

131. Wittgenstein, *Philosophical Investigations*, paragraph 217.

132. Grayling, "Wittgenstein on Scepticism and Certainty."

133. DCB, 86. MacIntyre makes a similar point in LS, 184. There are echoes of Newman's argument for the illative sense in MacIntyre's argument here. See Newman, *An Essay in Aid of a Grammar of Assent*, chapter 9.

the standards which we believe a being worthy of worship must satisfy, and so on.[134]

MacIntyre notes that the convergence of our moral insight with other criteria provides a rational basis for the act of trust in Christ, by disposing of some factors which might militate against such trust. This is not the same as *demonstrating* the rational legitimacy of an act of trust in Christ, as MacIntyre acknowledges, but he suggests that such complementarity underpins the coherence of faith by excluding inconsistencies between our religious commitments and our ethical presuppositions. "[These criteria] do provide some test, even if only a negative one: they do preserve a place for reasoning even in our choice of ultimate criteria."[135]

This argument from the complementarity of our moral insight to our spiritual desires points to the relationship between our beliefs about human nature and our ethical beliefs. MacIntyre suggests that the complementarity of our spirituality and our ethical concerns rests in their relationship to the achievement of our ultimate happiness. The point of Christian worship and ethics lies in their relevance to the pursuit of happiness for me and for other people.[136] This, MacIntyre suggests, is the purpose of morality: "... the point of morality is that if we follow moral rules we shall get for ourselves and others authentic happiness."[137]

This link between ethics and happiness is also the basis for his justification of the cogency of adopting a Marxist perspective, as we will see in section 1.5. The difference between a religious person and the secular materialist may, therefore, lie in how each conceptualizes happiness, and how each understands the shape of the moral life. For the Christian that shape culminates ultimately in a final union with God, and therefore God must be central to our morality in a way that is alien not only to a materialist ethic, but also to a Kantian account of moral imperatives as principles that exist independently of human needs and desires. From a Christian perspective "God must play a role because he created our nature and he alone knows what in the end will make us happy."[138]

MacIntyre concludes from this argument not that the Kantian or secular moral perspectives are wrong, but that they represent alternative conceptions of ethics to the Christian understanding of morality.

---

134. DCB, 86.
135. DCB, 86.
136. DCB, 102–6.
137. DCB, 106–7.
138. DCB, 107.

The implication of this argument, that there are alternative moralities, is important. Just as in religion there is no standpoint beyond both belief and unbelief, beyond all different types of belief, no neutral standpoint from which we can judge between Christianity and its alternatives, so in morality also we have no neutral standing ground between Christian morality and other moralities.[139]

Crudely put, the outcome of MacIntyre's explorations of the justification of religious faith during the 1950s was that the answer to the question of religious belief depended on one's psychological makeup. If the world can only be rendered intelligible for you through a teleological perspective, if your moral sense required a hope of eternal happiness for its coherence, you should adopt religious faith. If you are content with a materialist model of explanation in terms of efficient causes and have no reason to found morality on an idea of eternal happiness as the ultimate telos, then one might legitimately adopt an atheist or agnostic stance. Once one had committed oneself to such a position one had obligations to ensure that one's position was developed in ways that could be defended rationally, but the adoption of one's starting point could not be rationally justified.

1.5 Marxism and Morality

In LS MacIntyre appeared to embrace an interpretation of religious faith in which commitment depends on non-rational choice. Such a notion of religious commitment is paradoxically analogous to the liberal notion of moral autonomy that MacIntyre repudiates. It is also inconsistent with a Marxist understanding of the relationship between belief, and historical and economic circumstances. What led him to this fideist position was the recognition that traditional attempts to justify religious faith were both incoherent and theologically unsound. But given MacIntyre's analytic rigor, such a fideist perspective was inherently unstable and by 1961 MacIntyre had stopped being a Christian.

However, MacIntyre continued to be a Marxist and his concern with the nature of justification became focused on the legitimacy of Marxism and the cogency of its ethical perspective. In "Notes from the Moral Wilderness 1 and 2" (NMW) MacIntyre explored the ethical position of those who had rejected Communism in the 1950s after they had become aware of the excesses of Stalinism. MacIntyre criticizes these apostates for failing to justify their moral position, and his critique is accompanied by a statement of the

---

139. DCB, 107–8.

characteristics that a metaphysical position must possess if it is to provide an adequate foundation for morality and human development. These papers prefigure his attempt to defend an Aristotelian ethic in *A Short History of Ethics* (SHE), and the more developed position on the nature and foundations of ethics he articulates in AV.

The critic of Stalinism advocates a particular ethical viewpoint, but, MacIntyre asks, what is the justification of this moral perspective? "[The critics] repudiate Stalinist crimes in the name of moral principle; but the fragility of their appeal lies in the apparently arbitrary nature of that appeal. Whence come these standards by which Stalinism is judged and found wanting and why should they have authority over us?"[140] In raising this question MacIntyre was seeking to illuminate the relationship between theoretical presuppositions about human nature and moral judgment, and to expose the fragility of every ethical perspective that has become detached from its theoretical moorings. Stalinism had dismissed questions of moral justification by claiming that the laws that govern historical development mean that human beings are simply participants in an inevitable historical process. Their actions are predetermined[141] by the laws that underpin this process.[142] What should be considered to be right is simply that which "is actually going to be the outcome of that historical development."[143] Our moral preferences are irrelevant to the judgment of history. However, the critic of Stalinism passes an independent moral judgment on events in that history, on the basis of standards which reflect her autonomous moral perspective. What justifies these standards?

This may seem to be a strange question to ask, because contemporary moral philosophy claims that moral standards are logically independent of matters of fact.[144] One corollary of this claim is that moral standards cannot be justified on the basis of reasoned argument from factual premises, but have to be adopted. As a result, systems of thought such as liberalism and existentialism project an image of the autonomous individual formulating their moral perspective by the exercise of "unconditional and arbitrary choice."[145] But such a position fails to give any satisfactory account of why one set of moral standards should have authority over us rather than any others. If this is the case, then the apostate's condemnation of Stalin-

---

140. NMW, 32.
141. NMW, 32.
142. NMW, 35.
143. NMW, 32.
144. NMW, 32–33.
145. NMW, 33.

ism can only be the expression of her personal preferences, rather than the outcome of evaluation in accordance with principles which are binding on everyone.[146]

MacIntyre argues that what is required to address this deficit is an alternative theory of morality which avoids the rigidity of Stalinism but which nevertheless "provide[s] us with some conception of a basis for our moral standards."[147] One can repudiate a Stalinist perspective, Macintyre argues, by presenting an accurate interpretation of Marx's theory. Stalinism overemphasizes the determining power of history, at the expense of denying the possibility of human freedom and control over events. Stalinism is correct in recognizing that human freedom is always limited by the form of society in which the individual is embedded, but socialism offers the opportunity of liberating humanity from the determining forces of history.[148] MacIntyre therefore rejects the mechanistic notion of historical development characteristic of Stalinism,[149] and argues that the contrary is true. "That liberation that Marx describes . . . is a freeing of our relationships from the kind of determination and constraint hitherto exercised upon them."[150] And precisely because socialism is about the realization of human freedom, it is not something which can be established through the operation of impersonal laws. Marxist "prediction" is not the claim that social development *must* happen, but an affirmation of the belief that human beings will choose to take the new step towards freedom that the emergence of socialism offers.[151] This understanding of history, MacIntyre suggests, provides a basis for clarifying the authority of moral rules:

> If we bring out as central to Marxism the kind of points which I have suggested, may this suggest a third alternative [to Stalinism and liberalism] . . . which treats what emerges in history as a basis for our standards, without making the historical process sovereign or its progress automatic? In order to ask this question properly we ought to re-examine some of the traditional questions about human nature and morality. What is the relation between what I am, what I can be, and what I want to be and what I ought to be?[152]

146. NMW, 34.
147. NMW, 7.
148. NMW, 40.
149. NMW, 37–39.
150. NMW, 39.
151. NMW, 40.
152. NMW, 40.

Providing an account of human nature leads MacIntyre to consider issues that are more fully addressed in AV. Understanding human action may involve the type of causal explanation that a physiologist may provide, or it may be require reference to human purposes and goals: a teleological explanation which links human behavior to particular preferences and desires. It is this understanding of desire that enables us to make the behavior of others intelligible to ourselves.[153] Liberalism, however, divorces the meaning and authority of moral concepts from history and from the facts of human nature. As a result "the 'ought' of morality is utterly divorced from the 'is' of desire."[154] In consequence Liberalism renders morality unintelligible as a motive for human action, because it assimilates ethical principles to the status of primitive taboos for whose force no explanation can be given, except that of authority within a particular community.

For MacIntyre the link between morality and the fulfilment of human desires is central to the evolution and intelligibility of moral notions. Some behavior can be understood in terms of desires interpreted as drives aimed at ensuring that out basic animal needs are met, such as the response to hunger or fear. But MacIntyre argues that the desires that morality serves are not such crude psychological or physiological drives. Human reflexivity means that it is possible to make a distinction between what a person may want (in the short term) and what may benefit and meet their needs and interests in the longer term. Recognizing and fulfilling these longer term desires is made possible through participation in community, and the role of morality is to shape our desires in ways which couple them to our longer term interests. Morality is, therefore, concerned with the transmutation of human desire into forms which realize human potentiality. MacIntyre asserts that "morality expresses the most permanent and long-run of human desires,"[155] and points out that this connection is explicit in Aristotle and in the Bible, where the point of morality is to lead to our happiness, through the complete realization of our human potential. The interpretation of the nature of that potential will be shaped by the history and distinctive conceptual resources of each community. The purpose of the community's ethical code is to shape human desires into forms which direct action towards the achievement of human potential as conceptualized by each community.

MacIntyre argues that the understanding of the logical connection between socially transformed desire and morality has been lost today, because the erosion of religious belief and the search for a secular foundation to

---

153. NMW, 41; see also AV, 161–62, and section 2.3 below.
154. NMW, 41.
155. NMW, 42.

morality has disrupted the relationship between moral injunctions and a prior understanding of the potentiality of human nature, and has left behind only the imperatives, "do this" or "do not do this."[156] With the loss of an understanding of the connection between morality and the transformation of desire, human desire has become conceptualized in individualist terms "which tends . . . to the war of all against all."[157] Paradoxically, this Hobbesian outcome does not lend itself to individual freedom, because the self may become dominated and controlled by its unmoderated desires to the extent that it loses all autonomy,[158] given that autonomy implies the ability to evaluate and choose between different goods. The individual who is driven by their immediate and selfish desires has no capacity to identify and select higher goods.

The class structure of communities at different points in their history will lead them to conceptualize human potentiality in ways which reflect the interests of the dominant class, but MacIntyre argues that it is only by identifying our desires with the communal needs and desires of the social class of which we are part that we can come to an understanding of our needs and identity.[159] The class –driven conflicts which characterize the evolution of human history will embed each of us in new forms of social life that reveal to us new elements of our potential: " For Marx the emergence of human nature is something to be comprehended only in terms of the history of class-struggle. Each age reveals a development in human potentiality which is specific to that form of social life."[160]

But the forms of economic production that characterizes each age also limit the extent to which human potential can be achieved. Life under capitalism allows people to become conscious of the extent to which the expression of their potential is limited by these forms of production. As a result, it reveals the possibility of human beings re-appropriating that nature by creating alternative forms of production and patterns of social relationship. MacIntyre argues that this account closes the gap between morality and desire because the discovery of their deprivation under capitalism can enable people to "discover . . . that what they want most is what they want in common with others . . . [and] that certain ways of sharing human life are indeed what they most desire."[161] This rediscovery of common desire allows

---

156. NMW, 42–43.
157. NMW, 44.
158. NMW, 44–45.
159. NMW, 45–47.
160. NMW, 46.
161. NMW, 46.

the emergence of "a new moral standpoint" by providing new answers to the question "what do I really want?" which can lead to social change. In this process the Marxist *discovers* her values, as opposed to the Liberal who merely invents them.[162]

I want to draw three conclusions from this discussion. Firstly, the account of morality that MacIntyre articulates through this notion of fulfilled desire (albeit satisfaction of desires that have been transmuted through participation in a community) is teleological without requiring the definition of some ultimate human good. The human telos is not a fixed end-point that can be known and defined once and for all time. Rather the understanding of this telos will be shaped by changing economic and social relationships, and by the changing conceptual resources that a community can use to understand human nature and community. In NMW MacIntyre argues that it is only when humanity is fully liberated from the consciousness-limiting conditions of particular modes of social and economic relationship that people can become aware of their true potentiality—although one might equally say that it is only in this historical process of change that they have the opportunity to invent the concepts and practices that *create* different forms of human potentiality.

The second point I want to bring out is that MacIntyre's position implies that different histories will shape different communities, conceptual resources and understandings of human potentiality, and will therefore shape different associated moralities. As a result, each ethical system will be coherently related to its community but distinct from the ethics characteristic of other societies who have experienced a different history. MacIntyre's account of the evolution of human freedom in NMW is shaped by a Marxist interpretation of historical development as following a trajectory that is common to all societies. But if Stalinist determinism is an error, as MacIntyre argues it is,[163] societies may follow radically different histories and as a result radically different ethics may emerge, together with radically divergent understandings of human nature. One question which MacIntyre's account leaves unanswered is the basis on which one such ethic might be judged superior to another. If he is unable to answer this question, his position is not an advance on the position of the liberal critic of Stalinism, because MacIntyre's position is equally open to the challenge that he is unable to offer a broader justification for his ethical preferences.

My third point is related to the fact that MacIntyre's account of the emergent understanding of human nature and telos that develops through

---

162. NMW, 47.
163. NMW, 37.

historical change, described in NMW, is conceptualized as a progressive movement in the direction of liberation and newly realized potentiality. But if one rejects Marxist historical determinism (as MacIntyre does) historical change is also potentially regressive. Some societies may develop and express an understanding of human potentiality which is not expressible in the concepts available to another culture, and develop social relationships that foster the achievement of that potential. But other cultures may lose the concepts that underpinned their notions of human potential and freedom in the process of social change, and as a result the social relationships which were directed towards the realization of that potential may also vanish. Despite these changes, the words that once expressed these concepts may continue to be used in such a culture even though their original meanings have been forgotten.

AV begins with an account of cultural amnesia in contemporary Western culture which MacIntyre argues has been created by the fragmentation of our understanding of the relationship between human nature, human telos and moral language. For the MacIntyre of AV we live in a time in which "the language and the appearances of morality persist even though the integral substance of morality has to a large degree been fragmented and then in part destroyed."[164] How could such conceptual and ethical dislocation have occurred? MacIntyre's early studies of secularization and social change, and his analysis of the impact that these processes of cultural change have had on the understanding of morality in Western culture, anticipates and illuminates the account of our conceptual amnesia he gives in AV, as I will show in the next section.

1.6 Conceptual Change, Morality, and Religious Belief

Theism and Morality

The secularism and individualism that marks the ideology of Western capitalist societies underpins contradictory images of human nature. On the one hand the individual is conceived as autonomous and pre-formed, existing prior to any engagement in community. On the other hand the individual is also seen as "extremely malleable"[165] shaped by social forces into a variety of different roles and masks. As a result the identification of a determinate human nature which exists independently of social interaction becomes problematic. In the 1960s MacIntyre argued that the contemporary image

164. AV, 5.
165. RSA, 44.

of human nature has been denuded by the corrosion of the conceptual scheme that had originally supported both theism and a determinate moral code. During this decade MacIntyre produced two works which developed an interpretation of the relationship between social change and change in theoretical, religious, and ethical beliefs, and which articulate an account of how this erosion of conceptual resources had taken place.[166] These works provides the basis for his mature view that in our society moral debate has been rendered irresolvable.by our forgetfulness of the original meaning of moral concepts, and by the loss from our conceptual resources of the theoretical moorings that had secured that original sense.

In these works MacIntyre contrasts our contemporary culture with what he perceives to be the culture of pre-industrial Britain. MacIntyre visualizes such a culture as characterized by fundamental agreement on a set of moral principles and a set of religious beliefs. These beliefs provide the basis for an integrated society, notwithstanding the economic and social differences between different classes.[167] MacIntyre claims that in such a culture morality and religion represent interdependent spheres of thought that together underpin social relationships and practices. Despite their interdependence in such a culture, MacIntyre denies that morality can be equated to a subset of religious beliefs, such as obedience to the will of God, as in that case ethical concepts would simply be redefined to mean "what God commands."[168] As a result "injunctions such as 'Do this because God commands it and what God commands is right and obedience to his commands produces certain goods' collapse into injunctions in which 'Do this because God commands it' are being reiterated in certain disguised and misleading ways."[169]

If ethical imperatives are identified with commands it becomes impossible to distinguish morality from the exercise of power.[170] There must therefore be an independent set of moral criteria through which that culture can determine that God's commands are appropriate.[171] These moral criteria relate to the role played by both moral imperatives and God's commands in the realization of an essential human nature. The point of conformity to the dictates of morality and of obedience to God's commands is that such

---

166. SMC (The Riddell Lectures: delivered 1964, published 1967) and RSA (The Bampton Lectures: delivered 1966, published1969).

167. SMC, 12.

168. RSA, 33.

169. RSA, 34.

170. RSA, 34–35.

171. RSA, 35.

submission leads to the fulfilment of human needs and desires. What would destabilize such a culture is a lack of agreement about what constitutes human nature and its fulfilment, as this would lead to a failure to agree on the meaning of moral propositions within that culture, and this in turn would weaken any connection between such propositions and their fulfilment through adherence to religious beliefs and injunctions. The point of both moral and religious beliefs would be lost with the loss of their interconnection with the achievement of human happiness and potential.

MacIntyre therefore argues that the coherence of such a culture depends on the universal acceptance of its moral principles and beliefs, an acceptance that will be reinforced by three cultural convictions. Firstly, by the belief that the community's moral code "is at least as well justified, and probably better justified than, any [other] particular theory about morality."[172] Secondly that within the community what counts as ethical practice only varies marginally (at worst) from what is laid down in the moral code, so that there is consistency between belief and behavior. And thirdly, that any suggestions that the moral code is mistaken are summarily dismissed, so that the nature and content of morality is not questioned.[173] Where there is a morality of this kind MacIntyre suggests that

> Theism furnishes an explanation for the authority and the fixed character of the rules, both by according them divine status and by providing grounds for the underlying belief in a single determinate human nature. God created men with just those goals, wants and needs which a way of life embodying the given rules will enable them to achieve. To the natural morality of men theism adds rules concerned with man's supernatural end, and a set of beliefs and practices concerning guilt, repentance, and forgiveness to provide for moral, as well as religious, failure. Theism and morality of this kind naturally and easily reinforce one another.[174]

MacIntyre thus envisages a society in which the moral code is rendered intelligible by an underlying naturalistic conceptualization of human needs and ends. Theism complements this picture of morality by locating the origins of that nature in the actions of a wise and good creator. However, the justification of the moral code does not lie in the fact that God wills us to obey (although he does) but because it is the means by which we can achieve the ultimate end of beings of our nature. The point of morality lies in its

---

172. RSA, 37.
173. RSA, 37.
174. RSA, 38.

relevance to our telos. Such beliefs about morality, human nature and God naturally support each other, and MacIntyre suggests that a loss of belief in one will destabilize belief in others.[175]

The Impact of Social and Conceptual Change

MacIntyre argues that prior to industrialization British society was united by a set of shared religious and ethical beliefs, notwithstanding the economic and cultural differences between different social groups.[176] But the evolution of capitalism has resulted in this social unity being dissolved into a set of distinct classes each with its separate and fragmented understanding of the moral life. As a result "in our society the notion of moral authority is no longer a viable one. For the notion of authority can only find application in a community in areas of life in which there is an agreed way of doing things, according to accepted rules."[177] This is because unless there is general agreement on the rules that govern a practice, there can be no appeal to authority to resolve disputes. This is true of games such as chess, but it is also true of ethical practices.[178] In our society the practices and agreements that underpinned moral authority have broken down, with different groups and classes formulating notions of morality and authority in different ways. As a result our culture is disunited. Enlightenment liberalism accommodates this diversity of perspective, but for MacIntyre it is not a solution to this problem: it is a symptom of our lack of moral direction.[179] One corollary of this lack of consensus on morality is the emergence of a range of diverse views of human nature. MacIntyre argues that within our society the view has developed that there is

> not just a single determinate human nature; that human nature is intensely malleable; and that around the relatively unchanging biological core society and culture may weave very different

---

175. There is a similarity between MacIntyre's analysis here and his diagnosis of our original moral framework in AV. In AV he writes with approval of Kant's postulates of practical reason in the Second Critique: "if my thesis is correct Kant was right; morality did in the eighteenth century, as a matter of historical fact, presuppose something very like the teleological scheme of God, freedom and happiness as the final crown of virtue which Kant propounds. Detach morality from that framework and you will no longer have morality, or, at the very least, you will have radically transformed its character" (AV, 56).

176. SMC, 12.

177. SMC, 53.

178. SMC, 53.

179. MC, 1–2.

The Roots of *After Virtue*

patterns, resulting in widely varying wants, needs, and goals. It is just because this belief is dominant now that no ultimate shared criteria can be invoked by which moral disputes may be resolved.

[As a result] theism has lost the morality which it logically presupposed; and the lack of social contact between theism and contemporary morality is at least partly to be explained by the lack of connection between theistic beliefs and modern moral beliefs.[180]

Social and conceptual change has rendered theism irrelevant to contemporary moral perspectives. But this lack of a coherent relationship between theism and morality means that for those who are not theists there is no longer a vocabulary in which they can ask and answer fundamental questions of meaning and purpose.[181] The development of secularism within Western Societies has resulted in the loss of a capacity to formulate questions about God, immortality, morality, freedom and the ends of human life in a coherent way.[182] As he puts it in SMC:

The consequence of this [process of secularisation] is that there remains no framework within which the religious questions can be systematically asked. For different classes the loss of a religious framework proceeds in different ways ... but for all there are left at last only fragments of a vocabulary in which to ask or to answer these questions.[183]

How has this conceptual erosion taken place? In RSA MacIntyre argues that theism faced two successive crises in entering the modern world.[184] The first crisis of theism was created by the emergence of the falsificationist perspective which is characteristic of natural science. Falsifiability became a criterion of significance in many areas of discourse and this created a crisis precisely because religious belief had previously been held in a form which implied that it was irrefutable by any set of events. "Theism was elaborated in the light of that pre-scientific culture where the anomalous and the exceptional are not permitted to falsify existing beliefs."[185] However, the emergence of falsifiability as a criterion of epistemic justification meant that theism had either to adopt a form in which it met that criterion

180. RSA, 44.
181. RSA, 52.
182. MC, 2.
183. SMC, 30.
184. RSA, 9–10.
185. RSA, 10.

of significance, or repudiate the relevance of that criterion to the special area of belief represented by religion. The first type of response required the reconstruction of theistic beliefs into the form of a deist hypothesis which could be defended in the same way in which any scientific hypothesis might be defended. The second type of response required the adoption of a fideist interpretation of the nature of belief, and the refusal to engage in debate about religion in accordance with the standards of the secular world.[186] In practice, the first crisis of theism encouraged the development of deistic reinterpretations of religious belief in an attempt to make these beliefs conform to the requirements of falsifiability.

However, MacIntyre argued that the evolution of the critical standards of modern culture meant that, by the middle of the nineteenth century, refutability had become "a necessary standard of warrantable belief at every point."[187] At the same time belief in the deist God invented in the seventeenth and eighteenth centuries, was being eroded by the emergence of new kinds of scientific findings.[188] These changes resulted in a further and more acute crisis of faith, which led to renewed attempts to construct a theological and communal space in which theistic commitments could be sustained. For MacIntyre, this second type of response has been characterized by "a total rejection of the attempt to adapt theism to the climate of secular thought, and an endeavour to preserve a theistic enclave in both thought and life. Rationally, this takes the form of insisting on the idiosyncrasy of religious concepts and beliefs."[189]

Both the deist and fideist strategies represented the characteristic responses of a culture in which the question of belief or unbelief remained of central importance. However, the intense crises of faith described in Victorian literature[190] have become increasingly irrelevant to a contemporary society in which the number of people who are either committed Christians or atheists is dwarfed by the numbers who are indifferent to both religion and its atheist alternative. The consequence of this process of secularization is that our received moral code has lost its original theistic anchor, an anchor which originally emphasized the relevance of ethical behavior to realizing our potential nature. This tendency has been reinforced by the growth

---

186. RSA, 11.

187. RSA, 14.

188. RSA, 14.

189. RSA, 15; there is a striking resemblance between MacIntyre's description of this strategy and his own position in LS.

190. In RSA MacIntyre discusses the crisis of faith of the eponymous hero of Mrs. Humphrey Ward's novel *Robert Elsmere* as an example of the intense concern around belief and unbelief in the Victorian period.

The Roots of *After Virtue*

in liberal individualism in moral thought, the impact of industrialization and urbanization, and the consequent disruption of communities and social relationships.[191] These factors have resulted in a diversity of moral views and the development of the cultural assumption that "rival moral views are essentially irreconcilable, that there are no shared criteria to which men may appeal in order to settle fundamental disputes."[192]

As a consequence of these social and conceptual changes, theism is looked upon as an "alien cult."[193] Members of that cult may find their moral principles and religious beliefs mutually reinforcing, but their belief in the coherence and complementarity of these beliefs will appear incomprehensible to the non-theistic majority. But the loss of theistic conceptual resources in secular society has not been replaced by an alternative vocabulary which enables that society to address the issues of human purpose. As a result that society still exhibits dependence on "a strong vestigial Christianity, manifested whenever at times of birth, marriage, and death questions about meaning, purpose, and survival become inescapable."[194] However, this dependence on religion at times of ritual importance could not hide the fact that

> What our children are left with is on the one hand a vestigial Christian vocabulary of a muddled kind and on the other an absence of any alternative vocabulary in which to raise the kind of issues which it is necessary to raise if there is to be no mere assessment of means, but some kind of explicit agreement or disagreement about social and moral ends ... It is the product of the history of the whole of our society, and the whole of society shares the same fate.[195]

Christianity has faltered in the face of urbanization and the resultant processes of social and moral change. MacIntyre argues that two theological responses to these changes have become apparent in the modern world. On the one hand there has been a further retreat into fideism. At the other extreme an adoption of religious liberalism which has resulted in the loss of "any distinctive theological content"[196] to belief, and which has created a religion whose formal content has become indistinguishable from atheism.[197]

191. RSA, 40–43.
192. RSA, 44.
193. RSA , 45.
194. SMC, 30–31.
195. SMC, 36.
196. SMC, 68.
197. SMC, 69.

But this secularization of religion has left behind a lacuna in our moral life which is filled by a religiose return to Christianity at the major turning points of life because there is no coherent alternative:

> The suggestion which I have made in these lectures, that we cannot do with Christianity in the modern world, but often cannot do without it entirely either, because we have no other vocabulary in which to raise certain kinds of questions, could be framed once more in terms of our inability to respond to the facts of death ... This is one of the great cultural and social gaps in our lives, but it is quite clear that in face of this particular crisis Christians have been in the same difficulty as everyone else.[198]

Marxism and Christianity

The denuded ability of mid-twentieth century Christianity to articulate a response to the reality of death, and its apparent transformation into a secular and arguably non-theistic version of religion left people in Western societies with a fragmentary and inadequate means of articulating an understanding of their nature and destiny. Marxism had provided an alternative to this religious worldview because:

> [Marxism is] the only systematic doctrine in the modern world that has been able to translate ... the hopes men once expressed, and could not but express in religious terms, into the secular project of understanding societies and expressions of human possibility and history as a means of liberating the present from the burdens of the past, and so constructing the future.[199]

But the problem for MacIntyre was that, by the time he came to revise MI for its re-publication as *Marxism and Christianity* in 1968, he held that neither Marxism nor Christianity could be accepted as true in any unproblematic sense. In MC MacIntyre suggests that Marxism has to be treated as "a doctrine that we cannot adhere to because there are truths which it cannot accommodate, yet also a doctrine we cannot entirely discard because it embodies truths inseparable from their connection with Marx's general theoretical formulations."[200]

---

198. SMC, 69–70.
199. MC, 115.
200. MC, 117.

For MacIntyre, both Marxism and Christianity embody truths not otherwise available to contemporary culture, but the difficulty with holding Marxism to be true as a description of social and economic development is that its predictions have been falsified by historical events, notwithstanding the attempts by some adherents to modify its doctrines to accommodate such challenges.[201] This process of modification had, for MacIntyre, destroyed the organic relationship between Marxist theory, Marxist prediction, and Marxist moral imperatives and values. Once this organic connection is denied, there is no fundamental justification for adopting a Marxist perspective.

> Theory is precisely not a set of opinions which individuals may or may not happen to choose to adopt. But just this is what Marxism has become: a set of "views" which stand in no kind of organic relationship to an individual's social role or identity, let alone his real position in the class structure. And in becoming like this, Marxism has been "practiced" in precisely the same way as that in which religion has been practiced . . . as . . . a private talismanic aid for the individual . . .[202]

Implications

Whatever the merits of the schematized cultural history Macintyre sets out in SMC and RSA, he expresses a vision of a pre-modern society in which religion and morality reinforce each other so that neither is thrown into doubt. Such a society cannot be recreated in the modern world, even if this were considered desirable. And the desirability of such a return to a pre-modern culture is questionable, given the dependency of such a culture on the unquestioned authority of its culturally determined moral standards and practices. There may be widely differing cultures in which moral code and religious belief are mutually reinforcing, each society reflecting contrasting views of human nature and destiny. On what basis would we choose between the merits of the beliefs embodied in such different cultures? MacIntyre's sociological claim that such cultures support a stable belief system does nothing to substantiate their conflicting claims to legitimacy. MacIntyre may have a personal preference for the moral certainty that characterizes such a society but without further argument this certainty is unlikely to be attractive to those who value individualism.

201. MC, 118–22.
202. MC, 122–23.

Christianity or Marxism might provide the foundations of such arguments, but if they are reduced to the status of beliefs which are arbitrarily adopted, they would also appear to lack any rational justification. They may provide an attractive and satisfying way of conceptualizing the relationship between the individual and society, but the adoption or rejection of such a perspective would appear to depend on choices to which argument and justification are irrelevant. But this is not the end of the story. MacIntyre argues that those who entirely reject Marxism and Christianity tend to do so from a perspective which rules out of court not merely Marxist theory or Christian belief, but any definitive account of human nature, and any naturalistic account of ethical concepts based on a teleological understanding of that nature. This rejection of teleology will frustrate all attempts to provide a wider justification for a moral perspective:

> Not only are the moral attitudes of Marx, or the analysis of past history, or the predictions about the future abandoned; so is the possibility of any doctrine which connects moral attitudes, beliefs about the past, and beliefs in future possibility. The lynch pin of this rejection is the liberal belief that facts are one thing values another—and that the two realms are logically independent of each other. This belief underpins the liberal rejection of Christianity as well as the liberal rejection of Marxism . . . But for both Marxism and Christianity only the answer to questions about the character of nature and society can provide the basis for an answer to the question: "But how ought I to live?" For the nature of the world is such that that in discovering the order of things I also discover my own nature and those ends which beings such as myself must pursue if we are not to be frustrated in certain predictable ways. Knowledge of nature and society is thus the principle determinant of action.[203]

For MacIntyre, what is required for a coherent and convincing account of morality is a justification of the ontological presuppositions which underpin a set of beliefs about human nature, the nature of society, and the nature of the world in which they are located. If I am able to discover the nature of that world I will also be able to discover my own nature and my telos. I will be able to make a justifiable distinction between the person that I am now and the person that I should strive to become in the future. My descriptions of these facts will close the logical gap between "is" and "ought," because what I ought to do will be determined by my account of my nature and its telos. The creation of a rationally justified and widely accepted account of

---

203. MC, 123–24.

human nature will render moral arguments resolvable. But this way of reconstructing the intelligibility of moral discourse is convincing only if there is some essential human nature to be discovered, a question that MacIntyre eventually addressed first in AV and then (more successfully) in DRA, as we will see in chapter 2.

1.7 A Short History of Ethics

MacIntyre's analysis of the relationship between social structure, theistic belief and morality suggests that confidence in the justification of a moral code will be a contingent feature of a particular form of society. Cultures in which all groups share the same ethical and religious presuppositions and principles will accept the authority of their moral framework. Other societies that are characterized by religious and ethical diversity, such as our own, will debate the justification of different moral perspectives, but will not be able to turn to shared criteria in order to resolve these debates. However, the theistic society that MacIntyre envisages in RSA and SMC does not possess criteria for determining the justification of a moral perspective that are superior to those available to our own culture. Rather, an unquestioned consensus over the truth of its moral judgments means that there is no need for such criteria to be formulated. Once the question of the justification of these judgments is raised, the culture may discover that it lacks the resources needed to deal with such a challenge, precisely because its beliefs have previously been accepted without question. And once the battle to formulate justification commences, the society will begin to engage in the same irresolvable debates that characterize our own moral discourse. The implication of MacIntyre's account of the interdependency of religious and ethical beliefs in RSA and SMC is that an ethical perspective cannot be justified on compelling rational grounds, but only in terms of its authority for a particular cultural group. If this is the case, we appear to be left with a position in which cultural conditioning, moral individualism or existential choice are the only grounds for adopting one morality rather than another. If moral concepts are shaped by culture and history, are there any grounds for holding one set to be superior to another?

The relationship between social structure and the evolution of ethical concepts was explored in the most significant publication of MacIntyre's first period of philosophical development, *A Short History of Ethics* (1966).[204] The argument of SHE can be summarized as follows. Analytic moral philosophy has conceptualized itself as exploring the significance of moral notions, as

---

204. MacIntyre, *A Short History of Ethics*—henceforth SHE.

if such notions exist in some timeless transcendental realm of universal and invariable meaning. In this realm, it is legitimate to answer questions such as "What is good?" "What is the nature of a moral imperative?" without reference to the cultural context in which these terms are embedded. MacIntyre argues against this position by pointing out that moral concepts change as social life changes and develops. Moral concepts are embodied in and partly constitutive of forms of social life, and therefore understanding a moral concept is part of the process of understanding the society and historical milieu in which it is embedded—and vice versa.[205] The history of ethics illustrates the way in which moral concepts change and evolve in response to social change and how in turn they influence that change. Moral concepts are not therefore semantically independent of social and cultural facts, but nor are they logically entailed by any set of such facts.

Analytic moral philosophy in the twentieth century had ignored the dependency of moral concepts on cultural context, but in doing so it created for itself the problem of giving a coherent account of moral discourse without reference to the facts of social life. As a result this type of moral philosophy was characterized by three main approaches which assumed that moral judgments must be logically independent of matters of fact. Intuitionist approaches claimed that the significance of moral concepts is derived from their capacity to act as names of simple non-natural qualities that defy further definition, as in the work of G. E. Moore.[206] Emotivism, characterized particularly by the work of C. L. Stevenson, conceptualized moral concepts as expressing feelings of approval or disapproval and as enjoining the listener to share these responses.[207] The prescriptivism of R. M. Hare argued that the essence of moral judgments lay in their formal structure as universally applicable imperatives (including being applicable to the person uttering the judgment).[208]

All three approaches denied that moral argument can be resolved by reference to the facts of social life. The intuitionist's claim that ethical concepts are the names of unanalysable moral qualities implies that rational argument is irrelevant in moral debate: one simply intuits what is good or right. Argument is equally irrelevant to emotivism: a moral judgment is the expression of a preference, combined with an encouragement to the listener to adopt the same attitude. Prescriptivism allows for moral argument, but only for arguments in which an evaluative major premise is already included

---

205. SHE, 1–2.
206. SHE, 242–44.
207. SHE, 249–50.
208. SHE, 252–55.

in the set of premises from which the evaluative judgment is derived. Moral judgments, cannot, therefore, be derived from non-evaluative premises. As a consequence, all three theories deny the possibility of demonstrating the truth of ethical judgments by reference to factual premises.[209]

If evaluative judgments are logically independent of factual judgments, the adoption of particular evaluative premises cannot be justified except by reference to further evaluative premises. These fundamental evaluative premises must simply be adopted by the individual. Ultimately, therefore, intuitionism, emotivism, and prescriptivism all lead to an individualism in which the sole source of ethical standards is the expression of a person's own arbitrary moral choice. Such individual choice is conceptualized as entirely free, undetermined by other non-evaluative criteria, and implies a strong relativism with respect to ethical judgments. As a result, MacIntyre suggests that twentieth-century analytic moral philosophy ends in a position which is similar to that of Sartre's existentialism.[210]

MacIntyre argues that what is required for rational argument and resolvable debate in any discourse is the capacity to determine which assertions are true and which are false, and ultimately this requires some accepted criterion for determining which statements embody correct judgments and which do not.[211] For example, to ask the question "What is the good for man?" in the way that Aristotle and Plato asked that question, is to presuppose that there is some criterion against which such a good can be identified. If there is no such criterion then the question itself ceases to have a point, as there is no basis for choosing between competing answers. He acknowledges that it does not follow from this that there *is* such a criterion but the intelligibility of the question and the possibility of identifying such a criterion stand or fall together.[212]

In SHE MacIntyre argues that there have been societies (such as that of Homeric Greece)[213] in which evaluative concepts, expectations of social roles, and the ends presupposed in these roles are so organically linked that there is indeed a shared capacity to determine the truth of evaluative judgments, because such evaluation can be tightly linked to the performance of these roles. In this context what counts as a good man or a good woman is a matter of conformity to the rules implicit or explicit in moral language

---

209. See SHE, 241–61.
210. SHE, 260.
211. SHE, 85.
212. SHE, 84.
213. SHE, chapter 2; MacIntyre explores the relationship between understanding of human nature and moral code in Homeric Greece in greater detail in WJWR, chapter 2.

and the corresponding social structures.[214] However, there may be considerable variation in evaluative standards between different cultures. Different cultures that have adopted similar social practices, as is the case in mathematics, will have similar concepts of correct performance. Such cultures will show consistency in their judgments of performance and truth in these shared areas of practice. However, other, more complex, evaluative judgments may relate to evaluative criteria that are specific to the distinctive forms of social life which are unique to a particular culture. The intelligibility and justification of such judgments will depend on familiarity with that culture and its particular practices, and these judgments will not necessarily be comprehensible to an observer unfamiliar with these practices. To assert that someone is a good cricketer would appear to be nothing but an arbitrary expression of approval to someone from a culture which lacked the concept of games and the practices that surround them, for example.[215]

On this interpretation of moral language, the intelligibility of a moral judgment depends on identifying the social practices with which those judgments are associated, and on understanding the criteria for appropriate performance associated with those practices. Such criteria may of course differ with respect to the different practices in question. As a result of this, MacIntyre suggests that the idea that there could be a *single* criterion of truth for all moral questions is incorrect. Indeed, he suggests that this was a mistake made by both Plato and Aristotle:

> Both assume that if the chain of justifications which are constituted by answers to questions about the good for men is to be a chain of rational argument, there must be essentially only one such chain and there must be one essential point at which it reaches a final conclusion (the Form of the Good or eudaemonistic contemplation). This is of course a mistake.[216]

The reason that this is a mistake is because what counts as the human good (for example) depends on the particular social structures and practices in which the question is raised, and their associated activities and ends. Arguments and judgments as to the human good will therefore differ from culture to culture. Particular social structures have different moralities, and each morality also carries with it a corresponding vision of human nature.[217]

The problem with this formulation is that, once again, it is a position that is open to the challenge of relativism. If moral concepts vary in their

---

214. SHE, 256.
215. SHE, 86.
216. SHE, 84–85.
217. SHE, 259.

meaning from culture to culture and can only be understood in terms of that cultural context, then there appears to be no set of ethical judgments that can be demonstrated to be logically and ethically superior to any other. We are always open to the challenge that we are simply promoting the values of a particular culture. MacIntyre sought to deflect the charge of relativism by suggesting that the commonalities of human life mean that "there are certain evaluative truths that cannot be escaped . . . In any human group some notions of truth and justice necessarily find some foothold. Moreover . . . in any human group it is almost inconceivable that certain qualities such as friendliness, courage and truthfulness will not be valued."[218]

The collaborative nature of human living, the need for language to be used consistently to be intelligible means that rule following has to be embedded in any human society. But as he points out, this fact gives us no criteria for distinguishing between the very different concepts of justice and truth (for example) that may operate within disparate societies, linked to their different practices, rules, and evaluative criteria. As a consequence the MacIntyre of SHE can sound very like any other relativist and individualist citizen of a Western liberal society: "Conceptual conflict is endemic in our situation because of the depth of our moral conflicts. Each of us therefore has to *choose* both with whom we wish to be morally bound and by what ends, rules, and virtues we wish to be guided."[219]

MacIntyre evaluated the position he had adopted in the first edition of *A Short History of Ethics* in his Preface to the Second Edition[220] which was published in 2000. MacIntyre acknowledges that he may have inadvertently given the impression of relativism in the first edition and suggests that this impression related to his inability to reconcile two points. The point that led to the impression of relativism was his recognition that there is no external criterion by which one can justify a belief in the fundamental principles that underpin each ethical theory. However, the point which was not given sufficient weight is the fact that each theory *also* claims to be presenting a universal rational truth about the nature of moral judgment and obligation, and therefore has to be taken seriously with respect to the evaluation of that claim. However, if there is no universal criterion of justification that can be applied to each moral standpoint, the assessment of their claims to universal truth must be undertaken from the standpoint either of the standards of some competing viewpoint, or from the perspective of the internal standards of the tradition making the claim to universal validity. He suggests

---

218. SHE, 92.
219. SHE, 259 (emphasis added).
220. Preface to SHE, 2nd Edition, xiv–xv.

that it was his failure to articulate this point in the first edition that had led to the accusation that he was relativist:

> What I had certainly been unable to do was to reconcile two positions, to each of which I was committed. The first was that which gave the appearance of relativism. Each fundamental standpoint in moral philosophy not only has its own mode of conceptualising and understanding the moral life, which gives expression to the claims of some actual or possible type of social order, but each has its own set of first principles, to which its adherents appeal to vindicate the claims of their own standpoint to universality and to rational superiority over its rivals. What I had failed to stress adequately was that it was indeed a claim to universality and to rational superiority—indeed a claim to possess the truth about the nature of morality—that had been advanced from the standpoint of each particular culture and each major moral philosophy. And what I had not therefore taken account of was that these philosophical attempts to present rationally justifiable universal claims to moral allegiance . . . had generated for each major moral philosophy its own particular difficulties and problems, difficulties and problems sometimes acknowledged, and sometimes not. The subsequent history of each such moral philosophy revealed the extent to which each possessed or lacked the resources necessary to become aware of and to resolve those difficulties and problems—each by its own particular standards. And by this standard the major claimants in modern moral philosophy seemed to me then and to me now to fail.[221]

This passage provides a summary of his mature philosophy, and it is perhaps misleading of him to claim that his position in SHE only gave the appearance of relativism, given that it was written before he had formulated that mature position. The MacIntyre of SHE is clearly relativist in the unproblematic sense of acknowledging that ethical frameworks and judgments vary from culture to culture and are relative to the conceptual resources and standards embedded in the social practices of each culture. And if there is no generally (and legitimately) accepted criteria by which one which can assess the competing claims to universal truth and the internal standards used to justify these claims then one appears to be left with a more fundamental version of relativism in which the norms that underpin judgment are also relative to each culture. MacIntyre's repudiation of relativism in his mature philosophy is based on his view that one can hold both that there are no

---

221. Preface to SHE 2nd Edition, xv–xvi.

transcendent criteria of justification but that, nonetheless, one perspective can be held to be superior to another on grounds that have more than tribal validity. This book evaluates and seeks to strengthen that claim.

1.8 Implications

This chapter has reviewed a number of attempts made by the early MacIntyre to provide an account of how belief in a "rational myth" might be legitimately embraced as a framework for living a good life. MacIntyre's aim in his earliest published work (MI) was to respond to the anomie of a society fragmented by the growth of secularism, by re-creating a religious and political framework that could underpin a community in which human potential could be realized. Such a project required change to the contemporary understanding of human nature. The three (quasi-Aristotelian) elements of that revised interpretation are human-nature-as-it-is-now, human-nature-as-it-would-be-if-perfected, and some account of how this change could be achieved. From a Marxist viewpoint, human-nature-as-it-is-now is a nature restricted and deformed by the political and economic relationships that characterize a capitalist society. From a Christian perspective it is a nature deformed by sin which can only begin to change through God's grace.

In MI MacIntyre attempted to integrate these perspectives by re-conceptualizing Marxism as a deviant, materialist, form of Christianity that had smuggled the salvific capacity of Christian belief into the twentieth century. In doing this it made the vision of salvation available to a society which had otherwise lost the ability to understand itself in the radical, liberationist terms of early Christianity. MacIntyre's dissatisfaction with the ability of the established Churches to free themselves from their compromises with contemporary forms of social and political life led him to call for new forms of community which could embody Christian and Marxist ideals. MI therefore presages some of the social diagnosis that is embedded in AV, and MI also calls for a solution similar to that proposed in the mature work, through the establishment of new forms of community in which forgotten virtues could flourish once more.

MacIntyre describes Christianity and Marxism as "rational myths." He argues that such myths are rational because they have formulated rigorous internal standards of argument and justification, but this leaves unanswered the question as to whether their founding presuppositions are themselves open to justification, and if so, in what way. His work on the nature of religious belief provides a window onto his attempts to address this question. MacIntyre, like George Lindbeck, was critical of liberal theologies and their attempts to establish the plausibility of belief by re-defining the essence of the Christian religion in terms that were intended to be plausible to contemporary sensibilities.[222] As we saw in section 1.4 above, he also rejected arguments that attempted to justify religious belief on experiential grounds. He was equally skeptical of the deist strategy of seeking to ensure the conformity of religious belief to post-Enlightenment criteria of significance.[223] He therefore rejected accounts of the justification of religious belief that relied on evidence that was external to the Christian belief system. In DCB he suggested that a gain in the intelligibility of a person's experience of the world as a result of the adoption of a religious belief system could be one ground for belief. However, whether such a gain occurred depended, he acknowledged, on the kind of person you happened to be,[224] but this appears to point towards contingent facts about personality as comprising the most significant basis for religious conviction.

The inability to offer cogent arguments to justify religious belief led MacIntyre to adopt a form of fideism in LS, in which the act of commitment to a religion has become a matter of passion rather than reason. MacIntyre, however, subsequently rejected this account of the grounds of belief on the falsificationist basis that it rendered religion irrefutable by any set of events, and that any irrefutable belief system must be vacuous. However, when this rejection of fideism is linked to his prior rejection of the idea that there might be universal standards of justification, it suggests that the standards of justification to which one can appeal can only be internal to the belief system itself. But this observation then raises the question, "How is it possible to have a non-vacuous account of the justification of a position where the criteria for justification are internal to that position?"

Similar difficulties around the question of justification arose in his discussion of Marxist beliefs, and in his discussion of the nature of ethics. The belief in a metaphysical perspective that is sufficiently robust to underpin a coherent account of the moral life appears to depend on the prior acceptance of presuppositions about the nature of the universe, human nature and telos that characterize particular cultures at particular points in their historical development. But the nature of these assumptions will embody and reflect the specific characteristics of that society's cultural and conceptual history. As a result, there will be many different moralities. Each will reflect different assumptions about the nature of the world and of human beings, and

---

222. See RSA, 25ff. This theme is one which MacIntyre also explores in several other publications including SMC, 67ff. and MacIntyre "God and the Theologians."

223. See DCB, 64–65 and chapter 8.

224. DCB, 80–81.

provide different accounts of the goals which that nature presupposes. Unless these ontological presuppositions can be held to be justified in some way—or at least held to be superior to other rival notions—the associated ethical position will appear to be arbitrarily adopted. As a result, MacIntyre's position not only gives an impression of relativism but also leads to an image of the individual adopting their principles on a-rational grounds. Social, cultural and psychological factors shape the individual's choice of their ethical perspective, but ultimately that choice is as unjustifiable as the choice of a liberal individualist ethic or a Sartrean existentialism.

What I have shown in this chapter is that MacIntyre's early development can be understood in terms of the tension between two philosophical imperatives. The first imperative was to establish a comprehensive metaphysical position which could integrate an understanding of human nature, community, and ethics, and which could therefore underpin social action designed to promote the realization of human potential. The second imperative was the need to provide a rational justification for such a position. His inability to provide such justification led him to temporarily embrace a form of fideism, but by the end of the 1960s he was unable to accept the relativism implicit in such a position. The incompatibility between these two imperatives reflected the fact that commitment to such comprehensive metaphysical positions could not meet the requirements of an Enlightenment concept of universal standards of rationality. What MacIntyre needed in order to resolve this problem was, firstly, a persuasive Aristotelian account of human nature and potentiality; and secondly, an alternative account of rationality to the dominant Enlightenment model. MacIntyre sought to construct these alternatives in the works that embody his mature position, and these works are considered in the following chapter.

2

MACINTYRE'S MATURE POSITION

2.1 Overview

As noted in section 1.3 above, the consequence of MacIntyre's inability to legitimize belief in any comprehensive metaphysical position was that, by 1968, he had found himself incapable of identifying with any substantive religious, political or philosophical viewpoint.[1] This profound uncertainty resulted in the period of painful self-reflection that MacIntyre described in his interview with *Cogito*.[2] This re-evaluation of his philosophical standpoint ultimately led to the construction of the mature position which he set out in his works from *After Virtue* onwards. MacIntyre's personal lack of certitude reflected the broader uncertainties of a culture defined by two intellectual crises. The first crisis had been created by the irresolvable character of modern moral debate. The second crisis was created by the recognition that analytic philosophy had been unable to resolve the fundamental questions of ontology and epistemology.

For MacIntyre, both crises had emerged from the collapse of the Christian theistic framework which had underpinned ethical discourse and the understanding of knowledge in pre-Enlightenment European thought. The ontological, epistemological, and ethical certainties that had characterized this framework were challenged in post-medieval philosophy by the demand for rational justification. Enlightenment philosophy had sought to

---

1. Introduction to MC 2nd Edition, xix and xxiii.
2. MacIntyre, "Interview with Cogito," 268–69.

replace received beliefs with incorrigible foundations for both knowledge and ethics, but the failure of these Enlightenment projects had replaced certainty with doubt, and had encouraged an epistemological and ethical relativism that contemporary philosophy lacked the resources to repudiate.

Formulating a coherent and persuasive account of ethics in the cultural context defined by these crises required not only the construction of a renewed understanding of the foundations of morality; it also required a reconstruction of the notions of rational justification that characterize our culture.[3] The four major works of MacIntyre's mature period therefore constitute a complex meditation around three themes. Firstly, the (re)construction of a coherent ethic which can underpin human flourishing and community. Secondly, the (re)construction of an account of human nature that can underpin such an ethical framework; and thirdly, the construction of an account of rational justification that can warrant belief in the presuppositions about human nature that give such an ethical position its coherence.[4]

These themes are each addressed in two or more of the main publications of his mature period. AV and DRA set out MacIntyre's substantive ethical position, and together with WJWR and TRV, they also present his reconstruction of an Aristotelian account of human nature. AV and TRV provide an analysis of the crisis of rational justification, while WJWR in particular articulates his alternative to Enlightenment accounts of rationality. Given the complex interaction between these different works a wholly chronological exposition would be repetitive. Therefore, while this chapter seeks to maintain a historical perspective on the major works of MacIntyre's mature period, it also follows a thematic approach.

Firstly, it provides an exposition of the nature of the twin crises of modernity that precipitated MacIntyre's personal epistemological crisis, drawing on AV and TRV (section 2.2). Secondly, it provides a summary of his attempt to reinstate an Aristotelian ethics in AV (section 2.3), and his revision and development of that account in DRA (section 2.4). The discussion of DRA evaluates the extent to which MacIntyre's position provides a successful response to the moral relativism implicit in modern moral philosophy, and articulates his considered response to the second major theme

---

3. AV 2nd Edition Postscript, 266–67.

4. MacIntyre is not, of course, alone in addressing the issue of the modern denial of a factual basis for moral judgment on the one hand and the need to construct an alternative account of justification on the other. For example Charles Taylor has also sought to construct an account of ethics which focuses on a naturalistic account of the good and an alternative account of epistemology which rejects Enlightenment foundationalism (see Taylor, *Sources of the Self* and "Overcoming Epistemology").

identified above: the (re)construction of an account of human nature that can underpin an Aristotelian ethics.

In promoting Aristotelianism and criticizing alternative ethical systems, MacIntyre is utilizing some implicit account of the superiority of one philosophical position to another. This account is adumbrated in AV and made explicit in WJWR, and section 2.5 provides an analysis of this alternative account of superiority and justification. Section 2.6 summarizes the overall architecture of MacIntyre's final position, and identifies some unresolved issues, which will be addressed in the rest of this book.

2.2 Two Crises of Contemporary Thought

The Crisis of Moral Debate

In AV MacIntyre develops arguments which are similar to those first put forward by Elizabeth Anscombe in a seminal paper published in 1958, whose influence MacIntyre has acknowledged.[5] In this paper Anscombe argues, *inter alia,* that

> the concepts of obligation, and duty—*moral* obligation and *moral* duty, that is to say—and of what is *morally* right and wrong, and of the *moral* sense of "ought," ought to be jettisoned [from our ethical vocabulary] if this is psychologically possible; because they are survivals, or derivatives from survivals, from an earlier conception of ethics which no longer generally survives, and are only harmful without it.[6]

Anscombe argues that our ethical concepts have changed their meaning over the centuries, while the words used to express these concepts have remained unchanged.[7] Some elements of our ethical language have evolved within an Aristotelian/Thomist framework, such as discourse about virtue and natural law. However, the language of virtues which derives from such a framework is only intelligible on the basis of an understanding of human nature and its telos that has almost disappeared from contemporary Western culture. And once the concepts that underpin that linguistic framework have been modified or discarded, the bones and sinews that connected the Aristotelian elements of our moral vocabulary have vanished. Similarly, the

---

5. AV, 53.
6. Anscombe, "Modern Moral Philosophy," 1; emphasis original.
7. AV, 10.

erosion of a law conception of ethics has left concepts such as "ought" isolated from the conceptual framework which originally gave them their point.[8]

Anscombe argues that one consequence of this disintegration of conceptual coherence is that modern moral philosophy is built around conceptual problems which would be dissolved if ethicists understood the historical context within which our ethical language has evolved. She contends that there is a need to rehabilitate an Aristotelian ethic in order to overcome the malaise of contemporary ethical theory. If such rehabilitation is to be successful, Aristotle's ethical concepts would need to be reinterpreted within the conceptual resources available to modernity. Anscombe suggests that this requires the construction of an adequate contemporary philosophy of psychology[9] in order to address the "huge gap, at present unfillable as far as we are concerned, which needs to be filled by an account of human nature, human action, the type of characteristic a virtue is, and above all [an account] of human 'flourishing.'"[10]

In AV MacIntyre develops and extends the philosophical agenda Anscombe had identified.[11] MacIntyre elaborates on Anscombe's position to argue that contemporary ethical debates reflect two incompatible characteristics. Firstly, different moral perspectives are characterized by conceptual incommensurability. As a result, each moral perspective is able to proffer arguments which proceed logically from its specific premises, but the premises which underpin different perspectives "are such that we possess no rational way of weighing the claims of one as against another. For each premise employs some quite different normative or evaluative concept from the others, so that the claims made upon us are of quite different kinds."[12]

Thus premises which are constructed in terms of some notion of "rights" as the fundamental moral concept, for example, cannot be expressed in terms of a set of statements about "success and survival,"[13] and nor can they be translated into propositions couched in other moral concepts (such as justice, freedom or innocence) without change in meaning. Our adopted premises may justify our moral arguments, but these premises are not in themselves justifiable with respect to some broader criterion of validation which has been established within our society. MacIntyre points out that "from our rival conclusions we can argue back to our rival premises,

---

8. Anscombe, "Modern Moral Philosophy," 5.
9. Ibid., 15.
10. Ibid., 18.
11. AV, 53.
12. AV, 8.
13. AV, 8.

but when we do arrive at our premises argument ceases and the invocation of one premise against another becomes a matter of pure assertion and counter-assertion."[14]

But if I am unable to offer good reasons for the adoption of my premises to others then we seem to be unable to demonstrate the rational superiority of one starting point over another, and it must appear that our selection of fundamental principles is the product of a non-rational decision or act of the will.[15] On this account, substantive moral positions occupy the same logical space as religious belief occupied in LS.[16] Once a set of beliefs has been adopted, rational argument becomes possible, but rational argument cannot precede commitment to the presuppositions of an ethical position.

MacIntyre identifies a second, conflicting, characteristic of modern moral debates. Such debates appear to presuppose the existence of universal and impersonal moral imperatives to which participants can appeal to support their argument, notwithstanding the incommensurability of their conflicting ethical perspectives. Thus in claiming that x is under an obligation to do Y, I am not simply asserting that I *want* her to do Y, as I may do if I am in a position of authority over her, but I am asserting that she is subject to some binding requirement that is independent of my will. Therefore our discourse both asserts the existence of universal and impersonal criteria of moral obligation, at the same time as that discourse emphasizes the arbitrary nature of the choice of underlying principles.[17] There is therefore an *aspiration* towards rational moral discourse within our culture, although our theoretical beliefs militate against the justification of these aspirations.[18]

The difficulties which MacIntyre identifies are rooted in social, cultural and conceptual change,[19] but these changes have largely gone unnoticed. As a result, we have arrived at a point in our cultural history which is characterized by dysfunctional ethical discourse and inconclusive moral debate.[20] The difficulties that characterize contemporary moral discourse reflect the fact that we have passed from an earlier culture in which the language of morals and the conceptual framework that underpinned that language formed an ordered whole, to a culture in which there is a disordered and partial relationship between moral concepts and our ethical language and moral

---

14. AV, 8.
15. AV, 8.
16. See section 1.4 above.
17. AV, 9.
18. AV, 9–10.
19. AV, 10.
20. AV, chapter 2 passim.

argument. We assume that irresolvable ethical debate will be characteristic of any culture,[21] and fail to recognize that this characteristic is a contingent feature of our particular social and conceptual history.

MacIntyre identifies emotivism as the form of moral philosophy that best represents the malaise of Western culture in the twentieth century. Expressionist and emotivist accounts of moral language seek to assimilate moral judgments to the expression of personal preferences or emotive responses. But such positions fail to take seriously the rational element that underpins moral discourse, evidenced by the fact that we seek to argue to a conclusive resolution of competing ethical judgments by offering (what we consider to be) good reasons for our evaluations. Expressivist accounts of ethics do not appear to allow for such reasons to play a role in moral judgment, and they do not therefore allow for a distinction between manipulative and non-manipulative social relations.[22] Once the justification of an ethical perspective is reduced to "I prefer X; so do X" there is no longer an appeal to standards of judgment that are independent of the individual's will, and persuasion simply involves seeking conformity to those preferences. Emotivism reduces ethical argument to a "clash of antagonistic wills."[23]

Emotivism is, therefore, a close relative of Nietzchean genealogy,[24] and for MacIntyre both emotivism and Nietzsche's philosophy represent the outcome of the Enlightenment's failure to establish an objective and generally accepted justification for ethics and morality.[25] MacIntyre argues that the collapse of this ambition had led to the assumption that the foundations of morality must rest on personal preference and individual choice alone. Emotivism avoids the problem of justifying ethical judgments by re-defining ethics in terms of attitudes and desires. However, in doing so it rules out the possibility of the rational resolution of moral argument through reference to some shared beliefs about the nature of the world and the nature of humanity. More generally, the emotivist, intuitionist, and consequentialist accounts of ethics that characterize modern moral philosophy are unable to demonstrate the truth of their fundamental premises, and therefore they can neither create a shared basis for moral argument, nor repudiate the claims of moral relativism.

21. AV, 11.
22. AV, 23.
23. AV, 9.
24. AV, 22.
25. AV, chapter 5.

The Crisis of Rational Justification

In our culture the type of fundamental ontological beliefs that might afford a resolution of moral argument are as contested as our competing ethical perspectives, and this has left the theoretical foundations of our ethical judgments unclear, as we saw in the discussion of MI and NMW in chapter 1. The crisis that characterizes modern ethical discourse runs parallel to a second, epistemological, crisis of modernity. MacIntyre describes this crisis in the following terms:

> what the progress of analytic philosophy has succeeded in establishing is that there are no grounds for belief in universal necessary principles—outside purely formal enquiries—except relative to some set of assumptions. Cartesian first principles, Kantian a priori truths, and even the ghosts of these notions that haunted empiricism for so long have all been expelled from philosophy.[26]

MacIntyre develops his argument by quoting David Lewis. Lewis had asserted that "our 'intuitions' are simply opinions; our philosophical theories are the same."[27] If this is the case, then there cannot be a final resolution to arguments about fundamental philosophical presuppositions, except in a few cases where the position put forward is so incoherent as to be unintelligible.[28] As a result, ethical and epistemological debates will be characterized by the fact that none of the sides engaged can demonstrate the final superiority of their position over that of others. This situation reflects the failure of the second Enlightenment project, that of finding universal and rational justifications for all elements of knowledge.

MacIntyre developed his analysis of the crisis of Enlightenment epistemology in the third of his four major mature works, *Three Rival Versions of Moral Enquiry* (TRV). This work was based on MacIntyre's contribution to the annual Gifford lecture series on natural theology, which he delivered in 1988, the year that WJWR was published. These books are complementary responses to the crisis of rational justification he identified in AV, and TRV also provides an illuminating account of the nature of the assumptions that underpin the Enlightenment notion of justification.

The Gifford lecture series had been endowed by Adam, Lord Gifford in 1885,[29] and MacIntyre argues that the endowment of these lectures reflected

---

26. AV 2nd Edition Postscript, 266–7.
27. AV, 267; quoted from Lewis, *Philosophical Papers: Volume 1*, x–xi.
28. AV, 267.
29. Gifford Lectures.org; http://www.giffordlectures.org/overview.asp.

MacIntyre's Mature Position

a view of universal knowledge as a comprehensive and universally accepted framework into which all aspects of science, natural theology and ethics could be incorporated. Gifford and his contemporaries visualized the structure and content of the ninth edition of the *Encyclopaedia Britannica* as a demonstration of progress towards this ideal.[30] The foundation stone of this project was the belief in a "unitary concept of rationality and of the rational mind" which would provide the basis for agreement both on data and on the interpretation of data so that any disputes about truth were ultimately decidable.[31] This unity was to be achieved through the application of the methods of science to all branches of knowledge, including theology.[32] Ultimately, therefore, there was to be no separation between objective scientific knowledge and religious belief. All knowledge would be unified under more and more comprehensive laws which would eventually embrace everything under natural theology.[33] But a hundred and more years later the ambitions of encyclopedia are no longer plausible to the contemporary sensibility.

For MacIntyre, what divides our culture from Lord Gifford's is threefold. Firstly, the encyclopedists assumed that there was a single conception of rationality shared by all intelligent beings, while we have alternative and conflicting conceptions of rationality. Secondly, they saw knowledge as an ordered whole, while we see many different types of enquiry and interpretations of knowledge, so the very idea of an ordered whole is brought into question. Thirdly, where they saw inevitable progress in knowledge we see the history of knowledge as marked by the sort of ruptures and discontinuities identified by Kuhn (for example),[34] who argued that the history of science is characterized by revolutions which replace one dominant mode of understanding a discipline with another, alternative, paradigm.[35]

These ideas are now the commonplaces of postmodernity. For MacIntyre, the inadequacy of the epistemological and ethical foundations of the Enlightenment project was illustrated by the failure of the attempts by figures such as Hume, Kant and Kierkegaard (among others) to articulate rational foundations for ethics.[36] This ethical project was finally undermined by Nietzsche, who recognized that there was no final objective and independent Archimedean point from which one could demonstrate objec-

30. TRV, 18.
31. TRV, 16–17.
32. TRV, 22.
33. TRV, 23.
34. TRV, 23–24.
35. See Kuhn, *Structure of Scientific Revolutions*, 84–91 and passim.
36. AV, chapter 4.

tive truth. For Nietzsche, "what remains fixed and binding about truth (and knowledge and duty and right)...is an unrecognised motivation serving an unacknowledged purpose."[37]

What is real for Nietzsche is the way in which human beings manipulate the concepts of truth and right in order to serve their purpose, through what he characterized as the "will-to-power."[38]

> So we have matched against each other two antagonistic views. The encyclopaedist's conception is of a single framework within which knowledge is discriminated from mere belief, progress towards knowledge is mapped, and truth is understood as the relationship of our knowledge to the world, through the application of...the rules of rationality as such. Nietzsche, as a genealogist, takes there to be a multiplicity of perspectives within each of which truth-from-a-point-of-view may be asserted, but no truth-as-such, an empty notion, about the world, an equally empty notion.[39]

Neither relativism/perspectivism nor encyclopedic optimism with respect to the possibility of universal knowledge is acceptable to Macintyre. His philosophy seeks to construct an alternative account of rationality and justified belief, that is neither dependent on the assumption that there are universal standards of justification and knowledge (as in encyclopedia), nor vulnerable to the challenge of a genealogical relativism.

The disintegration of the concepts of knowledge, order, and rationality that characterized the encyclopedic ideal have already been exemplified in Macintyre's early failures to construct some account of the justification of a comprehensive ontological and/or ethical position, as reviewed in chapter 1. Neither the easy fideism of LS with respect to religion, nor the falsificationism expressed in MI, nor the apparent relativism of SHE provided an answer to the issues he had sought to address in NMW. If a version of Aristotelianism is necessary to the construction of a robust account of the origin and justification of our moral principles, how can one reinstate an Aristotelian understanding of ethics in the contemporary world? *After Virtue* seeks to provide an answer to this question by setting out an account of human nature and of Aristotle's teleology that might be plausible in the modern world.

---

37. TRV, 35.
38. TRV, 35.
39. TRV, 42.

2.3 After Virtue

The Aristotelian Ethical Framework

MacIntyre argues in both NMW and AV that the Enlightenment ethical project was doomed because it had attempted to find justifications for moral concepts after they had become detached from the Aristotelian perspective in which they had originally been formulated. Such an Aristotelian perspective includes three main elements. Firstly, it presupposes that there is an overall good to which human life is or should be directed. It is the realization of that good "in a complete life" which acts as the telos of human existence.[40] Aristotle identifies this good with human flourishing or happiness.[41] Secondly an Aristotelian perspective requires a distinction between human nature as it is prior to the process of moral development which is necessary for the realization of that good, and human nature as it is when transformed through the acquisition of the virtues.[42] Thirdly it describes the characteristics or virtues which have to be acquired if that good is to be realized.[43] Within this Aristotelian framework, such virtues are not simply a means to an end that might be achieved through some other form of action. Their possession in large part constitutes the achievement of the telos of a human life. MacIntyre expresses this in AV when he says that "the exercise of the virtues is not . . . a means to the end of the good for man. For what constitutes the good for man is a complete human life lived at its best, and the exercise of the virtues is a necessary and central part of such a life, not a mere preparatory exercise to secure such a life."[44]

MacIntyre argues that this Aristotelian schema was elaborated but not discarded when it was incorporated into the pre-modern Christian worldview. For Aristotle, the human telos had to be achieved within this world by the realization of our potentiality as rational beings.[45] Within the Christian framework the realization of that telos had to be underpinned by the transforming power of God's grace and the acquisition of the virtues necessary to obey the natural law. As a result of this elaboration, moral injunctions

---

40. Aristotle, *The Nichomachean Ethics* (henceforth NE); Book 1, 1098a15-b5.

41. AV, 148; NE Book I, 1097a15-1097b25; the nature of happiness is not self-evident, of course, and Aristotle spends much time seeking to clarify its nature.

42. AV, 149-50; Aristotle emphasizes that the virtues do not arise through nature per se, but are constituted by habits of virtuous action acquired through training (NE Book II, 1103a10-1103a33).

43. AV, 52-53.

44. AV, 149.

45. NE, Book I, 1097b25-1098b5.

came to have a dual meaning, both as the means through which human potentiality could be achieved and as expressions of divine law. In addition, the Christian perspective added a further level to the understanding of the virtues:

> The table of virtues and vices has to be amended and added to and a concept of sin is added to the Aristotelian concept of error. The law of God requires a new kind of respect and awe. The true end of man can no longer be completely achieved in this world, but only in another.[46]

Within this Christianized framework, ethical assertions have a threefold function. They act as factual assertions about what is required for the achievement of human potentiality, statements about what the divine law is held to be, and injunctions that specify what ought to be done. Such assertions are not therefore logically independent of assertoric propositions, in sharp contrast to the divorce of "ought" from "is" claimed by twentieth century analytic moral philosophy. Their prescriptive and evaluative content follows from their function as descriptions of what is required to realize human telos.

The contemporary claim that one cannot derive ethical conclusions from any set of factual premises symbolizes the rift between a pre-modern and a modern understanding of ethics. MacIntyre contends that the roots of this claim lies in a change in the understanding of the nature of reason. In the medieval world the divine law was considered to be discoverable by human reason as well as being embodied in revealed religion. A combination of reason and revealed religion therefore provided at least a limited understanding of humanity's true end. MacIntyre argues that the emergence of "Protestantism and Jansenist Catholicism"[47] in the Enlightenment resulted in the construction of an account of reason as being so damaged by sin that it can acquire "*no* genuine comprehension of man's true end."[48] This pessimistic assessment of the capacity of reason resonated with the Enlightenment rejection of Aristotelian scholasticism to render the idea of the possibility of knowledge of an essential human nature related to a human telos implausible. Human reason became conceptualized as purely "calculative; it can discern truths of fact and mathematical relations but nothing more.

---

46. AV, 53.

47. AV, 53.

48. AV, 53 (emphasis original). This argument is similar to those put forward in RSA and SMC which were discussed in section 1.6.

In the realm of practice therefore it can speak only of means. About ends it must be silent."[49]

As a result of this change in the understanding of reason, human telos has been conceived as unknowable, and without the concept of a telos moral argument has been rendered irresolvable. Nietzsche had correctly diagnosed the intellectual bankruptcy of modern moral theory,[50] but his dismissal of the intelligibility of ethical discourse is justified if and only if the rejection of Aristotle is justified.[51] If a return to a teleological viewpoint is possible then moral discourse can be made coherent again. As a result, "the key question ... becomes[s]: can Aristotle's ethics, or something very like it, after all be vindicated?"[52] MacIntyre continues: "if a premodern view of morals and politics is to be vindicated against modernity, it will be in something like Aristotelian terms or not at all."[53]

MacIntyre's attempt at vindication involves the reconstruction of a conceptual framework that addresses the incoherence of contemporary moral discourse, and which can provide the scaffold for the formation of societies that can foster individual and communal realization. MacIntyre is not seeking to provide a *proof* of the fundamental elements of Aristotle's philosophy in doing this. His earlier studies had convinced him that conclusive demonstration was not possible, except in a very small number of cases.[54] Where conclusive demonstration is not possible (and this applies to politics and ethics), vindication and refutation have to be interpreted within a historical framework. One position is vindicated over another at some particular point in time when it can provide a more coherent and comprehensive account of the relevant facts than the opposing position, and when it is able to provide arguments against the opposing position to which that position has no rejoinder. Whether a position has been vindicated or refuted has to be judged in accordance with the standards of justification that apply at the time the question is raised. However, these standards may change over time, and additional information relevant to the evaluation of a position may also become available. A position such as Aristotelianism, which has been held to be refuted, may be reinstated if it is demonstrated that the initial arguments used to discredit the position no longer have

---

49. AV, 54.
50. Nietzsche, *The Gay Science*, section 335.
51. AV, 117.
52. AV, 118.
53. AV, 118.

54. MacIntyre acknowledges that it may be possible to refute a particular position in a very small number of cases and cites Gettier and Gödel as examples (AV, Postscript, 267).

force. Macintyre's task is not to prove that Aristotle was correct, but to show that a number of the conceptual problems that vitiate contemporary ethics can be resolved if an Aristotelian framework is adopted; that there are no conclusive arguments to repudiate such a framework; and that the adoption of this framework can then provide the basis for communities that are more effective in realizing human potential than their contemporary rivals.

MacIntyre identifies three key issues which would have to be addressed if this objective was to be achieved, each of which parallels an element in Anscombe's analysis of the challenges facing modern moral philosophy. Firstly, he would need to provide a teleological account of human identity.[55] Secondly, MacIntyre would need to provide an account of the virtues which clarifies their relationship to contemporary social life.[56] Thirdly, he would need to construct a contemporary account of human telos that avoids three difficulties in Aristotle's account of telos. Aristotle's teleology is based on the principle that "every activity, every enquiry, every practice aims at some good, for by 'the good' or 'a good' we mean that at which human beings characteristically aim."[57] Aristotle assumes that the biological essence of living organisms endows each being with an overall good or telos towards which their actions and development are ultimately directed. This fundamental principle of Aristotle's ethics is unacceptable to the MacIntyre of AV who rejected it as exemplifying "Aristotle's metaphysical biology."[58] MacIntyre therefore needed to provide an alternative way of incorporating teleology into our understanding of human life. He also needed to overcome Aristotle's narrow identification of the polis as the only social setting in which human flourishing can be achieved.[59] Thirdly, MacIntyre's revised account of an Aristotelian ethics had to avoid Aristotle's denial that there can be irresolvable conflicts between different goods, and allow for the possibility of conflict between the different goals towards which human behavior may be orientated, if it were to be plausible to a modern sensibility.[60]

55. AV, 205.
56. AV, 186.
57. NE, Book I chapter 1, 1 (quoted AV, 148).
58. AV, 162 MacIntyre subsequently revised this position in DRA as we shall see in section 2.4.
59. AV, 163.
60. AV, 163.

Reinstating Teleology

The Enlightenment rejection of teleological explanation has fostered an understanding of human behavior in materialist terms, characterized by the pre-suppositions of empiricism and the methodology of the natural sciences. It has, therefore, been accompanied by a shift in the understanding of causation, from a model of explanation in terms of final causes to one in terms of efficient causes.[61] Within such an explanatory framework, the "facts" of human behavior have to be detached from the intentional states of the individual including their values, goals, and ends. "Facts become value free, 'is' becomes a stranger to 'ought' and explanation, as well as evaluation, changes its character as a result of this divorce between 'is' and 'ought.'"[62]

In line with this changed understanding of explanation, Willard Quine had claimed that the scientific explanation of human behavior must involve specifying genuinely universal laws in which concepts such as "intentions, purposes and reasons for action"[63] are excluded from the explanatory vocabulary. MacIntyre inverts the argument and suggests that "it follows from Quine's position that if it proved impossible to eliminate references to such items as beliefs and enjoyments and fears from our understanding of human behaviour, that understanding could not take the form which Quine considers the form of human science, namely embodiment in law like generalisations."[64]

On an Aristotelian model of human behavior these intentional terms are essential elements in the *explanans* of any action. MacIntyre's strategy is to demonstrate that the concept of an action necessarily involves reference to such intentional states, and that attempts to reduce the explanation of behavior to the level of Quinean causal laws and descriptions of bio-physical processes (for example) denudes the concept of a *person* of any significance. His approach builds on the position that he had argued in many of his papers on philosophical psychology in the 1950s and 1960s.[65]

In AV MacIntyre firstly argues persuasively that the characterization of an action can never be completed by reducing it to a set of descriptions that specify physical movements and identify their biophysical origins. This is because the same physical movement can embody many different types of

61. AV, 81–82.
62. AV, 84.
63. AV, 83.
64. AV, 84.
65. See section 1.2 and footnote 22 for MacIntyre's work in this area. MacIntyre's claim that the explanation of action is irreducibly teleological is supported by other philosophers. See, for example, Schueler, *Reasons and Purposes*.

action. The same motion of the hand might be a welcome or a dismissal, an insult or a gesture of friendship depending on the conventions that define the social context and on the intentions of the actor. What identifies and explains a physical movement as an action is its relationship to the actor's personal history, and to the social setting in which the action takes place. A single physical activity (such as digging in the garden) may have multiple correct characterizations as an action depending on the level of narrative explanation drawn upon to render the behavior intelligible. I may dig the soil with a spade in order to please my partner who is concerned that a lack of activity is detrimental to my health, or because it is part of my preparation for spring planting, or both and more. Each of these descriptions relates the pattern of physical movement to some social institution or practice which renders my behavior intelligible by providing an explanatory context: the institutions of marriage and domestic life, the practice of gardening and the annual cycle of the garden, for example.[66]

Secondly, a Quinean mechanistic approach to the explanation of human behavior erodes the distinction between voluntary action and involuntary movement. A blink of an eye requires only a causal explanation, because it is involuntary. A deliberate wink, however, has to be rendered intelligible as an action by explaining what the actor was trying to achieve by performing the movement. The difference between the involuntary blink and the voluntary wink is that the latter is open to evaluation, while the former is not. It does not make sense to talk about successful or unsuccessful or good or bad blinks (although they may be fortunate or unfortunate); but it does make sense to evaluate the actor's behavior in relation to a voluntary action. Did the actor achieve what she intended? Were her intentions appropriate or inappropriate? Should she be praised or criticized for having chosen to act in this way?[67] If a physical movement can be fully explained without reference to an actor's intentions, then it cannot be subject to moral evaluation. This is MacIntyre's third objection to Quinean reductionism. The possibility of moral censure, aesthetic criticism, and legal action is predicated on a teleological understanding of human behavior and a distinction between

---

66. AV, 206.

67. It might be argued that a physicalist causal explanation of action could be sustained if distinctive brain states (for example) could be identified, each of which is associated with every distinct action. One response to this suggestion is that if the action associated with each brain state has to be identified in terms of the social circumstances and history of the actor and her intentions, then the associated brain state will also have to be identified by reference to these features. It will, not, therefore be possible to eliminate the features of social life that render the action (teleologically) intelligible from the causal description, and this would mean that the project to define actions in terms of brain states alone would fail.

voluntary and involuntary action that Quine's reductivism would eradicate. We can be held accountable for our actions in a way that would be entirely inappropriate for involuntary movements. It is this notion of accountability that is central to the intelligibility of our framework for moral evaluation and, as MacIntyre points out, it is central to our understanding of what it is to be a human being.

> Human beings can be held to account for that of which they are the authors; other beings cannot. To identify an occurrence as an action is in the paradigmatic instances to identify it under a type of description which enables us to see that occurrence as flowing intelligibly from a human agent's intentions, motives, passions and purposes. It is therefore to understand an action as something to which someone is accountable, about which it is always appropriate to ask the agent for an intelligible account.[68]

Thus to abandon teleological explanation would be to abandon the basis on which we recognize a person as an agent capable of recognizing their needs and wants and taking action to meet those needs and wants.

MacIntyre's fourth objection to Quinean reductionism is that it would eliminate the concepts we use in order to understand moral choice. Our interpretation of decision making reflects our unconscious adherence to an Aristotelian model of practical reasoning. We render other people's actions intelligible by connecting them to the way in which that person interprets their desires, assesses how these desires might be met, and selects some course of action aimed at securing the desired end. Each element of this description has to be provided if the person's decision is to be rendered fully intelligible. If a person performs an action, but it is claimed that they did not desire the object of that action, and/or that their chosen course was irrelevant to the achievement of their goals, we would demand further clarification. Were they acting under constraint? Was there a hidden goal? Until the response meets the conditions implied by Aristotle's analysis of practical reasoning their action remains unintelligible. MacIntyre comments that "Aristotle's account of the practical syllogism can be considered as providing a statement of necessary conditions for intelligible human action and as doing so in a way that must hold for any recognizably human culture."[69]

Interpreting practical reasoning in this way assumes that human action can only be understood in intentional terms, as goal directed. Teleology therefore provides the basis on which we distinguish human beings and advanced animals from other types of being. As a result, the concepts that

68. AV, 209.
69. AV, 161.

we use to understand other people are irreducibly teleological. MacIntyre's arguments, therefore, demonstrate that teleological explanation is ineliminable from the conceptual scheme that underpins our social lives (although this does not rule out the possibility of constructing other conceptual schemes which exclude teleological explanation). In achieving this outcome he partly addresses Anscombe's demand for a philosophy of psychology that will underpin an account of moral reasoning. However, the reinstatement of an Aristotelian ethical system requires two further steps. Firstly, he has to provide an account of the virtues which is convincing in a contemporary context. Secondly, he has to demonstrate that it is coherent to postulate an overall telos of human life, without reliance on the metaphysical account of human nature and telos that he had rejected.

Practices and the Nature of Virtue

Aristotle's account of practical reasoning presupposes that an agent can correctly understand their needs and will be able to select the course of action that best meets those needs, but it also allows for the possibility that a person may be mistaken with respect to what is a good and what is not. This implies that one can make a distinction between what an agent may take to be a good and what is a genuine good is for that person.[70] This capacity to distinguish between real and apparent goods is a precondition of an ethical life and the central virtue for Aristotle is, therefore, "phronesis"—the capacity for right judgment or "practical wisdom."[71] The development of this capacity for judgment depends on a process of education in which individuals learn to discriminate between genuine and apparent goods. The judgment of a person who has been through such a process of formation will differ from that of someone who has had more limited opportunities for moral development. As a result, the individual who has developed the capacities to recognize and pursue different (and, in some sense, higher) goods will not conceptualize their needs and wants in the same way as an individual whose culture and upbringing does not afford such opportunities for development.

The morally developed individual will acquire the practical reasoning skills to discriminate between different types of good, and to direct their actions towards the acquisition of those goods which bring longer term benefits. Such a capacity will develop through a person's socialization into the moral framework endorsed by their community. This framework will enable the individual to classify and articulate their goals and needs, to

---

70. AV, 150.
71. NE, Book VI, 1140a20–1140b30.

recognize what is held to be genuinely good by that community, and develop the characteristics needed to pursue and achieve those goods—the virtues. But how are the virtues to be defined given the competing accounts of the concept of virtue that MacIntyre traces from Homer onwards?[72]

According to MacIntyre, a virtue in the Homeric epics is identified with excellence at some distinctive activity that is important to social life. For example, we may refer to someone in Homeric terms as having virtue as a warrior or as a story teller or as a counsellor. To possess a virtue is to possess the capacity to be successful in undertaking a social role, and the nature of the virtue cannot be defined independently of that role. And, MacIntyre argues, one thing that remains constant in the subsequent transmutations of the concept of virtue is that a virtue *always* requires some background feature of social life for its expression.[73] MacIntyre generalizes from this observation to argue that the concept of a social practice is fundamental to the conception of a virtue. MacIntyre suggests that "this notion of a particular type of practice as providing the arena in which the virtues are exhibited and in terms of which they are to receive their primary, if incomplete, definition is crucial to the whole enterprise of identifying a core concept of the virtues."[74] This is an important step in MacIntyre's argument, which is designed to provide an account of virtue ethics in which the concepts of virtue and telos are shaped by social structure rather than biology (a position which he revised in DRA—see section 2.4 below). He defines a practice as:

> any coherent and complex form of socially established cooperative form of human activity through which goods internal to that form of activity are realised in the course of trying to achieve those standards of excellence, which are appropriate to, and partially definitive of, that form of activity, with the result that human powers to achieve excellence, and human conceptions of the ends and goods involved, are systematically extended.[75]

This definition implies a teleological understanding of human behavior, as it presupposes that practices develop in order to enable human beings to invent and pursue certain goals. As a result, practices shape new and distinct social roles. Thus, the need to provide people with shelter from the elements shapes the social role of the builder, and the practice of building will foster the development of standards which underpin the judgment as to whether the builder's role has been executed well or badly. Such standards

72. AV, 185–6.
73. AV, 186.
74. AV, 187.
75. AV, 187.

therefore provide the basis for the evaluation of the performance of the role defined by the practice. The development and elaboration of these standards will specify new areas of potential achievement for human beings, and the builder who meets those standards will not only achieve goods which pre-exist the practice (such as securing the safety of individuals who require shelter). She will also obtain goods which could only be achieved through conformity to the standards developed within the practice (such as standards of architectural excellence), and which are, therefore, internal to it. Such internal goods are acquired only through the individual's contribution to the achievement of the telos of the practice.

MacIntyre illustrates his conception of internal goods with reference to the game of chess. We may play chess simply in order to enjoy some external goods that accrue to us through participation, as a child might do if she was rewarded for playing the game with an adult.[76] However, particularly as her skill in the game (or virtue as a chess player) develops and her understanding of the objectives of the game becomes clearer, the child would gain satisfaction from achieving the internal objectives of the game. In developing her skills she would also be acquiring excellence of a form which would not be possible unless this practice had been established, and the practice therefore acts to extend the understanding of what it is possible for a human being to achieve. These internal goods cannot be understood by someone who lives in a culture which does not possess the practice of chess, because the excellence or "virtue" of a chess master cannot be defined or understood without reference to the constitutive rules of the game.[77]

To acquire excellence in a practice requires one to submit to the authority of the rules that govern that practice and to the standards of performance that have evolved over its history, because such rules and standards are constitutive of participation in that particular practice. If I do not accept the authority of those rules and standards I am not participating in the practice, although I may be pretending to do so.[78] Moreover, it is only by submitting to the authority of the constitutive rules and accumulated lore of a practice that I can develop the skills required to meet the standards that govern the activities. Through the development of such skills I may also ultimately be capable of performance that transcends and extends those standards, thereby contributing to the development of the practice as a whole. For someone to achieve excellence in a practice extends the community's

---

76. AV, 188.
77. AV, 188.
78. AV, 191.

understanding of what achievements are possible and thereby benefits everyone in that community.[79]

The concept of internal goods enables MacIntyre to provisionally define the nature of virtue as follows, although he recognizes that this definition requires extension and modification:

> *A virtue is an acquired human quality the possession and exercise of which tends to enable us to achieve those goods which are internal to practices, and the lack of which effectively prevents us from achieving any such goods.*[80]

The acquisition of virtue so defined therefore requires membership of a community which has established social practices, with clear standards of achievement with respect to these practices. However, the acquisition of virtue defined in this way does not require a particular form of social organization, such as the polis, for its expression. Any community which is sufficiently complex to allow different practices and social roles to emerge will provide opportunities for an individual to participate in practices, and thereby to develop the virtues necessary to realize the internal goods characteristic of those practices.

It would be misleading to interpret MacIntyre as arguing that each practice has associated with it a unique virtue, as this would imply that an individual cannot acquire all virtues without participating in all practices. There is a distinction implicit in AV between virtue as a specific skill associated with a particular practice and the more general virtues that participation in a range of practices imbues. My skill in chess will be different from my skill as a carpenter. But in both cases my submission to the rules of a practice and the authority and requirements of other practitioners means that my participation in a practice has to be characterized by the virtues of justice, trust, truthfulness and courage (among others).[81] Thus while the internal goods achieved by participation and the associated skills will be identified in terms of the aims of the practice, the virtues that may be acquired by participation may have a more general relevance to all social participation. MacIntyre holds that these general virtues and the relationships that they underpin "are genuine excellences, are virtues in the light of which we have to characterise ourselves and others, whatever our private moral standpoint or our society's particular codes may be."[82]

---

79. AV, 190.
80. AV, 191; emphasis original.
81. AV, 191.
82. AV, 192.

MacIntyre suggests that his initial account of the virtues in terms of practices is teleological; it relates virtues to the characteristics of social life; and it allows for conflict between different goods. In this he suggests it addresses the difficulties that he had identified with respect to Aristotle's account.[83] He has constructed a notion of human virtues that is independent of the idea of the polis,[84] his account of human nature is teleological without relying on an Aristotelian metaphysical biology, and he has provided an account of the virtues in which the failure of individuals to achieve their good is not simply the product of some character defect, but can arise from the conflict between the incompatible goods that are embodied in different social practices.[85]

However, MacIntyre acknowledges that there are also certain limitations to his account of virtue in terms of the nature of a practice. There are too many practices and therefore too many actual and potential conflicts between goods to enable us to give a coherent account of the overall shape of a life and its telos. The claims of one practice may conflict with those of another,[86] and "without an overriding conception of the overall telos of a whole life, conceived as a unity, our concept of certain individual virtues has to remain partial and incomplete."[87] And there is at least one virtue which, MacIntyre argues, cannot be defined without reference to the concept of a whole human life: that of "integrity or constancy"; the dedication of a life towards a single end.[88]

In addition to the limitations that MacIntyre identifies in his account of virtues and practices, it is also worth raising here a question about whether social practices and what they achieve always produce outcomes that are good. As we shall see in the next section, it is arguable that some practices may produce evil outcomes. If this is the case defining virtue in terms of excellence within a practice does not provide an adequate criterion of moral worth, as we would have to distinguish between those practices in which internal goods are produced, from those practices which create wrongs. But to discuss this at this stage is to get ahead of the story, and to anticipate a discussion that will take place in section 2.4. Suffice it to say that the concept

---

83. The three difficulties in Aristotle's account were identified earlier in this section as: dependence on a teleological biology, a denial that there can be conflict between different goods, and a reliance on the polis as the only form of community in which the virtues can be realized (AV, 162–163).

84. AV, 193.

85. AV, 196–7.

86. AV, 201.

87. AV, 202.

88. AV, 203.

of a virtue specified in the way that MacIntyre defines it gets us part of the way towards an account of the good life—but only part, at best.

In order to complete his account of the good life MacIntyre seeks to establish three further theses. Firstly, he attempts to establish that it is legitimate to speak of the unity of a human life, because such a unity is a precondition both for the exhibition of the virtues as longstanding dispositions to act in certain ways and for the coherence of the assertion that a human life may have a single overriding purpose. Secondly, he argues that the pursuit of such a telos is not sustainable by an isolated individual but requires a community which can support that individual in conceptualizing and pursuing their good. Thirdly, such a community is only able to sustain the individual's pursuit of the good if its practices embody some developing (albeit limited) understanding of that good and of the virtues. Such an understanding will have developed over the history of the community and will come to embody a tradition of enquiry into the nature of the good.

The Nature of the Human Telos

MacIntyre argues that the contemporary understanding of human action results in a Humean view of a human life as a concatenation of discrete actions with no overriding connection between each of those events.[89] From this perspective the unity of a life becomes invisible. This atomistic concept of the person leaves no place for the virtues because virtues are continuing dispositions which will be exhibited in a range of situations over a long period of time. It might be argued that criteria of personal identity in terms of physical and psychological continuity can underpin a concept of the unity of a life that is sufficient to enable someone to ascribe dispositions to the same person over time. However, constructing an account of personal identity in terms of spatio-temporal continuity tells us nothing about the way in which that individual understands the psychological and biographical identity of themselves and others. This requires a complementary notion of personal identity, conceived in terms of how an individual constructs the unity of their own life, and how in turn they conceive of the unity of other people's lives.

MacIntyre argues that we understand our own and other people's lives by constructing a narrative around them. The concept of a unitary self that underpins the concept of the virtues in AV is "the concept of a self, whose unity resides in the unity of a narrative, which links birth to life to death as

---

89. See Hume, *Treatise of Human Nature*. Book 1 Part 4 Section 6.

narrative beginning to middle to end."[90] MacIntyre observes that our actions have a fundamentally historical character[91], because we have to understand our own and other people's actions by embedding them in the context of a life story that (implicitly at least) has a narrative form.[92] Our lives may be unpredictable, but as a result of this narrative structure they have.

> a certain teleological character. We live out our lives . . . in the light of certain conceptions of a possible shared future. There is no present which is not informed by some image of some future, and an image of the future always presents itself in the form of a *telos*—or of a variety of ends or goals—towards which we are either moving or failing to move in the present.[93]

MacIntyre's account therefore combines two notions of personal identity; the physical and psychological continuity that is required to correctly ascribe dispositions to a person and the idea of personal identity as the ascription of a narrative unity to our own lives and the lives of others, in which we understand those lives as imbued with a teleological order, directed towards some end. This underpins his notion of an overall telos. He asks:

> In what does the unity of an individual life consist? The answer is that its unity is the unity of a narrative embodied in a single life. To ask "what is the good for me?" is to ask how best I might live out that unity and bring it to completion. To ask, "what is the good for man?" is to ask what all answers to the former question must have in common.[94]

MacIntyre suggests that it is the systematic asking of these questions throughout life that can provide that personal history with its overall identity: its unity is the unity of a narrative quest.[95] But this formulation immediately raises the question: "a quest for what?" MacIntyre suggests that we must have some general idea of the overall good that we are seeking, and it is our developing understanding of that good throughout our life, that will enable us to prioritize all the other specific goods which are associated with the different social practices in which we are engaged. This developing appreciation of the good therefore underpins the virtue of phronesis.

90. AV, 205.
91. AV, 212.
92. AV, 213.
93. AV, 215–16.
94. AV, 218–19.
95. AV, 219.

I want to pause here for a moment to consider what these arguments of MacIntyre demonstrate. Firstly, it is clearly not the case that conceiving one's life as a narrative unity directed towards some notion of the good is a logical necessity. It is perfectly (logically) possible for someone to live on a day to day basis and never consider whether their life constitutes some overall unity or whether it has an overall goal. Indeed, this is the image of modern life that emerges from Macintyre's critique of liberal individualism.[96] Nor is MacIntyre's contention an empirical hypothesis to be tested by psychological tests to measure the degree to which individuals and populations conceive of their lives as a unity. Macintyre's arguments are in essence *moral* arguments that are intended to persuade the reader that one cannot render one's life fully intelligible and worthwhile without considering it in terms of an overall unity, and to conceive of that unity in terms of some overall purpose that we are seeking to realize. Incorporating the Aristotelian notion of an overall telos into our conceptual armory enables one to make sense of the language of morals, and to direct our actions towards some overall purpose.

He is therefore, seeking to equip the contemporary reader with the conceptual resources necessary to understand and live a good life. However, in our contemporary culture, the abandonment of an Aristotelian perspective means that there is little cultural endorsement for conceiving of one's life in the way that MacIntyre suggests is necessary if virtue ethics is to be revived. What is required to make a life lived in pursuit of some ultimate telos an option for the contemporary person is a community that embodies the understanding of that life as a unity, and which provides its members with the practical and conceptual support necessary for them to make progress in the task of understanding and realizing such a telos.

The Role of Community

If an individual is to be able to consistently conceive of their life in terms of a unity directed towards the achievement of some telos they will require the support of others to maintain a focus on their developing understanding of the good, and on the development of the virtues required to achieve that good. MacIntyre's account therefore extends the concept of virtue beyond the characteristics of the individual, to the social virtues necessary to create and sustain the type of community which can support the individual in their pursuit of the good:

---

96. AV, 228.

> The virtues therefore are to be understood as those dispositions which will not only sustain practices and enable us to achieve the goods internal to practices, but which will also sustain us in the relevant kind of quest for the good, by enabling us to overcome the harms, dangers, temptations and distractions which we encounter, and which will furnish us with increasing self-knowledge and increasing knowledge of the good. The catalogue of the virtues will therefore include the virtues required to sustain the kind of households and the kind of political communities in which men and women can seek for the good together and the virtues necessary for philosophical enquiry about the character of the good. We have then arrived at a provisional conclusion about the good life for man: the good life for man is the life spent in seeking for the good life for man, and the virtues necessary for the seeking are those which will enable us to understand what more and what else the good life for man is.[97]

It might be argued that defining the good in this way is so vague as to be entirely unsatisfactory, but it is not MacIntyre who needs to provide a more adequate definition. This is the philosophical task of the community that espouses some notion of a human good, and it is the task of that community to progressively construct an adequate definition of that good and develop those practices which will enable its members to pursue the good life. This does not mean that all communities will define the good in the same way. But it does imply that the conceptual scheme that such a community uses to underpin its understanding of the moral life will be incomplete and therefore not entirely intelligible without some interpretation of the nature of the good. The debates and arguments through which a community constructs such an understanding of the good lead to the development of a tradition, and it is through her participation in such a tradition that an individual can be sustained in her pursuit of the good.

Participation in a Tradition

An individual has no control over the social position and community into which she is born and in which she develops, and in whose practices she participates. But this community and these practices have a history and this history constitutes a particular tradition or set of traditions. As a result of her participation in these practices the individual will become "one of the

---

97. AV, 219.

bearers of a tradition."[98] As a bearer she will not merely act as a passive recipient of the practices and beliefs transmitted through the tradition, she will also play a part in shaping these practices. She will engage in a more or less limited way in debates about the fundamental aims of the tradition, which defines the good towards which it is directed. She will learn the history of the debate, and help shape its future, because such debates continue through generations. In participating in the practices endorsed by the tradition she will both seek to achieve the goods that are internal to the practice, and also contribute to the pursuit of the overall good of the tradition of which it is a part. The practice is both illuminated by and illuminates the history of that tradition and points towards its future: "practices always have histories and . . . at any given moment what a practice is depends on a mode of understanding it that has been transmitted often through many generations."[99]

Traditions therefore support and embody practices, and these practices make possible the virtues. The virtues fostered by these practices serve to strengthen the tradition and preserve it from decay, because unless participants exhibit the virtues that are necessary for the preservation of the integrity of social life, such as truthfulness, justice and courage, the practices of a tradition and the tradition itself will wither away. Thus virtues, practices and traditions are mutually inter-dependent and provide the resources required for the coherent pursuit of the good life.[100]

The Virtues in Contemporary Life

The good life envisaged by Macintyre has at its heart the idea of a community that is engaged in a range of social practices that characterize a particular tradition. Individuals contribute to a communal pursuit of the good through their involvement in these practices. This image of a communal pursuit of the good has only a limited relevance to contemporary life. Industrialization has meant that "where the notion of engagement in a practice was once socially central, the notion of aesthetic consumption . . . is [now central], at least for the majority."[101] Instead of participating in a set of practices which integrate us into a social group defined by a tradition, we

---

98. AV, 221.
99. AV, 221.
100. AV, 223.
101. AV, 228.

are now more likely to be passive observers and consumers of the actions and creations of others, except in relatively restricted environments.[102]

For MacIntyre, this shift away from participation in communally valued practices is both a consequence of the fragmentation of the individual's life, and a feature of modernity which reinforces that fragmentation. In a community which exemplifies an Aristotelian ethic, the virtues are those dispositions which enable the citizen to contribute to the pursuit of a communally defined good. However, we live in a society in which people are considered to naturally pursue their self-interest and their personal notions of what is good for them, and where they will engage in whatever activities they deem to be relevant to those interests. As a result, we no longer possess a shared understanding of the common good. The nature and status of the virtues have therefore become problematic because we have lost such a communal notion of the good.[103] As a consequence "there are no longer any clear criteria [by which one could identify what was to count as a virtue]. It is unsurprising that the adherents of virtue began to look for another basis for moral belief and that various forms of moral rationalism and intuitionism reappear."[104]

The individualism of the 18th century led philosophers to see community as simply the forum in which individual goals are pursued, and to exclude from their understanding of society any view of community as creating a shared vision of the good for humanity that is independent of individual interests.[105] However, this understanding of community has not entirely disappeared. The tradition of the virtues has continued into the contemporary world, but in an attenuated form. MacIntyre points out that "in the conceptual mélange of moral thought and practice today, fragments from the tradition—virtue concepts for the most part—are still found alongside characteristically modern and individualist concepts such as those of rights or utility. But the tradition also survives in a much less fragmented, much less distorted form in the lives of certain communities."[106]

Such communities are, however, small and marginalized and MacIntyre concludes that the range of disparate moral concepts means that moral consensus is not possible today.[107] The result has been the growth of moral individualism on the one hand and Nietzschean genealogy on

---

102. AV, 228.
103. AV, 235–36.
104. AV, 236.
105. AV, 236.
106. AV, 252
107. AV, 252.

the other. MacIntyre believes that his arguments have shown that this individualist concept of the self-sufficient moral authority is incoherent.[108]

> For if the conception of a good has to be expounded in terms of such notions as those of a practice, of the narrative unity of a human life and of a moral tradition, then goods, and with them the only grounds for the authority of laws and virtues, can only be discovered by entering into those relationships which constitute communities whose central bond is a shared vision of and understanding of goods.[109]

This observation undermines moral individualism. If the conceptualization and understanding of morality is dependent on participation in a community which is engaged in constructing and realizing a notion of the human good, then the individualist who chooses her own "morality" effectively isolates herself from the possibility of realizing such a good. The notion of the Sartrean individualist who can establish his or her own morality from a perspective of unconditioned choice is incoherent, because the individualist severs herself from the social relationships, practices and standards that are essential to the creation of the virtues.[110] Such a person's self-isolation denies to her the resources necessary to formulate an understanding of the moral life. Moreover, such social engagement is essential to the fulfilment of even the most basic human needs at many points in our lives (a point which MacIntyre develops further in DRA—see section 2.4). Our understanding of what can count as a moral viewpoint has to be framed and shaped by our prior commitment to a community and its social practices.[111] The genealogical critic articulates an effective *reductio ad absurdum* of liberal moral individualism, but such criticisms have no power to undermine MacIntyre's account of virtue ethics.

Challenges to MacIntyre's Position in AV

MacIntyre argues that individualist perspectives are manifestations of, and responses to, the disordered ethical vocabulary characteristic of the modern world. This observation reinforces his claim that a return to an Aristotelian tradition is a plausible way of regaining a coherent conceptual framework to underpin our morality. However, his position is open to two major

---

108. AV, 256–57.
109. AV, 258.
110. AV, 205.
111. AV, 259.

challenges, each of which is related to either the crisis of rational justification or the crisis of moral debate that I identified at the beginning of this chapter. The first challenge is that MacIntyre's advocacy of an Aristotelian perspective is simply the expression of a personal preference, because his repudiation of Enlightenment standards of justification means that he cannot offer any compelling arguments to the individual who does not share his enthusiasm for virtue ethics. MacIntyre's arguments are constructed from *within* the Aristotelian tradition itself, and his assessment of the validity of these arguments presupposes an understanding of the nature of rationality and justification that is derived from that tradition. These standards of justification cannot therefore legitimate the decision to commit oneself to that tradition, because these standards can only be acquired through that commitment. Without some account of the nature of rationality that can replace the Enlightenment account, MacIntyre has no way of repudiating the critic who does not share his judgment of the cogency of the different arguments. And if this is the case he has no way of repudiating the claim that his rejection of Enlightenment standards of rational justification licenses epistemological relativism. His response to this challenge has to be to construct an alternative account of rational justification to replace the Enlightenment model. As he points out

> my negative and positive evaluations of particular arguments . . .presuppose a systematic, although here unstated, account of rationality.
>
> It is this account—to be given to a subsequent book—which I shall hope to deploy . . . against those whose criticisms of my central thesis rests chiefly on an incompatible evaluation of the arguments.[112]

This subsequent book was to be WJWR, and a purely chronological account of his work would move on to consider the account of rationality and justification that he sets out in that work. However, to move directly to WJWR would leave incomplete my account of MacIntyre's development of an Aristotelian ethics that might be persuasive to the modern world. Completing that account will also provide a response to the second challenge, which is related to the crisis of moral debate. It is arguable that MacIntyre's account of virtue ethics endorses moral relativism: the view that what counts as right or wrong is culturally determined. His account of the virtues is dependent on his account of practices. If one community endorses practices that another community considers to be evil and identify as virtues characteristics that the second community would consider to be vices, how

---

112. AV, 260.

can moral argument proceed to resolve the underlying disputes about good and evil, virtue and vice? If MacIntyre is unable to construct arguments to show that the position adopted by one community is superior to another, his Aristotelianism would appear to allow an unacceptable relativism in terms of what may be judged to be good or evil.

In AV he had sought to repudiate a biologically based interpretation of human telos. In *Dependent Rational Animals* (DRA—first published 1999) he reverses his position and seeks to reinstate such a biological account of human telos. This represents a significant strengthening and development of his moral philosophy, because this biologically based account of telos completes Macintyre's account of virtue ethics and strengthens his position against the claim of moral relativism. It is, therefore, helpful to discuss DRA to complete an account of Macintyre's Aristotelian ethics before considering the extent to which he provides an effective alternative to Enlightenment standards of rationality.

2.4 Dependent Rational Animals

Limitations of AV

MacIntyre's objective in AV is to reconstruct an Aristotelian conceptual scheme which he believes can remedy the incoherence of our contemporary understanding of ethics. His arguments do not present this scheme as demonstrably true, but as a way of conceptualizing the human condition which can render our moral experience more intelligible. Macintyre also seeks to show that Aristotelianism is superior in coherence to the rivals represented by contemporary moral philosophy, but this does not demonstrate that it would be impossible for some alternative conceptual scheme to make our understanding of morality equally or more coherent. As he acknowledges in both AV and DRA, he is arguing his case from a committed Aristotelian perspective and his standards of justification are derived from this prior commitment.[113] Someone who does not share that commitment will not be compelled to accept the Aristotelian standards of superiority and justification that he applies and may argue that his position is simply the expression of his own personal preferences. Thus MacIntyre's appeal to the alleged superiority of the Aristotelian moral tradition cuts no ice for critics such as Robert Wachbroit, because, as Wachbroit points out, such a claim would simply be rejected by the adherent of a different ethical tradition.[114]

113. AV, 277–78; DRA, 77–78.
114. Wachbroit, "Relativism and Virtue," 1560.

However, MacIntyre's account of rationality in WJWR is intended to respond to this type of challenge, and I consider this response in section 2.5 and chapter 4.

The problem I have described above reflects a form of *epistemological* relativism in which what is cast into doubt is the justification of the standards by which we seek to demonstrate the superiority of one theoretical position to another. What I want to address in this section is a different, although related, problem that arises from his position in AV, which leaves him open to the criticism that his version of Aristotelian ethics legitimates *moral* relativism. MacIntyre's account of such an ethic in AV represents the human telos as a concept *constructed* by human beings and their communities, through their culturally distinctive practices, rather than something that is determined by our biological nature, as Aristotle had asserted. But without the anchor of a biologically determined human nature that shapes the human telos, it is arguable that MacIntyre's version of Aristotelianism in AV allows far too much variability to the interpretation of his core ethical concepts. The conceptual elements of an Aristotelian ethical schema may simply act as variables that can be fulfilled in diverse and conflicting ways by different cultures.

This issue can be illustrated by the fact that some practices that are approved in one culture may be considered to be morally wrong in another, even though both cultures might embody an Aristotelian understanding of ethics. MacIntyre links the concept of virtue to the internal goods that can be realized through social practices, and he acknowledges in AV that it is possible in principle for some practices to be evil, although he reserves judgment as to whether this is ever actually the case.[115] This would appear to leave his version of Aristotelianism open to the claim that it endorses moral relativism, because the personal characteristics required in order to realize the internal "goods" of that practice would be considered a virtue by the culture that approves the practice, although this "virtue" may be judged to be a vice by other cultures. This is a point that Wachbroit makes in his perceptive review of the first edition of AV, where he argues that the appeal to practices as the basis on which virtue can be defined must lead to such relativism[116] unless there is some basis on which one can judge the moral status of different practices. The underlying difficulty here is that in order to judge a practice or associated "virtue" as evil, one requires some criterion of value that is external to the practice itself, and independent of the standards of the culture that approves that practice.

115. AV, 200.
116. Wachbroit, "A Genealogy of Virtues," 572.

MacIntyre argued in the Postscript to the second edition of AV that such criticisms fail to take into account the fact that his account of the virtues has three stages, only the first of which is the provisional definition of a virtue in terms of a capacity to achieve the internal goods of a practice. Whether such a capacity is in fact a virtue depends on its relationship to two further stages of the moral life which are defined as "the notions of the good of a whole human life and of an on-going tradition . . . no human quality can be accounted a virtue unless it satisfies the conditions specified *at each of the three stages*.[117]

This observation however does not resolve the problem of moral relativism because there can be rival traditions of the virtues[118] and rival conceptualizations of the good life embodied in such traditions. The cultures that embody such traditions may also embody practices and institutions which would be judged evil within our contemporary Western culture—a culture characterized by the philosophy of the Nazis, or a society built on slavery and the subjugation of women, for example. On MacIntyre's arguments in AV such cultures might still embody some understanding of the human telos, and might sustain and develop this understanding within its tradition and institutions, teaching its citizens habits which we would view with repugnance. I want to say "rightly view with repugnance," but MacIntyre's account of ethics in AV does not provide any culturally independent account of the nature of "right" that can form the basis of this evaluation.

The claim that MacIntyre's position in effect endorses moral relativism is a challenge to its internal coherence. As initially formulated in AV, MacIntyre's account does not provide a sufficiently developed account of the nature of the human telos to set boundaries around what might be counted as a virtue. His notion of a narrative unity of a human life leaves open the question of the genre within which such a unity can be constructed, and how the quest for a telos may be shaped by that construction. My argument in this section is that these difficulties are a consequence of MacIntyre's initial repudiation of a biologically based account of telos and that this deficit is addressed in DRA. DRA therefore represents the completion of his construction of a coherent contemporary Aristotelianism. As a result, this section also articulates the importance of DRA to an assessment of MacIntyre's overall position, an importance which has not always been acknowledged. For example, as I noted in section 1.1 above, Christopher Lutz appears to reject the overall significance of DRA in his otherwise excellent book *Tradition in the Ethics of Alasdair MacIntyre*. He does not mention DRA in the

---

117. AV, 275; emphasis original.
118. AV, 276.

body of the text and in the "Preface to the Paperback Edition" he comments that "*Dependent Rational Animals* does not seem to address the metaphysical issues of truth, teleology, and natural law directly and for this reason it does not appear in the argument" of his book.[119] This disregards the fact that DRA addresses some fundamental deficits in MacIntyre's moral philosophy, and thereby helps defend Macintyre's position against the charge that it endorses moral relativism—an issue that in fact forms one of Lutz's central concerns.

What the charge of moral relativism puts into question is whether there are any logical or other constraints which restrict what can be counted as virtues. Wachbroit has argued that the virtues can be considered as particular character traits which are approved by different cultures. However one culture may approve of some characteristics as virtues which are considered to be vices in another society.[120] An acceptance of such relativism would undermine MacIntyre's aim, which is to establish a version of Aristotelian ethics in which there is a single coherent account of telos and virtue. For MacIntyre the possession of the virtues in large part *constitutes* the achievement of the human telos, and if the virtues vary from culture to culture then so does human telos. If this relativism of the virtues were accepted then his attempt to use Aristotelianism to overcome the contemporary incoherence of moral debate would fail. However, if the nature of the virtues and telos can be anchored in biological aspects of human nature that are independent of culture, the nature of flourishing and the virtues that constitute such flourishing will possess characteristics that must be evidenced in all cultures. Consequently, this will define some constraints on what may be counted as a virtue and specify some of the virtues which must characterize any viable community. This in turn would provide a basis for moral dialogue. Specifying the nature of these constraints is the task MacIntyre undertakes in DRA.

The Importance of Dependence

By the time he came to write DRA MacIntyre had recognized the need to reconsider his earlier rejection of a biologically based account of human telos.

> I now judge that I was in error in supposing an ethics independent of biology to be possible . . . for two distinct, but related reasons. The first is that no account of the goods, rules and virtues that are definitive of our moral life can be adequate that

---

119. Lutz, *Tradition in the Ethics of Alasdair MacIntyre*, "Preface to the Paperback Edition," xi–xv and xiii–xiv.

120. Wachbroit "Relativism and Virtue," 1563–64.

does not explain . . . how that form of life is possible to beings who are biologically constituted as we are, by providing us with an account of our development towards and into that form of life. That development has as its starting point our initial animal condition. Secondly, a failure to understand that condition and the light thrown upon it by a comparison between humans and members of other intelligent animal species will obscure crucial features of that development. One such failure . . . is the [lack of attention given to the] nature and extent of human vulnerability and disability.[121]

DRA emphasizes the way in which our dependence on others shapes the nature of community. We require care and sustenance as babies and children and when we are ill or disabled through age or infirmity. We also have to offer care to others who require support. The relationships that govern our communal life must, therefore, be grounded in the facts of our mutual interdependence and vulnerability, although our culture appears to ignore the facts of this biological determined dependency in its consideration of ethical issues. MacIntyre therefore raises the question of what would happen if "we were to treat the facts of vulnerability and affliction and the related facts of dependence as central to the human condition?"[122]

He identifies three tasks that must be addressed in the consideration of this question. Firstly, he argues that the failure to acknowledge the significance of our vulnerability is accompanied by a failure to recognize that this vulnerability is a product of the nature that we share with other animals. It is therefore necessary to give an account of virtue that takes account of that animality. Secondly, we are born as animals and remain animals throughout our lives, but as we grow we develop into creatures that are capable of practical reasoning and moral choice. It is therefore important to consider the neglected question of the relationship between our animal nature and the development of practical reason. The neglect of this question has been encouraged by those philosophers who have posited a radical disjunction between human nature and animal nature because "philosophical theories about what it is that distinguishes members of our species from other animal species . . . may seem to provide grounds for the belief that our rationality as thinking beings is somehow independent of our animality."[123]

MacIntyre challenges this assumption and argues that our reasoning has to be understood as related to the needs determined by our animal

121. DRA, x.
122. DRA, 4.
123. DRA, 5.

nature, albeit a nature that is transformed through our social development. The third task is to clarify the relationship between our animal dependency and the nature and functions of community. The needs that spring from our biological nature define our telos and through this shape the form of our social life because, MacIntyre argues, "it is only because human beings have an end towards which they are directed by reason of their specific nature, that practices, traditions and the like are able to function as they do."[124]

The Virtues and Human Telos

MacIntyre argues in DRA that the virtues that we must develop if we are to become independent practical reasoners are one and the same virtues as those that are required to respond to vulnerability in ourselves and others. That is, they are "the distinctive virtues of dependent rational animals, whose dependence, rationality and animality have to be understood in relationship to each other."[125] Each of the three terms "dependent" "rational" and animal" has to be given due weight if we are to conceive of human nature appropriately. And because they are interdependent, our rationality cannot be understood without reference to these other characteristics. This observation enables MacIntyre to argue persuasively that our rationality is continuous with the rationality exhibited by other higher animals. If this is the case, then it must be possible to apply the concepts we use to elucidate human action to other animals, and much of the book is devoted to justifying the claim that it is legitimate to ascribe characteristics such as beliefs, reasons for action and the possession and acquisition of concepts to animals other than human beings.[126] MacIntyre's arguments are convincing and underpin his claim that the sophisticated conceptual and collaborative capacities of human beings grow from the less sophisticated capacities that we share with other animals. He concludes that:

> adult human activity and belief are best understood as developing out of, and are still in part dependent upon, modes of belief and activity that we share with some other species of intelligent animal . . . and that the activities and beliefs of members of those species need to be understood as in important respects approaching the condition of language-users.[127]

---

124. MacIntyre, "Prologue" to After *Virtue* (3rd Edition), ix–xvi and xi.
125. DRA, 5.
126. DRA, chapters 3–6.
127. DRA, 41.

At birth our engagement with the world is a wholly animal engagement, and this is only modified, distilled and refined through the processes of socialization which lead to the development of language and our ability to participate in community. Our language capacity transforms human nature, but this transformation is a modification of our animal nature and not a replacement of it.[128]

MacIntyre defines the telos of all animal species in Aristotelian terms, as flourishing, and argues that the nature of the human telos can be revealed by an examination of what counts as flourishing in other species, because the concept of flourishing has the same sense whether it is applied to an animal or a human being. This does not mean that what it is to flourish is exactly the same for each species, but that "what a plant or animal needs is what it needs to flourish qua member of its particular species. And what it needs to flourish is to develop the distinctive powers that it possesses qua member of that species."[129]

The ability to flourish will require an ability to identify and pursue those goods which promote the development and exercise of an animal's distinctive powers, and the capacity to flourish therefore needs to be underpinned by processes of practical reasoning. Human beings share similar pre-linguistic reasons for action to those possessed by other animals (hunger, thirst, a need for protection for example), and these reasons for action are essential precursors for the development of human and animal practical rationality. However, the development of our linguistic capacities means that a human being can evaluate the desirability of different goods, and the acquisition of this capacity means that we can reflect on and pass judgment on our reasons for action in a way that is not shared by other animals.[130] Through our social development we can learn to identify those goods that should be valued for their own sake and which can provide the basis for judgments "about how it is best for an individual or a community to order the goods in their lives."[131] The development of this reflective capacity underpins a transition from the pre-ethical pursuit of the goods required for flourishing that characterizes animal behavior, to the ability of individuals to order these goods hierarchically and form notions of what might constitute some overall good for humanity. It is this understanding of the relative merit of different goods and of an overall telos that guides practical decision making. This transition to reflexive awareness makes the formulation of an explicit moral code possible, but the origins of such a mo-

128. DRA, 49.
129. DRA, 64.
130. DRA, 56–58.
131. DRA, 67.

rality remains rooted in its relevance to meeting needs that emanate from our animal nature.

The Nature of Practical Reasoning

The capacity for reflexive practical reasoning is essential to the pursuit of human telos because what will count as flourishing for a human being will vary from situation to situation, and what is required to promote such flourishing is a developed capacity to select the action that maximizes the general good within that situation, balancing both individual and communal interests. Thus defining the nature of human telos is not a question of identifying a set of individual or community characteristics which represent individual perfection and social utopia, but of identifying a set of reasoning capacities which enable individuals and their communities to select the correct path among conflicting goods. MacIntyre suggests that "if we want to understand how it is good for humans to live, we need to know what it is to be excellent as an independent practical reasoner, that is, what the virtues of independent practical reasoning are."[132]

MacIntyre argues that the virtues of practical rationality can only be acquired by participation in a community which is characterized by patterns of giving and receiving. These patterns reflect the fact that at certain points in our lives we are both dependent on others and that at other points we will also provide the source of care to those who are in need. We first experience such patterns of care as children, but these patterns continue throughout our lives.[133] As our autonomy develops, we become increasingly capable of fulfilling our own desires. However, our developing rationality means that we learn to stand back from our immediate desires to consider what our longer term good really requires, and learn to make rational choices between realistically imagined alternative.[134] In this process we are also modifying what we desire away from the objects that may provide immediate gratification into a desire for what is really good.[135] What must underpin this process are the virtues:

> the qualities that a child must develop, first to redirect and transform her or his desires, and subsequently to direct them consistently towards the goods of the different stages of her or

132. DRA, 77.
133. DRA, 82.
134. DRA, 83.
135. DRA, 67.

his life . . . are the intellectual and moral virtues. It is because failure to acquire those virtues makes it impossible for us to achieve this transition that the virtues have the place and function that they do in human life.[136]

This transformation of desire is not simply the development of self-control. Rather it is a process of redirecting our desires towards the good so that we no longer desire what is inappropriate. Someone who acquires the virtue of temperance will not need to resist a desire for excessive food and drink, because their desire has become a desire for moderation.[137] Moral development is therefore a process of personal transformation in which we learn to stand back from our immediate impulses, so that "the child moves beyond its initial animal state of *having reasons for acting in this way rather than that* towards its specifically human state of *being able to evaluate those reasons, to revise them or to abandon them and to replace them with others.*"[138]

MacIntyre argues that we become effective practical reasoners through our participation in a set of relationships in which we are given and receive nurture. These relationships continue from our birth to our death, reflecting our animal nature and needs and they also form the foundations of our moral education. Throughout our lives we are in debt to those people who provide care for us, and in turn we respond to those who need care from us. And because we may have to give care to people other than those from whom we receive care, we cannot respond to others through strict reciprocity by calculating what is due and delivering this and no more, but must be prepared to give freely.[139]

Human beings are therefore embedded in communities in which networks of uncalculating care-receiving and care-giving are central. The serial patterns of dependency and nurture embedded in these networks are a constitutive element of human flourishing, and therefore of the human good:

> If I am to flourish to the full extent that is possible for a human being, then my whole life has to be of a certain kind, one in which I not only engage in and achieve some measure of success in the activities of an independent practical reasoner, but also receive and have a reasonable expectation of receiving the attentive care needed when I am very young, old and ill, or injured. So each of us achieves our good only if and in so far as others make our good their good by helping us through periods

---

136. DRA, 87.
137. DRA, 88.
138. DRA, 91, emphasis original.
139. DRA, 100.

of disability to become ourselves the kind of human being—
through acquisition and exercise of the virtues—who makes the
good of others her or his good.[140]

The human telos is not therefore secured through the pursuit of my own personal flourishing alone but through both an unselfish commitment to the flourishing of others, and through contributing to the formation and maintenance of a community which responds to the needs of people who are temporarily or permanently unable to meet their own needs. In this process analytic abilities are developed so that practical reasoning becomes focused on achieving a good that integrates both individual and communal needs and goals. As a result, the individual finds her "place within a network of givers and receivers in which the achievement of [her] individual good is understood to be inseparable from the achievement of the common good."[141] This fusion of the individual good and the common good is necessary to our flourishing, and as a result the concept of "flourishing" for human beings has to incorporate and acknowledge a response to our mutual dependence.[142]

This acknowledgment shapes the form of a moral life. If I am to act justly (for example) I must not only respond in accordance with another person's desert. I must go beyond the requirements of distributive justice and respond with immediate concern to the needs of others:

> that individual [who responds appropriately to another's need] at once acts liberally, from the beneficence of charity, justly, and out of taking pity ... what the virtues require from us are characteristically types of action that are at once just, generous, beneficent, and done from pity. The education of dispositions to perform just this type of act is what is needed to sustain relationships of uncalculated giving and graceful receiving.[143]

Aristotle emphasized the importance of the virtues that underpin independence.[144] These remain important, but MacIntyre argues that we also need to develop a complementary set of virtues, which he describes as "the

---

140. DRA, 108.
141. DRA, 113.
142. DRA, 102–3.
143. DRA, 121.

144. MacIntyre criticizes Aristotle's approval of the "megalopsychos" who fails to recognize the reality of their dependence on others. See DRA, 127 for MacIntyre's comments and NE, Book IV chapter 2 for Aristotle's image of the "magnificent man."

virtues of acknowledged dependence."[145] The central virtue of acknowledged dependence is that of "just-generosity" and involves an individual acquiring the disposition to respond appropriately to the mutual patterns of obligation which characterize a society in which people at different points in their lives will be both care providers and care receivers. The development of this virtue enables the possessor to respond to those who require help to meet their needs, and to accept support when their own needs have to be met.[146] Developing such dispositions requires the development of a capacity for affection and regard for others as the basis of our actions of just generosity.[147] We may act from duty, but the primary driver of acts of just-generosity are our affections, just as what drives a response to someone in pain is not a sense of duty but our pity—and more generally our consciousness of, and response to, a shared humanity.[148] We need the virtue of "pity" or "*misericordia*"[149] to ensure that the responses we give are proportionate to the extent of the person's need, rather than determined by the extent of our obligation to that individual. The grounds for this response are our identification and empathy with the person in need.[150]

The reunification of the concepts of telos, practice and virtue with an account of a biologically shaped human nature enables Macintyre to reaffirm some of the principles defined by his early commitment to socialism. He argues that the type of society which can embody the virtues of acknowledged dependence has to embody two principles enunciated by Karl Marx.

> Between independent practical reasoners the norms will have to satisfy Marx's formula for justice in a socialist society, according to which what each receives is proportionate to what each contributes. Between those capable of giving and those who are most dependent and in most need of receiving—children, the old, the disabled—the norms will have to satisfy a revised version of Marx's formula for justice in a Communist society, "from each according to her or his ability, to each, so far as is possible, according to her or his needs."[151]

In such a society even the most disabled are contributors to the common good, by illustrating what it is for someone to be wholly dependent on

145. DRA, 120.
146. DRA, 120.
147. DRA, 121–22.
148. DRA, 122–23.
149. DRA, 124.
150. DRA, 124–25.
151. DRA, 129–30.

others, a state in which we began our lives, and a state to which we may return if illness or severe disability affect us.

The Justification of Moral Judgments

How would the type of community which MacIntyre envisages justify ethical judgments? MacIntyre argues that in becoming independent practical reasoners we have to overcome a number of obstacles to self-understanding: for example our limited knowledge and capacity for self-delusion—and the key to overcoming these obstacles is openness to being questioned by others.[152] In responding to such questioning we try to make ourselves intelligible to others by disclosing just enough of our personal history to provide a context which makes action understandable, and which explains how we could have come to the type of judgments that underpin that action. In doing this we also make ourselves intelligible to ourselves. Indeed, as MacIntyre points out, the questioning to which we respond is often "how on earth could you do *that*?" He argues that the only adequate answer will be an account of the good at which we aimed, or an account of our mistaken judgments with respect to that good.[153] In such dialogue, MacIntyre argues that we have to become accountable to others, to treat ourselves as duty bound when challenged to truthfully answer the question as to nature of the good we were pursuing in our actions.[154] Thus within a flourishing community there will be reasons that are accepted as being sufficient and final justifications for the actions taken by an individual. Such justifications are not arbitrary; they are endorsed by the standards of justification that have emerged within that community. But are the standards of justification that emerge within a community any more than a set of "shared prejudices" by which that community, my fellow citizens and myself are governed?

MacIntyre argues that by participating in such a community we are not only committed to the pursuit of the goods that are endorsed by the community but we are also accepting a set of commitments to other members of that community as a consequence of our mutual dependency. This commitment appears to render impractical my consistent adoption of an ironic and distanced critique of the bases of obligation in the community, while I remain a member of that community:

---

152. DRA, 148.
153. DRA, 149.
154. DRA, 149.

> ... both the moral and political relationships that are required for the achievement of the common good involve commitments that are in some respects unconditional not only to a certain range of goods, but also to those particular others together with whom we attempt to achieve that common good. Those commitments seem to preclude us from putting seriously in question that practical understanding of goods, virtues, rules, and relationships which is presupposed by our commitments and which we share with many of those same others. For to assume the standpoint of the serious questioner seems to involve standing aside from, separating ourselves from, prior commitments.[155]

It is easy to misunderstand MacIntyre at this point. These commitments do not require unquestioning commitment to every expectation of the community. One may critically respond to some aspect of the community's ethics and priorities. Indeed, as we shall see in the discussion of WJWR, MacIntyre argues that critical debate and challenge is the driver of all development within a tradition. But the standards of argument and justification I employ in engaging in such argument are those that I have learned as a member of the community. If I bring into question the legitimacy of the fundamental commitments that constitute the identity of that community, I am both employing and undermining these standards, and in doing this I have denuded myself of the resources required for coherent moral dialogue. A corollary of this observation is that critical rational enquiry cannot be undertaken alone; it is essentially a communal and collaborative activity: "rational enquiry about my practical beliefs, relationships and commitments is ... not something that I undertake by attempting to separate myself from the whole set of my beliefs, relationships, and commitments and to view them from some external standpoint. It is something that *we* undertake from within *our* shared mode of practice."[156]

The process of such rational enquiry involves looking collaboratively at the strongest objections to this or that belief or concept. Such enquiries may lead us to revise our specific judgments and the standards which underpin these judgments, but MacIntyre argues that it would be a mistake to infer that *anything* can be reasonably and justly put in question. In particular, I cannot participate in a shared process of enquiry if at the same time I challenge and reject the ties of mutual obligation that forge my participation in the community. Participation in a community requires a response to the dependency of others and recognition of my own dependency, which together

---

155. DRA, 156.
156. DRA, 157.

lead to an understanding of an overall good which is not confined to the satisfaction of my immediate desires. The achievement of such a good also requires the acquisition of the virtues required to subordinate my personal desires to communal values. This process of moral development underpins the legitimacy of practical reasoning:

> there can be a chain of sound justificatory reasoning that runs from the nature of the human good to the need for the virtues and from what the virtues require to answers to the particular question of what action should be performed . . . And the soundness or otherwise of that chain of reasoning is what makes it practically rational or irrational to act in this way or that.[157]

If I do not possess these virtues, I will not appreciate the force of the pattern of practical reasoning used to justify particular forms of action. The ironic stance of someone such as Nietzsche indicates a failure of moral learning and a failure to acquire the virtues that are required for the effective evaluation of moral argument. While moral action may be justified by practical reasoning, the grounds for our actions are not normally patterns of inference. What we respond to as a reason for action depends in large part on the virtues that we have acquired and our response to need does not normally require arguments and formal justification. If I have failed to acquire the virtue of just-generosity I will not be moved to respond to the plight of a person who is in dire need. The person who asks for rational justification of the claim that she should help a person in extremis exhibits not only their failure to learn the nature of the commitments required by membership of a mutually dependent community, but also their failure to acquire the virtues that make the response to need an immediate response rather than the outcome of a process of justificatory argument.[158]

MacIntyre's Achievement in DRA

In AV there is no biologically determined human nature which defines what counts as the ultimate good for a human being. In that book the quest for a telos becomes in itself the telos of human existence. The argument of DRA changes the parameters of MacIntyre's position by making an ethics of the virtues necessarily associated with our dependency, and defines our telos in terms of flourishing as a member of an animal species. However, such flourishing is not defined in terms of any particular state of being, but rather

---

157. DRA, 159.
158. DRA, 157–58.

in terms of a capacity for appropriate moral judgment, and an appropriately nuanced response to our needs and to the needs of others. This makes the possession of the virtue of "just-generosity" an essential element of our moral life if our needs and the needs of others are to be consistently met. The particular ways in which that virtue and other virtues are expressed will, however, be shaped by the nature of the community and culture in which the individual is embedded. Expressing the virtue of just-generosity will take a different form in the community formed by a religious order than it would within the day to day life of an extended family or a fishing community. There will however be family resemblances (in the Wittgensteinian sense) which make all these different actions expressions of that virtue. The virtue of an excellent practical reasoner is the capacity to make appropriate judgments as to what particular action is an expression of virtue in each particular social context.

The claim that MacIntyre's Aristotelianism implicitly endorses moral relativism was premised on the view that variability in practices and cultural expectations would result in different and incompatible virtues being endorsed by different communities. DRA formulates a version of Aristotelianism which avoids this criticism by making the virtues of just-generosity and effective practical reasoning central to the achievement of human flourishing. This does not mean that communities will come to precisely the same judgment as to what actions are required to promote flourishing: this will depend on the distinctive context of the practices and institutions that exist in that specific community. However, the judgments made by an effective practical reasoner have to remain anchored and explicable in terms of a coherent response to human dependency, rationality and animality, and the limits of the ability to construct a coherent justification of action in these terms set boundaries around what can be considered to be an ethical action.

As a result of these arguments, MacIntyre has defined significant limits to what might count as a coherent ethical position within an Aristotelian perspective. Any community that is capable of ensuring human survival and development would need to exhibit uncalculating care-giving to (at least some classes of) vulnerable people and would tend to approve of and foster the disposition towards just-generosity towards such individuals. Certain types of justification for action will become culturally accepted as a consequence of the endorsement of this characteristic, and one would anticipate that those who have acquired the virtue of practical reasoning in such communities would respond to need without requiring some deductive chain of practical reasoning. Those who participated in the community would benefit from the patterns of mutual care that had emerged and might be accused of inconsistency if they sought to question the legitimacy of these obligations at the same time as they received such benefits. But how far does this take us?

It would certainly be the case that there would be similarities between different cultures in terms of what actions are approved as good and those which are considered wrong. But one can also imagine societies (such as Nazi Germany) where classes of individual are excluded from the status of citizens and can not only be denied care but can be killed by the state. Patterns of mutual obligation and uncalculating care may exist among those whom such a society considers to be persons, but these features may be coupled with a morally repugnant denial of humanity and human rights to other groups of people by the dominant classes. It is beyond the scope of this book to do more than suggest the direction in which one could construct an argument to show that such societies are morally corrupt from a MacIntyrean perspective. I would suggest, however, that one could use MacIntyre's conceptualization in DRA of human nature in terms of dependency and animality to show that such communities are illegitimately narrowing the concept of a person. This would serve to show that from a MacIntyrean perspective such societies do not have to be held to be justified by their own moral framework (as would be the case if moral relativism proved unavoidable) but, that they can be legitimately condemned as corrupt.

The argument here is an argument about the definition of what counts as a human animal, and MacIntyre's general argument is written from a declared Aristotelian perspective. Within this framework it provides a coherent and persuasive account of the place that just-generosity must play in communal life. If MacIntyre's version of Aristotelianism in DRA is correct, then it also provides a much more coherent and effective account of the nature of the telos and virtues than that provided by his position in AV, and, I have suggested, it provides a coherent basis for a repudiation of the criticism that his position endorses moral relativism. However, the facts of human need and dependency to which MacIntyre appeals in constructing his argument might also be accommodated in terms of alternative ethical frameworks—such as consequentialism, for example.

DRA argues from Aristotelian premises about human nature and telos to Aristotelian conclusions,[159] and by anchoring those assumptions in human biology it enhances the overall logical coherence of MacIntyre's position. Nevertheless, his approach may appear to be question begging, because it takes for granted the superiority of Aristotelianism to other philosophical

---

159. DRA, 77–78.

positions, a point that MacIntyre acknowledges. He argues that this aspect of his work is inevitable: because in philosophy "there is no presupposition-less point of departure. What vindicates this or that starting point is what comes next, the enquiry thus generated and its outcome in the achievement of some particular kind of understanding of some subject matter."[160]

DRA has shown that MacIntyre's ethics can be developed to enable it to resist the accusation that it endorses moral relativism, but can the initial adoption of the presuppositions of such an Aristotelian position be justified? Does MacIntyre's claim that the outcomes of enquiry ("what comes next") can act to vindicate the presuppositions that underpin a tradition provide the basis for an effective rebuttal of epistemological relativism? This is the question that MacIntyre explored in WJWR.

2.5 Tradition, Rationality, and Relativism

The Need for an Account of Superiority

MacIntyre's arguments suggest that a teleological understanding of human behavior is central to the coherence of our inherited conceptual scheme, and his Aristotelian ethics are strengthened by his development of a biologically based account of human nature and human telos in DRA. However, his arguments do not show that it would be impossible in principle to formulate alternative conceptual schemes that could provide a coherent non-teleological account of human nature, perhaps drawing entirely on causal and materialist concepts. And even if teleology is ineliminable from our language, MacIntyre's arguments do not demonstrate that human beings must share the same goals or that they share some single over-arching end to which other ends are subordinate. Nor does his argument rule out the possibility that alternative ethical traditions could address the issues raised by our animal dependency as effectively as Aristotelianism. Utilitarian principles, for example, would have some plausibility as a basis for arguing that the recognition of mutual dependence and the need for action in accordance with the principle of just-generosity are essential components of any society which might effectively promote the greatest happiness of the greatest number.

The absence of arguments intended to *prove* the truth of Aristotelianism is not a failure or an omission on MacIntyre's part. It reflects his assessment of our intellectual condition. There is no consensus on ethical beliefs and their associated accounts of human nature within our culture. We live in a world in which there are multiple and conflicting epistemological and

---

160. DRA, 77.

ethical traditions and anti-traditions.[161] Indeed, it is our culture's inability to resolve the conflicts between these different traditions that undermines the Enlightenment belief in unitary and universally acceptable standards of rationality. The history of Enlightenment and post-Enlightenment thought is marked by the construction of multiple accounts of the nature of reason, none of which have been able to command consensus.[162] Nonetheless, the argument of AV is not only that a quasi-Aristotelian account of ethics is implicit in our language and conceptual frameworks, but also that it can be defended as superior to the alternatives. Indeed, without an account of how one tradition might demonstrate its superiority to others, MacIntyre's position in AV would become simply an expression of his personal preference for an Aristotelian ethic. This would be to adopt his ethical perspective on non-rational grounds, and this choice would exemplify the type of liberal individualist approach to ethical commitment that MacIntyre repudiates. His overall position therefore requires the construction of a general account of how it is possible for one tradition to demonstrate its superiority to another, so that he can repudiate the claim that his philosophy is simply an example of contemporary liberalism in action, and that in practice his position endorses both ethical and epistemological relativism. MacIntyre noted the importance of this challenge In the Postscript to the second edition of AV.[163] His arguments in WJWR are intended to show that it is possible for one tradition to demonstrate its rational superiority to other traditions without recourse to the claim that there are universal principles of justification which can be used by an individual to evaluate the legitimacy of different traditions, in advance of making a commitment to one tradition or another.

The Rationality of Traditions

In WJWR MacIntyre argues that the demand for the identification of universal standards of rational justification is self-defeating, because it is only by committing oneself to a particular tradition that it is possible to come to any reasoned view as to the merits of one tradition over another:

> it is an illusion to suppose that there is some neutral standing ground, some locus for rationality as such, which can afford rational resources sufficient for enquiry independent of all

161. Emotivism and the philosophies of Nietzsche and Sartre are examples of such anti-traditions cited by MacIntyre in AV, 21–22.
162. WJWR, 6–7.
163. AV, 276–77.

traditions. Those who have maintained otherwise either have covertly been adopting the standpoint of a tradition . . . or else have simply been in error. The person outside all traditions lacks sufficient rational resources for enquiry and *a fortiori* for enquiry into what tradition is to be rationally preferred. He or she has no adequate relevant means of rational evaluation and hence can come to no well-grounded conclusion, including the conclusion that no tradition can vindicate itself against any other.[164]

The person who tries to construct some tradition-independent claim to justified belief has to rely on some set of universally demonstrable propositions in order to construct their position. Logical principles such as the law of non-contradiction meet this requirement, but the concepts embodied in such principles are not rich enough to provide the basis for substantive theories in either ontology or ethics. First principles that are substantive enough to initiate fruitful enquiry always have to include additional premises which include beliefs about the nature of the world and about the nature of humanity whose truth cannot be known prior to the commencement of that enquiry.[165] The justification of such a process of enquiry cannot, therefore, lie in the pre-existing justification of its elementary beliefs, but rather in the dialectical elaboration of its assumptions, principles of investigation and substantive claims over time, and the demonstration of their consistency with unfolding experience. In this process, questions will arise as to whether conflicting formulations of its position are correct or incorrect, more or less justified. The standards which guide such judgments are created within the process of debate that characterizes the development of the tradition. It is these standards of justification and accepted modes of argument that constitute the emergent rationality of a tradition. The Enlightenment project has, therefore, obscured from view the role that has to be played by the concept of a tradition in underpinning a proper understanding of rationality.[166]

---

164. WJWR, 367. Many of the points made by MacIntyre about the nature of tradition and its influence on understanding reflect the influence of the hermeneutics of Hans-Georg Gadamer. Gadamer emphasized both the inevitability and the beneficence of the fact that our understanding of any aspect of the world is shaped by the beliefs and concepts that we acquire from our historical situation. Such "prejudices" are essential preconditions of dialogue and understanding. There is therefore "no neutral standing ground" from which we can commence enquiry. See Gadamer, *Truth and Method*, 354–55. MacIntyre notes the influence of Gadamer on his work in "An Interview for *Cogito*," 269.

165. WJWR, 173.

166. WJWR, 6–7.

> What the Enlightenment made us for the most part blind to . . . is . . . a conception of rational enquiry as embodied in a tradition, a conception according to which the standards of rational justification themselves emerge from and are part of a history in which they are vindicated by the way in which they transcend the limitations of and provide remedies for the defects of their predecessors.[167]

The question of whether a substantive ethical, epistemological or faith position is justified therefore depends on the application of standards of justification which are formulated within the tradition itself, a claim that MacIntyre had first adumbrated in LS.[168] But if a tradition need only justify its position in accordance with its own internally constructed standards, has it not rendered itself immune to falsification, and therefore become vacuous as a claim to truth, a criticism that MacIntyre had directed at his own account of the justification of Christianity when he published the second edition of LS in 1970?[169] If his mature position is to defend itself against the claim that it is as vacuous as his original defense of Christianity, MacIntyre needs to show that a tradition may become demonstrably false, even though it establishes its own standards of truth and justification. MacIntyre argues this point through his account of the development of a tradition.

The Evolution of a Tradition

Tradition based enquiry is rooted in the unreflective acceptance of beliefs by a particular community at some specific point in time because "every such form of enquiry begins in and from some condition of purely historical contingency, from the beliefs, institutions, and practices of some particular community which constitute a given."[170] Initially these beliefs may be unquestioned, but this situation cannot continue indefinitely, because every society changes and develops, and in this process received beliefs will come under challenge. Founding texts may be shown to be susceptible to multiple interpretations; inconsistencies in the system of beliefs may become apparent; external events may engender new questions and may expose a lack of resources within the tradition to answer these questions. The community may also come into contact with some previously unknown

167. WJWR, 7.
168. See section 1.4 above.
169. See Lutz, *Tradition in the Ethics of Alasdair MacIntyre*, 20.
170. WJWR, 354; See also MacIntyre, "Reply to Dahl, Baier and Schneewind," 175–76.

tradition through migration or invasion and this may result in challenges to established belief and expose the community to new concepts.[171] How communities respond to these challenges:

> will depend not only on what stock of reasons and questioning and reasoning abilities they already possess but also upon their inventiveness. And these in turn will determine the possible range of outcomes in the rejection, the emendation, and reformulation of beliefs, the revaluation of authorities, the reinterpretation of texts, the emergence of new forms of authority, and the production of new texts.[172]

The community's recognition of internal inconsistencies or its exposure to external challenges will result in a nascent tradition reaching a second, self-conscious, stage in which inadequacies in the formulation of its central beliefs and principles will have been identified, but not yet remedied. This awareness of defects will initiate a third stage in the development of a living tradition, in which the identification of inadequacies in its position leads to the reformulation of certain beliefs. When this third stage has been completed members of the tradition will be in a position to contrast their new formulations of belief with the old formulations, which will now be perceived as inadequate and therefore false. This represents a gain in knowledge, through a dialectical process in which specific aspects of the beliefs embodied in a tradition are brought into question by particular challenges or events. The awareness of this gain and the recognition of new challenges will generate continuing processes of enquiry and development. This process of enquiry will produce new formulations of beliefs which are superior to their predecessors in the specific and limited sense that these revised formulations are no longer vulnerable to the same criticisms. These formulations therefore do not represent some set of propositions that have been demonstrated to be unchallengeable, although some assertions may claim to express such eternal truths (and in principle may ultimately be found to deserve such a status). Any statement of belief is worthy of endorsement in so far as its formulation has successfully resisted the specific challenges that have been identified so far, but no such formulation can guarantee that it will not have to be modified or abandoned in the light of some new and unanticipated challenge:

> from the standpoint of tradition-constituted and tradition-constitutive enquiry, what a particular doctrine claims is always a

---

171. WJWR, 354–55.
172. WJWR, 355.

matter of how precisely it was in fact advanced, of the linguistic particularities of its formulation, of what in that time and place had to be denied if it was to be asserted, of what was at that time and place presupposed by its assertion, and so on. Nor does it follow that claims to timeless truths are not being made. It is rather that such claims are being made for doctrines whose formulation is itself time-bound and that the concept of timelessness is itself a concept with a history, one which in certain types of context is not at all the same concept that it is in others.[173]

Justification involves dealing with the immediate threats to specific formulations of belief. Some formulations of belief will be peripheral to the central concerns of the tradition but others will be part of a set of interrelated beliefs that are held to be the core elements of the tradition. In Aristotelianism, for example, the belief that there is a good towards which human live should be directed, and that the acquisition of the virtues is a precondition of the achievement of such a good, are examples of such core elements. The clarification, elaboration, and justification of these central presuppositions of the tradition will become a central topic of enquiry for a tradition that has become self-conscious in the face of challenge. These presuppositions will need to be formulated in a way which enables them to repudiate such challenges if they are to be considered justified, but the form that such justification will take is not independent of the success of the tradition as a whole in making progress in its areas of enquiry. What justifies the "first principles" of the theory is the whole structure of the theory of which they are a part, and in particular "the rational superiority of that particular structure to all previous attempts within that particular tradition to formulate such theories and principles; it is not a matter of those first principles being acceptable to all rational persons whatsoever."[174]

This implies that a community that is developing a tradition of enquiry will be engaged in a process of theory construction which meets two requirements. The first is that the theory should consist of a set of statements which are coherent in the sense of forming an internally consistent system. The second requirement is that the system as a whole must be defensible against internal and external challenge: "it is the success or failure of the theory as a whole in meeting objections posed either from its own or rival points of view which vindicates or fails to vindicate."[175] This does not mean that the theory will be invulnerable to every challenge: only that it is robust

---

173. WJWR, 9.
174. WJWR, 8.
175. WJWR, 252.

enough to repel the challenges that have been identified so far—or, where challenges remain unresolved, that no more coherent alternative is available. What counts as knowledge is that position which to date has withstood all attempts to repudiate it, as assessed in accordance with the standards of adequacy that have emerged in the development of the tradition.

Can a Tradition's Claim to Knowledge Be Challenged?

Such an account of the progress of rational belief invites the criticism that it identifies truth with what is merely *held* to be knowledge by some specific social group. The evolution of tradition-specific standards of rational justification enables a community to construct ever more developed statements of its position in response to specific objections, but this process does not enable the community to demonstrate that they have established truths that transcend the limits of their tradition. MacIntyre emphasizes that "Progress in rationality is achieved only from a point of view"[176] and this formulation suggests that one may only be able to speak of truth-from-a-particular-perspective, rather than of an objective truth that is independent of all perspectives

In discussing Plato's model of enquiry, MacIntyre notes that one of the key issues for epistemology is the possibility of maintaining a substantive distinction between what *is* the case and what *appears* to be the case to some group or individual.[177] Identifying progress in rationality with progress from a particular viewpoint faces MacIntyre with the criticism that he has eroded this Platonic distinction, leaving room only for the notion of truth-from-a-particular-viewpoint and has eliminated a notion of objective truth that exists independently of the specific perspectives of particular traditions. This issue can be described in terms of the distinction between warranted assertability and ontological models of truth. On the warranted assertability account the legitimate assertion of truth is primarily a matter of the internal relationships between the statement asserted and the standards of justification appropriate to that type of assertion.[178] There is no conception of truth-in-itself which enables us to transcend the framework of our web of concepts and standards and achieve a perspective from which these beliefs can be evaluated: "for on this view we can have no criterion of truth beyond the best warrants that we can offer for our assertions . . . So the concepts of truth and reality are defined internally to our scheme of

---

176. WJWR, 144.
177. WJWR, 79.
178. WJWR, 169.

concepts and beliefs."[179] But who are the "we" who define these concepts of truth and falsity? MacIntyre suggests that an underlying assumption of such a warranted assertability model of truth is that there is

> one and only one overall community of enquiry, sharing substantially one and the same set of concepts and beliefs. But what if there appears a second community whose tradition and procedures of enquiry are structured in terms of different, largely incompatible and largely incommensurable concepts and beliefs, defining warranted assertability and truth in terms internal to its scheme of concepts and beliefs?.[180]

The assumption that our world consists of a single community, inhabiting a single conceptual framework is false. We exist in a world in which there are different traditions of enquiry each reflecting incompatible presuppositions and possessing distinctive methodologies of rational justification. MacIntyre argues that interaction can occur between these different communities at the points where their different traditions happen to overlap in terms of their "beliefs, images and texts."[181] Where this is the case, members of one tradition would ignore the arguments and contentions of another tradition only at the risk of ignoring substantive grounds for re-evaluating their own conclusions and beliefs.[182]

But if separate traditions each formulate their own distinctive presuppositions and standards of rational justification how can such interaction take place? MacIntyre identifies two major barriers to achieving effective engagement and interaction between different traditions. Firstly, the beliefs expressed in different traditions may reflect incommensurable concepts, so that there is no way of constructing an account of the position characteristic of one tradition which could be seen as conceptually coherent from the perspective of the second tradition. As a result, their contentions will be untranslatable and un-interpretable by the other tradition. Secondly, there may be sufficient shared semantic resources for assertions to be rendered comprehensible in each tradition, but the meaning of these assertions will reflects the different presuppositions of each tradition, so that there is no neutral way of characterizing the points of contention in a way that allows for the possibility of conclusive debate. MacIntyre contends that such patterns of inconclusive argument are typical of contemporary moral debate.[183]

179. WJWR, 169.
180. WJWR, 169.
181. WJWR, 350.
182. WJWR, 350.
183. AV, chapter 1; WJWR, chapter 1.

MacIntyre's position on translatability and incommensurability has been a focus of considerable debate,[184] and I will consider this issue further in the following section. At this point I want to focus on MacIntyre's analysis of the second barrier, the lack of any common means of characterizing the matters under dispute. MacIntyre summarizes this difficulty as follows:

> When two rival large-scale intellectual traditions confront one another, a central feature of the problem of deciding between their claims is characteristically that there is no neutral way of characterising either the subject matter about which they give rival accounts or the standards by which their claims are to be evaluated. Each standpoint has its own account of truth and knowledge, its own mode of characterising the relevant subject matter. And the attempt to discover a neutral, independent set of standards or mode of characterising data which is *both* such as *must* be acceptable to all rational persons *and* is sufficient to determine the truth on the matters about which the two traditions are at variance has generally, and perhaps universally, proved to be a search for a chimera. How then can genuine controversy proceed?[185]

MacIntyre answers his question by identifying two stages to the progress of a controversy between traditions. In the first stage, each tradition may set out the contentions of the alternative tradition in its own terms, and sets out the reasons why it considers these contentions to be inadequate, perhaps conceding the value of the alternative position on some marginal issues. A second stage may be reached if the first tradition realizes that it cannot make some progress on its core problems in accordance with its own standards of achievement, and looks to the second tradition to provide some resources to assist it in resolving these issues.[186] If the tradition is able to make use of the resources potentially made available by the alternative tradition, it will be necessary to move beyond the concept of truth that has evolved within that tradition and to give some consideration to the alternative standards of truth and justification that characterize the opposing tradition.

But both the first and the second tradition will be able to claim warranted assertability for their own set of beliefs in accordance with their own standards, and this creates a dilemma. Either each tradition allows that the

---

184. See, for example, Fowl, "Could Horace Talk with the Hebrews?"; Roque, "Language Competence and Tradition–Constituted rationality"; Fuller, *Making Sense of MacIntyre*, 75 ff.

185. WJWR, 166.

186. WJWR, 166–67.

other tradition meets the requirement of warranted assertability within its own frame of reference, thereby conceding that there is no absolute claim to truth that "can be attached to the fundamental judgements underpinning their mode of enquiry"; or they must make "a claim of truth of a kind which appeals beyond their own particular scheme of concepts and beliefs, to something external to that scheme."[187] To adopt the second option is to recognize that each tradition asserts that something is true of a reality that is tradition-transcendent, and thereby makes a claim for ontological truth.

But if the assertions of each tradition genuinely conflict with each other, both sets of assertions cannot be true. And this observation indicates that both traditions are open to challenge in two ways. Firstly, the beliefs of tradition T_1 may contradict the substantive beliefs of the second tradition, T_2, and challenge that community to re-evaluate these beliefs. The consequence of this re-evaluation may be that the community that embraces tradition T_2 either constructs additional justifications of its own position which deal to its own satisfaction with the challenge of T_1, or it may decide that such a defense is not possible and come to modify or reject some of its original beliefs. Secondly, if the beliefs that are rendered doubtful in this process have previously been justified by the standards that have emerged in the tradition, the adequacy of these standards themselves will also be brought into question. Thus, the idea that traditions can be self-insulating, self-sustaining systems of thought founders on the fact that traditions do not exist in isolation, but are part of an intellectual ecology in which they may interact with rival systems of thought. In this process they may be forced to recognize that what they hold to be true is unsubstantiated and that their methods of rational justification are inadequate. And in this process the most fundamental presuppositions and founding principles of the tradition may be brought into question, as it falls into an epistemological crisis.

Epistemological Crisis

MacIntyre introduced the notion of epistemological crisis (EC) in a paper first published in 1977.[188] According to MacIntyre, an EC arises when the conceptual scheme through which we interpret our experience of the world no longer appears adequate to the evidence before us. As a result, we can no longer believe that our presuppositions, beliefs and expectations lead us to interpret reality correctly. Such crises may arise both for an individual and

---

187. WJWR, 170.

188. MacIntyre, "Epistemological Crisis, Dramatic Narrative and the Philosophy of Science"; henceforth ECS.

also for particular cultures or traditions, and, indeed, the crisis experienced by an individual may be an expression of a broader crisis within a tradition of enquiry.[189] An EC may, therefore, involve an irresolvable philosophical problem, but it may also arise in everyday experience, when someone is suddenly faced with the collapse of her assumptions about herself or her relationships.

The events that might precipitate such an individual EC are many and varied. A person who regards themselves as a valued member of a company is suddenly fired; another person is betrayed by a longstanding lover who they have trusted implicitly on the basis of what they believed to be excellent reasons; a third person might be accused of a crime and is then abandoned by those friends she believed would support her. What is brought into question by these examples is not only what one had come to believe, but also the individual's confidence in the processes through which they had come to accept that their belief was justified. MacIntyre refers to these patterns of interpretation and evaluation of evidence as "schemata."[190]

For the person faced with an EC the collapse of their confidence in the way in which they interpret their experience and make judgments about what is the case means that the predicted relationship between evidence and belief no longer holds. The challenge to the legitimacy of the conceptual scheme through which the individual had previously interpreted her experience may force that person to reassess and reconstruct her preconceptions. In this process she may be faced with competing ways of interpreting what is happening around her, with no clear basis on which she can choose which is correct.[191] As a result, the familiar distinction between the world as it *seems* to us; and the world as it actually *is* will become a central concern of the individual faced by an EC.[192]

MacIntyre's initial examples, and my additions to these examples, center on our interpretation of the intentions, emotions and beliefs of other people—in philosophical terms, our knowledge of other minds. MacIntyre argues that the basis for our interpretation of other minds is our capacity to construct a narrative which links that interpretation to preceding events and which enables us to predict future events and actions. The collapse of this narrative explanatory framework precipitates the EC, and the resolution of this sort of personal EC involves "the construction of a new narrative

---

189. MacIntyre cites Descartes as an example of a philosopher who describes the personal experience of an epistemological crisis. See ECS, 8–10.

190. ECS, 4.

191. ECS, 4.

192. ECS, 3.

which enables the agent to understand both how he or she could intelligibly have held his or her original beliefs, and how he or she could have been so dramatically misled by them."[193]

MacIntyre argues that the narratives through which we begin our attempts to order our experience are the stories we learn in childhood. These provide us with a template for the process of understanding the relationships between people. Such stories may be fairy stories or myths, but as we grow and learn these stories will be replaced by more sophisticated accounts of the individual's place in the world.[194] The ways in which we render our experience intelligible therefore share similar origins to those of traditions of enquiry, which also, we recall, begin in myth. And in the same way that children acquire more adequate explanatory narratives through education, traditions make progress towards a more robust understanding of their subject matter through the discovery of deficits in their previous accounts, and the construction of more adequate and sophisticated explanatory narratives which also account for the inadequacies and failings of the previous narratives.

An individual faced with an EC has to construct new schemata which both explain the new facts in a satisfactory way and explain how the previous schemata the person had developed had led to a false interpretation. The individual faced with an EC must question their epistemic competence and if necessary reconstruct the standards that underpin her judgments. This challenge also arises when a tradition is faced by an EC. Failure to make progress may make the tradition aware that it lacks the resources required to address its core concerns. At this stage it may require conceptual innovation to establish new methods of enquiry and new standards by which the tradition can make judgments about what is and is not the case.[195] Such innovation must rewrite the history of the tradition from a new perspective which shows the reasons for its earlier vicissitudes and for its failure to resolve internal debates.

Tradition, Change, and Identity

However, rewriting the history of the tradition is not the same as abandoning that tradition. There has to be continuity between the identity of the tradition as it was prior to the crisis and the identity of the newly reconstituted tradition as it has become after the crisis. I may be utterly changed

---

193. ECS, 5.
194. ECS, 7–8.
195. ECS, 10–11.

following a personal EC, but I can only know that *I* am utterly changed because I recognize that I am also the same person as I was before. There is a similar issue of change and identity that arises in relation to the transformation of a tradition. A community engaged in a scientific enquiry (for example) may come to recognize that the theories and methodology that it has constructed are entirely inadequate to resolve the problems that have emerged in the process of enquiry. What is required is the construction of an alternative theory which resolves these problems in a particular way.

> [A] successful theory . . . enables us to understand its predecessors in a newly intelligible way. It . . . enables us to understand precisely why its predecessors have to be rejected or modified and also why, without and before its illumination, past theory could have remained credible. It introduces new standards for evaluating the past. It recasts the narrative which constitutes the continuous reconstruction of the scientific tradition.[196]

This recasting of the narrative allows the tradition to manage the tension between continuity and change. MacIntyre criticizes Thomas Kuhn for failing to acknowledge the degree to which continuity is sustained through the process of paradigm change, and, therefore, for failing to give an accurate account of the nature of scientific revolutions. Kuhn claimed that "the transition from a paradigm in crisis to a new one from which a new tradition can emerge is far from a cumulative process. . . . Rather it is a reconstruction of the field from new fundamentals, a reconstruction that changes some of the field's most elementary generalizations as well as many of the paradigm methods."[197] MacIntyre argues that this account of paradigm change fails to give an account of the nature of the rationality that underpins the move from the first perspective to the second. That rationality is embodied in the construction of a historical narrative which enables the participants to understand the problems associated with the preceding paradigm in a new way and which therefore renders intelligible the change of perspective associated with the new model of explanation.[198] The continuity of the tradition in the process of such change is not guaranteed, but if it survives the EC that continuity is embodied in the continuation of the guiding aim of the enquiry and a capacity to understand its history as constituting a significant whole:

---

196. ECS, 11.
197. Kuhn, *Structure of Scientific Revolutions*, 85.
198. ECS, 18.

> What is carried over from one paradigm to another are epistemological ideals and a correlative understanding of what constitutes the progress of a single intellectual life. . . ..Kuhn and Feyerabend recount the history of epistemological crises as moments of almost total discontinuity without noticing the historical continuity that makes their own intelligible narratives possible.[199]

In WJWR MacIntyre formalizes these points into a statement of three conditions that must be met if the response to an EC is to be effective. Firstly, the solution must resolve the problems which have proved previously irresolvable in the tradition "in a systematic and coherent way"[200]. Secondly it must explain what it was that previously rendered the tradition incapable of solving these problems; and thirdly, the first two tasks must be carried out in a way which demonstrates continuity with the previous elements of the tradition. The theory that is constructed in order to resolve the crisis will require some form of conceptual change and elaboration, as otherwise it would not escape from the limitations which the tradition previously faced. "Imaginative conceptual innovation will have had to occur."[201] MacIntyre continues:

> To have passed through an epistemological crisis successfully enables the adherents of a tradition of enquiry to rewrite its history in a more insightful way. And such a history of a particular tradition provides not only a way of identifying continuities in virtue of which that tradition of enquiry has survived and flourished as one and the same tradition, but also of identifying more accurately that structure of justification which underpins whatever claims to truth are made within it.[202]

Response to Relativism and Perspectivism

When an individual (or a tradition) makes an effective response to an EC she (or it) will also become more conscious of the limitations of the human capacity for knowledge. The individual will be sensitized to the fact that the criteria they use to distinguish truth from falsity may prove unreliable.[203]

---

199. ECS, 19.
200. WJWR, 362.
201. WJWR, 362.
202. WJWR, 363.
203. ECS, 9.

While new criteria will have been formulated which address the deficits of the previous schemata, the individual will become conscious that these revised schemata may also prove inadequate in future:

> The agent has come to understand how the criteria of truth and understanding must be re-formulated. He has had to become epistemologically self-conscious and . . . he may have come to acknowledge two conclusions: the first is that his new forms of understanding may themselves in turn come to be put in question at any time; the second is that, because in such crises the criteria of truth, intelligibility and rationality may always themselves be put in question . . . we are never in a position to claim that we now possess the truth or know we are fully rational.[204]

Further challenges may arise and it is always possible that we will be unable to maintain the coherence of our revised schemata in the future. Such observations may give rise to extreme skepticism with respect to the possibility of knowledge. One response to such skeptical challenge is to commence the search for unassailable criteria of truth that had characterized Cartesian epistemology. But the failure of such projects may lead to the type of epistemological crisis which affected MacIntyre in the 1960s, and which undermined his ability to adopt any substantive philosophical perspective at that time. Another response to the sceptic's challenge is to adopt the type of fideism MacIntyre appeared to advocate in LS. But the mature MacIntyre repudiates such fideism because it excludes the epistemological openness that is necessary for genuine enquiry—for, he suggests, only a "degenerate tradition" will construct the type of epistemological defenses that will prevent it from ever being brought into question.[205]

For MacIntyre, an awareness of the possibility of falsification and of the limitations of human intellectual capacity is a pre-requisite for any legitimate (albeit provisional) claim to knowledge. Such openness to challenge is a sign of a sophisticated rationality which acknowledges the historical limitations of any claim to justification, but does not allow such an awareness to inhibit the pursuit of truth. Such openness demands that the individual and tradition expose their beliefs and theories to the tests of experience and internal debate, and listen to the voices of rival traditions. The degenerate tradition can preserve its presuppositions and safeguard its conceptual scheme by evading such challenges, but in doing so it denies to itself a distinction between *seems* and *is*, and simply assimilates truth to warranted assertability. The epistemological openness of a living tradition

---

204. ECS, 5.
205. ECS, 12.

rests on recognition of the limitations of human knowledge. Such recognition does not exclude the adoption of the goal of achieving a comprehensive understanding of all aspects of the world as a telos of enquiry, but it also acknowledges that this telos will never be fully realizable.

The implications of these points enable MacIntyre to deal with the relativist challenge, to his own satisfaction at least.[206] The standards of rationality that emerge within a particular tradition cannot deliver an understanding of a final and absolute truth, but progress can be made in human knowledge because we can discover that some beliefs are demonstrably false, while others are (provisionally) defensible as true. In the process of dealing with challenges to these beliefs, we can construct a series of statements of a position, each of which is demonstrably superior to the previous statement in specific respects. But while a tradition can make progress in accordance with its own standards of rational justification, this process also contains within it the seed of a tradition's ultimate falsifiability. For a tradition may reach a point where its progress is halted. At that stage it may need to call on the insights, beliefs and arguments of another tradition to enable it to move forward.[207] In doing this it may be forced to recognize the superiority of the insights offered by that alien tradition to its original beliefs. This awareness will reinforce the recognition that warranted assertability is not a sufficient criterion of ontological truth, and that the insights of the alien tradition are closer to disclosing the nature of reality than its own original formulations.

> What the explanation afforded from within the alien tradition will have disclosed is a lack of correspondence between the dominant beliefs of their own tradition and the reality disclosed by the most successful explanation, and it may well be the only successful explanation which they have been able to discover. Hence the claim to truth for what had hitherto been their own beliefs has been defeated.[208]

The relativist accusation rests on the presupposition that any substantive philosophical position can defend its claims to truth by reference to its own standards of rationality and justification.[209] But this assumption is undermined by MacIntyre's account of tradition-constituted rationality, because it shows that a tradition may discover that its own standards of justification are inadequate, and that its previous claims to truth have to be revised or abandoned. A tradition's claims to knowledge and truth can

---

206. WJWR, 364.
207. WJWR, 364–65.
208. WJWR, 65.
209. WJWR, 352.

therefore be defeated and this is the possibility which the relativist challenge had failed to envisage.[210]

The perspectivist position builds on relativism by arguing that the meaning of "truth" should be modified so that the different worldviews advocated by different traditions can be seen to represent complementary attempts to express aspects of an infinitely complex ultimate truth. Contradictions between different formulations reflect the limitations of human semantics, rather than genuine conflict between ontological commitments. The perspectivist therefore does not see any difficulty in accepting that the viewpoints of many different traditions can all be legitimate, and in holding that each may be adopted when this is appropriate. Macintyre argues that this perspectivist claim fails to recognize that the power to make rational judgments about truth and falsity requires commitment to a particular tradition:

> The perspectivist . . . fails to recognize how integral the conception of truth is to tradition-constituted forms of enquiry. It is this which leads perspectivists to suppose one could temporarily adopt the standpoint of a tradition and then exchange it for another . . . but genuinely to adopt the standpoint of a tradition thereby commits one to its view of what is true and false and, in so committing one, prohibits one from adopting any rival standpoint . . .[211]

One can only make progress in distinguishing between truth and falsity by fully committing oneself to the enquiry embodied in one particular tradition, and rejecting other perspectives. The perspectivist therefore excludes herself from genuine engagement in the pursuit of knowledge. MacIntyre continues by asserting that "the multiplicity of traditions does not afford a multiplicity of perspectives among which we can move, but a multiplicity of antagonistic commitments, between which only conflict, rational or non-rational, is possible."[212] How might a relativist or perspectivist respond to MacIntyre's arguments? They might suggest that MacIntyre is correct in asserting that the adherents of a tradition may abandon their epistemic commitments in response to an unresolved epistemological crisis, but deny that this fact undermines a relativist position. The fact that a tradition lacks the resources to deal with a set of challenges at one point in time does not imply that an adequate response to those challenges is impossible. Its adherents may have been mistaken in giving up their beliefs. An appar-

210. WJWR, 365–66.
211. WJWR, 367.
212. WJWR, 368.

ently defeated tradition may be resurrected, as MacIntyre is seeking to revive the moribund Aristotelian tradition. If traditions do not die but only go into abeyance, and can flourish again when circumstances change, is there any position which cannot, in principle, be sustained? And if, as MacIntyre claims, all positions can be sustained "where . . . the adherents of each are willing to pay the price necessary to secure coherence and consistency"[213] can his position be clearly differentiated from that of the relativist?

MacIntyre argues that commitment to a tradition is necessary for epistemic progress because it is not possible to judge the claims of rival traditions from a tradition-neutral perspective, and on this latter point the relativist and perspectivist are in agreement with him. However, each of the protagonists draws a different conclusion from this thesis. The relativist takes it as indicating that there is no justification for adopting one tradition based perspective rather than another. The perspectivist takes this claim as a basis for accepting the legitimacy of all perspectives. MacIntyre takes this fact as demanding a commitment to a specific tradition as a precondition of constructing workable notions of enquiry, truth and knowledge. All three accept that the enlightenment notion of tradition-independent truth sets a standard for knowledge which is unachievable. MacIntyre, however, concludes that this standard must be abandoned and replaced with standards of truth and justification that flow from commitment to a particular tradition. The relativist and the perspectivist have abandoned enquiry and the pursuit of ultimate truth in response to their recognition that the human intellect cannot meet these Enlightenment standards of knowledge. For MacIntyre, in contrast, continuing enquiry is the only rational response to this recognition. Such continuing investigation is only possible within a tradition of enquiry, and every legitimate tradition therefore must open itself to uncertainty, challenge, and to the possibility that it will be falsified in the future.

These general observations about the limited ability of human intellect to formulate truth must also apply to MacIntyre's own perspective. There is no absolute and irrefutable justification for any of MacIntyre's major theoretical claims in his mature work—for that, he says, is the nature of the beast: any complex theoretical position and substantive approach to enquiry may prove to be mistaken as its history unfolds. MacIntyre claims that his account is superior to Enlightenment accounts of knowledge and ethics because it explains the failure of this rival account to resolve its epistemological crises, and therefore his account demonstrates its superiority in accordance with the standards established within MacIntyre's own position. And this, according to MacIntyre, is the only basis on which any

213. AV, 267.

philosophical position can show itself to be superior to another. Deciding whether MacIntyre's claim can be accepted will depend on an evaluation of his mature position. In this process of evaluation I will identify some weaknesses in MacIntyre's account, which must be addressed if his claim to have constructed a superior account of rationality is to be sustained.

2.6 MacIntyre's Relationship to the Enlightenment

Overview

In WJWR MacIntyre renders the decline of Aristotelianism intelligible by placing its history in the context of other philosophical and social changes. However, as a result of these changes contemporary social conditions are not those under which an Aristotelian understanding of ethics could thrive. MacIntyre's account of our cultural history emphasizes that the growth of industrialization and individualism has fragmented traditional forms of community. As a result, the belief that there are communal goods, which should shape the individual's understanding of their own needs and objectives and underpin ethical reasoning, has been eroded. Social life has been reduced to a forum in which individual goals are pursued, and the idea of a good for man that is shaped by communal practices has been excised from our ethical vocabulary.[214] Moral change has fostered the development of a society in which religious belief has become an isolated element of private experience, rather than the integrative framework within which all aspects of individual and social life must be understood. As a result it has become virtually impossible for us to think about goods except in terms of the various private interests of individuals, each of which is related to an independent aspect of their existence. Notwithstanding this, our cultural self-perception is one of progress in knowledge, and growth in ethical sophistication and tolerance. In AV MacIntyre attempted to pierce that cultural complacency by presenting contemporary society as a culture sleepwalking through two epistemological crises: a crisis of ethical theory and moral guidance, and a crisis of rational justification. MacIntyre offered an alternative vision of ethical renewal, through the establishment of communities in which it might be possible to rediscover the nature of the human telos, and in which small groups of people might recreate the life of the virtues, by rediscovering the Aristotelian tradition.

WJWR seeks to place this project in a broader theoretical framework in which the notion of tradition, and the rationalities associated with

214. AV, 172.

traditions, are central. The viability of such traditions can be tested by epistemological crises. The resolution of such a crisis requires conceptual innovation to address the unresolved problems, and this innovation will enhance the resourcefulness of the tradition, while maintaining continuity with its original elements of belief.[215] Although MacIntyre never makes this point explicit, his mature work acts as a demonstration of his thesis as well as an exposition of his theory. He not only offers a diagnosis of the ethical and epistemological crises of modernity in terms of the post-medieval abandonment of a Thomistic Aristotelianism, he also offers modernity a set of concepts drawn from Aristotle and Aquinas as a remedy to the disease. Whether one finds his position convincing depends, firstly, on whether one finds his narrative to be a plausible interpretation of the history of our culture and its current condition; secondly on whether one is convinced by his diagnosis of the impact of that culture on the human condition; and, thirdly, whether his theoretical constructs of the concepts of tradition, tradition-constituted rationality and epistemological crisis provide a defensible framework for analysis and action.

Evaluation

MacIntyre's mature position has provoked a considerable amount of controversy. Four important areas of criticism emerge in the secondary literature. Firstly, a number of authors have criticized the accuracy of MacIntyre's historical analysis,[216] and his interpretation of the work of some of the philosophers who are central to his account, thereby bringing into question the plausibility of his historical narrative[217] and his analysis of our contemporary situation.[218] A second line of attack is exemplified by criti-

---

215. WJWR, 362.

216. For a summary of this line of criticism, see Thomas, "Alasdair MacIntyre." Some examples of this type of criticism can be found in Baier, "MacIntyre on Hume," 3; and Annas, "MacIntyre on Traditions," 395–401. For a response to some of these criticisms see MacIntyre "Reply to Dahl, Baier and Schneewind," 172–74.

217. Wohler develops this type of criticism in his paper "Projecting the Enlightenment." MacIntyre also acknowledges the legitimacy of such criticism and the need for a more detailed charting of the intellectual history that he sketches out: see MacIntyre, "A Partial Response to my Critics." Other examples of this type of criticism can be found in Porter, "Tradition in the Recent Works of Alasdair MacIntyre"; Cohen, "In Defense of Nietzschean Genealogy"; Pakaluk, "A Defence of Scottish Common-Sense"; Dahl, "Justice and Aristotelian Practical Reason." However, MacIntyre's historical analysis has been supported by other commentators. See for example Curthoys, "Thomas Hobbes, the Taylor thesis and Alasdair MacIntyre."

218. Stout has criticized MacIntyre's account of the disorder of contemporary moral discourse in *Ethics after Babel*, 212–13.

cisms of MacIntyre's account of personal identity for failing to recognize that personhood is prior to and independent of community.[219] This aspect of the debate appears to illustrate the clash of incommensurable traditions, as the critics seek to defend a liberal political perspective from what they perceive to be an illegitimate "communitarian" critique,[220] thereby challenging MacIntyre's evaluation of the impact of contemporary culture on human potentiality. Thirdly, there is a debate about the relationship between MacIntyre's position and Enlightenment patterns of thought. One set of critics have questioned the legitimacy of MacIntyre's rejection of Enlightenment epistemology and ethics, and queried whether his alternative project is not, in fact, simply an extension of Enlightenment patterns of thought,[221] while a second group of critics have argued the converse position, that his rejection of Enlightenment principles is genuine, but that it commits him to relativism.[222] Fourthly, there have been a set of debates around the coherence of MacIntyre's theoretical perspective, addressing the questions of incommensurability and translatability,[223] the nature of a tradition[224] and the meaning and legitimacy of the associated notion of tradition-constituted rationality.[225] The first line of criticism questions the accuracy of MacIntyre's

219. See Cohen, "Does Communitarianism require Individual Independence?" 285; also Cochran, "The Thin Theory of Community: the Communitarians and their Critics," 426; for a more positive assessment see Gill, "MacIntyre, Rationality, and the Liberal Tradition."

220. I have used scare quotes because MacIntyre does not accept the description of himself as communitarian: see MacIntyre "Prologue" AV 3rd Edition, xiv.

221. Roque, "Language Competence and Tradition–Constituted Rationality," 611–17, claims that MacIntyre's position collapses into an assertion of universal standards of rational justification. Allen offers a similar criticism in "MacIntyre's Traditionalism," 521; Levy argues that MacIntyre's notion of a tradition gradually morphs into something which is virtually indistinguishable from the culture of modernity: See Levy, "Stepping into the Present: MacIntyre's Modernity," 471–90.

222. See for example: Clark, "Relativism and the Limits of Rationality"; Dahl: "Justice and Aristotelian Practical Reason"; Early, "MacIntyre, Narrative Rationality and Faith"; Fuller, *Making Sense of MacIntyre*, 28–29; Milbank, *Theology and Social Theory*; Ormerod, "Faith and Reason: Perspectives from MacIntyre and Lonergan," 11–22.

223. Fowl criticizes MacIntyre from a Davidsonian perspective in his paper "Could Horace Talk with the Hebrews?"

224. See, for example, Allen, "MacIntyre's Traditionalism," 511; Porter, "Tradition in the Recent Works of Alasdair MacIntyre"; Annas, "MacIntyre on Traditions."

225. Schneewind, "MacIntyre and the Indispensability of Tradition," challenges this notion, while Milbank emphasizes the limitations of reason with respect to the fundamental convictions that are at the heart of religious traditions (Milbank, *Theology and Social Theory*, 330). Herdt argues that MacIntyre's account of the rationality of traditions is itself a tradition-transcendent normative account of rationality; see Herdt, "Alasdair MacIntyre's 'Rationality of Traditions' and Tradition-Transcendental

reconstruction of the historical roots of the contemporary crises of Enlightenment thought. This is a significant test of his perspective, given MacIntyre's historicist approach. The debate on the nature of personal identity is more narrowly focused, but illustrates the opposition between a liberal individualist view of the relationship between individual and society, and the alternative perspective which sees communal practices as constitutive of that identity. It therefore symbolizes an important challenge to MacIntyre's critique of liberal individualism.

The third and fourth areas of criticism represent more fundamental objections to the coherence and legitimacy of MacIntyre's project as a whole, and these will form the focus of my evaluation. I will address the question of MacIntyre's relationship to Enlightenment thought in this section, and I will evaluate MacIntyre's theoretical constructs in chapter 4, drawing on my exposition of Lindbeck in chapter 3. In this section I will address three main issues. Firstly, is MacIntyre's philosophy a genuine alternative to Enlightenment thought or is it simply an unacknowledged variant of that epistemology? The resolution of this issue requires consideration of a second question, which is whether MacIntyre's account of traditions as mutually incommensurable and untranslatable is defensible. Thirdly I will consider the question of MacIntyre's alleged relativism.

MacIntyre and the Enlightenment

Some authors have argued MacIntyre's explicit rejection of Enlightenment epistemology disguises the fact that he implicitly imports elements of Enlightenment universal epistemological criteria into his position. This type of challenge can be illustrated by reference to papers by A. J. Roque and A. Allen. Roque argues that MacIntyre's claim that it is possible to understand another tradition through learning it as a "second first-language"[226] implies that human beings must have a "cognitive faculty" which provides them with such a learning capacity.[227] She contends that this innate capacity

> is nothing other than a variation of the Enlightenment view which MacIntyre rejects, that there is in humans a faculty of "common sense" which provides a universal and therefore neutral, context- and tradition-free, court to which we can appeal

Standards of Justification." Herdt's argument is challenged by Lott in his paper "Reasonably Traditional: Self-Contradiction and Self-Reference in Alasdair MacIntyre's Account of Tradition-Based rationality."

226. WJWR, 374.

227. Roque, "Language Competence and Tradition–Constituted Rationality," 617.

and which can provide the justification for claims of rationality
... MacIntyre has simply substituted "ability to acquire a second
first language" for the Enlightenment's "common sense."[228]

Roque's criticism appears to rest on either a trivial observation or a mistaken claim about the implications of MacIntyre's position. The first interpretation is that she is saying no more than that a person must have certain cognitive capacities in order to learn two or more languages. This is clearly correct, but the possession of such capacities says nothing about the nature of these languages or whether the cultures that use them embody different forms of rationality. The alternative interpretation is that she is asserting that the existence of a capacity for learning language implies that all languages must share some common characteristics and that these common characteristics imply the existence of a universal form of rationality. But it does not follow from the fact that a person can learn two different languages (or traditions) that these languages are commensurable and translatable and must embody common standards of evaluation.

MacIntyre has responded to Roque's criticism by suggesting that the idea of such a specific language-learning cognitive capacity is absurd.[229] He acknowledges that any language qua language must have certain features in common with other languages, and that any practice which can be understood to be a form of rationality requires conformity to the laws of logic.[230] However, these are necessary rather than sufficient conditions for the existence of translatability, commensurability and compatible processes of rational evaluation. These points do not undermine MacIntyre's contention that traditions may conceptualize issues in ways that are incommensurable with each other, and may have incompatible standards for judging truth and falsity.

Allen puts forward a similar but more sophisticated line of criticism to that of Roque. Allen claims that MacIntyre's account of the evolution of a tradition in effect establishes a universal standard of rationality to which all traditions must adhere, and that this implies that MacIntyre is unconsciously adhering to Enlightenment concepts of rationality. Allen interprets MacIntyre as claiming that the evolution of a tradition proceeds via a process of "determinate negation"[231] through which members of a tradition only modify a "few select tenets [at any one time] ... leaving a core of beliefs untouched. In the process of following this rational method, members of

---

228. Roque, "Language Competence," 617.
229. MacIntyre, "Reply to Roque," 619.
230. Ibid., 620.
231. Allen, "MacIntyre's Traditionalism," 521.

traditions may not negate all of their basic beliefs at any one time; they may only negate a determinate number of them."[232]

He suggests that MacIntyre sees this as a dialectical procedure common to all traditions, through which members of the tradition arrive at the truth. Macintyre's claim that one can only be rational through membership of a tradition therefore implies that all rational people must follow the principle of determinate negation. He continues:

> This sounds familiar because it is a description of the same kind of universalist standpoint which MacIntyre criticized Enlightenment thinkers for espousing. The view that MacIntyre espouses is itself one in which "*truth* is guaranteed by *rational method* and rational method appeals to *principles undeniable by any fully reflective rational person.*" Clearly then, MacIntyre's account of the rationality of traditions entails an implicit appeal to precisely those kinds of Enlightenment standards that he claims to reject.[233]

Allen's argument appears to assume that MacIntyre is establishing a deontological criterion of rationality to which all traditions must conform if they are to be considered rational. But MacIntyre would claim that he is *describing* what happens in the history of tradition, rather than prescribing standards to which all traditions must conform. The similarities in the evolution of different traditions will be underpinned by shared principles of argument (the laws of logic). However, such principles are necessary but not sufficient conditions to justify claims to rationality (see TRV p. 172 and TRV p. 326, for example). Each tradition will incorporate additional presuppositions and standards into its processes for evaluation and justification which will shape its rationality of the tradition into forms which are incompatible with those of other traditions.

Allen's "principle of determinate negation" points to the fact that membership of a tradition involves adherence to a specific set of beliefs and engagement in culturally endorsed practices. A tradition cannot maintain its identity if all of its precepts are questioned or rejected at the same time, although during its history every element of its beliefs may be subject to challenge and modification at different times. The conservative nature of Allen's principle of determinate negation reflects the fact that if all members were to reject every tenet the tradition would no longer exist. There must be elements of continuity in the beliefs and practices of any tradition

---

232. Ibid.

233. Ibid., emphases added by Allen; see WJWR, 353 for the MacIntyre quotation embedded in the passage from Allen.

if that tradition is to maintain its identity over time. Lindbeck's exploration of the identity of the Christian tradition in ND points to the role played by the regulative functions of doctrine in shaping the identity and stability of Christian traditions, and in section 4.3 I will apply this idea more generally to the question of the identity of a tradition.

The arguments by Roque and Allen do not demonstrate that MacIntyre's position endorses the Enlightenment belief in universal standards of rational justification. There are, however, two elements of MacIntyre's position that might support the contention that he is espousing Enlightenment universalism. The first is his assertion that any tradition must adhere to the laws of logic in constructing standards of rationality; the second, and more important feature, is MacIntyre's claim that only a degenerate tradition would allow itself to construct the type of epistemological defenses which would prevent its beliefs being put into question.[234] This implies that a living tradition must meet a standard of epistemological openness if it is to be considered a rational form of enquiry,[235] and this does specify a universal standard to which all traditions must conform qua traditions of enquiry. These universalist elements are however, balanced by two other elements of his account of rationality. These are, firstly, the claim that each tradition will develop unique concepts in its attempts to articulate its central concerns; and that, as a result at least some of its assertions will be untranslatable into the concepts available to rival traditions. Secondly, there is the claim that each tradition will have formulated distinctive standards of justification that reflect its conceptual development, its history of challenge and conflict resolution, and the nature of its enquiry. Even if assertions made in one tradition may be translated into the conceptual scheme of the other, these distinctive standards of justification may lead to incompatible judgments of truth and falsity.

MacIntyre's account of tradition-constituted rationality is therefore a hybrid position which combines two elements of Enlightenment universalism (logical consistency and the principle of epistemological openness) with two elements that are tradition specific (incommensurability and incompatible standards of justification). If these tradition-specific elements do not exist, and all traditions can be shown to be mutually translatable and commensurable, MacIntyre's position would collapse into a version of Enlightenment universalism. I will argue in the next sub-section that MacIntyre's claims for the untranslatability of different traditions are vulnerable to challenge. However, I will also argue that the claim that traditions have different

---

234. ECS, 12.
235. See section 2.5 above for a discussion of epistemological openness.

standards of justification is not vulnerable in this way, and that if this is the case, his claim that some traditions have distinct and incommensurable standards of rationality can be sustained.

Incommensurability and Translatability

The claim that different traditions form incommensurable systems of thought is central to MacIntyre's repudiation of Enlightenment notions of knowledge, truth and justification. If (at least some of) the concepts that can be used within one tradition cannot be translated into the concepts of another tradition, the two traditions will be "two radically different... conceptual schemes" and will not be mutually interpretable.[236] As a result a tradition will embody a distinct set of concepts, practices and beliefs which are not equivalent to the concepts, practices and beliefs of a rival tradition and which cannot, therefore be translated into the concepts available within that tradition.[237] Such incommensurable traditions could only be learned as one learns a new language, and only through this process of immersion could one learn that the concepts used in the new tradition are incompatible with the concepts used in one's original tradition. Incommensurability therefore can only be recognized by "someone who inhabits both conceptual schemes; who knows and is able to utter the idiom from within, who has become...a native speaker of two first languages."[238] Conversely, if incommensurable conceptual schemes do not exist, MacIntyre's critique of the Enlightenment would be subject to challenge. If all conceptual schemes are commensurable then assertions[239] made in one tradition could be fully translated into the idioms of another tradition without loss of meaning. However, even if all traditions were mutually translatable, this would not guarantee agreement on the truth status of assertions made in one tradition unless each tradition had identical criteria for testing the truth or falsity of such assertions.

---

236. TRV, 43.
237. WJWR, 327–28.
238. TRV, 114.

239. I am using the term assertion to be concise but it is potentially misleading if it is identified with the claim that every significant sentence corresponds to or asserts a particular proposition. I do not believe that there is a set of propositions which constitute the meanings of sentences uttered in different languages and which form the basis of translatability. My position is similar to that of Stout, Diamond and MacIntyre who (following Wittgenstein) emphasise that meaning is about communication in a language-in-use; see Stout, *Ethics after Babel.*, 63; Diamond, "Losing your Concepts"; WJWR, 372–73.

There are therefore two questions which need to be addressed in testing whether MacIntyre's position provides a genuine alternative to Enlightenment epistemology. Firstly, there is the question of whether incommensurable conceptual schemes can ever be rendered mutually interpretable. Secondly, there is the question as to whether this mutual interpretability also implies common standards of rational evaluation. If the answer to both questions is "yes" the combination of universal translatability and consensus concerning judgments of truth and falsehood would make the encyclopedic aim of identifying and connecting all aspects of knowledge into a single interdependent network a realistic possibility, and the ambitions of the Enlightenment could be revived.

The notion that it is possible to have separate, incommensurable and therefore mutually untranslatable, conceptual schemes has been criticized, most famously by Donald Davidson.[240] This controversy still continues,[241] and it would be beyond the scope of this book (and the abilities of its author) to seek to finally resolve this debate. However, defending the coherence of MacIntyre's position does not require the complete resolution of the question as to whether fully incommensurable conceptual schemes can exist or not, because MacIntyre is primarily concerned with limited or partial incommensurability and untranslatability in relation to some specific elements of tradition. Davidson does not reject the possibility of this type of incommensurability and MacIntyre himself suggests that his position and that of Davidson are at least potentially reconcilable. He comments that Davidson's perspective "can be interpreted as saying no more than would be conceded . . . by anyone; that there will always be something in common between any two languages or any two sets of thoughts. But he has sometimes at least been understood to be asserting claims incompatible with the account which I have given."[242]

Davidson's seminal article is concerned primarily with the possibility of conceptual schemes that have no shared elements. He contends that if such schemes existed, we would be unable to recognize the supposed rival conceptual framework as a means of communication or as a way of understanding reality. This is because we cannot interpret an alien language as a form of communication unless we can assume that the speaker is generally asserting what she believes to be true (the principle of charity),[243] and that

---

240. Davidson, "On the Very Idea of a Conceptual Scheme."

241. See, for example, Wang, "On Davidson's Refutation of Conceptual Schemes and Conceptual Relativism."

242. WJWR, 371.

243. Davidson, "On the Very Idea of a Conceptual Scheme," 18–19.

the speaker's judgments about what is the case will generally match our own. There will therefore be consistency in the type of judgments that are held to be true notwithstanding the use of different languages. This implies that all intelligent beings live in the same reality, and have to be assumed to be asserting a similar set of judgments about that shared reality. The process of communication has to begin by mapping elements of the set of true assertions in each language against each other. This assumption would enable one to establish "a systematic correlation of sentences held true with sentences held true"[244] in each language. Davidson does not deny the possibility of conceptual differences and disagreements about truth arising between the groups who use these different languages, but such differences and disagreements presuppose a background of general agreement with respect to what is held to be true. It is only the background of shared understanding about what is true that "make[s] meaningful disagreement possible."[245]

MacIntyre may or may not believe that it is possible to have completely independent (and thereby incommunicable) conceptual schemes. But this is not the type of incommensurability with which he is primarily concerned in his arguments about tradition. His incommensurable rival traditions exist in human societies in which different groups may hold disparate belief systems, but these groups will also share many conceptual elements with the other social groups with whom they interact. At worst, therefore, he is concerned with conceptual worlds in which some elements, but not all, may be incommensurable with others. As a result, MacIntyre allows that traditions may interact, either because some person or persons has been sufficiently immersed in the conceptual schemes of different traditions to compare their different perspectives; or because different traditions share an overlapping stock of texts, images and beliefs which provides a basis for communication. In this latter case, the similarities may enable each tradition to recognize and consider their differences.[246] MacIntyre is therefore concerned with only partial incommensurability and untranslatability.

Davidson considers the issue of partial untranslatability, and suggests that "we improve the clarity and bite of declarations of difference, whether of scheme or of opinion, by enlarging the basis of shared (translatable) language or of shared opinion."[247] Davidson's point here is that where differences arise they may be treated as either differences of belief as to what is the case (disputes about truth) or differences in the conceptual resources

---

244. Ibid., 19.
245. Ibid.
246. WJWR, 350.
247. Davidson, "On the Very Idea of a Conceptual Scheme," 19.

used to interpret reality (a clash of incommensurable perspectives). In some circumstances we may understand such differences of perspective as arising from the use of the different and incompatible concepts embodied in each tradition, in which case the task of understanding may involve constructing new concepts to express the insights of the alien tradition within the language of our own tradition. But once conceptual innovation has enabled the insights of that alien tradition to be expressed, we may still disagree with what the alien tradition holds to be true, because other elements of our belief system lead us to judge the truth or falsity of what is asserted by the rival tradition in a different way. This point can be exemplified by drawing on a thought experiment constructed by Jeffrey Stout.

Stout appears to share similar views on partial incommensurability to Davidson and MacIntyre, despite the claim by some critics that his views on this issue are opposed to those of MacIntyre.[248] Stout's account of translatability in *Ethics after Babel* is consistent with and adds detail to MacIntyre's description of the process of understanding an alien tradition. Stout imagines two isolated communities who come into contact with each other and seek to understand their respective moral frameworks; the Corleones (who emphasise the virtues of purity, honor and revenge) and the Modernists who possess a Kantian deontological concept of morality. Stout stipulates that neither side possess the concepts and vocabulary that would enable them to express the moral insights of their rivals when they first interact. Consider the following quotation:

> In our example, the Modernists cannot, by stipulation express most of the propositions of Corleone moral discourse in Modernese. That means they cannot do so now. But the Modernists may end their cultural isolation and send out their own ethnographers to study the Corleones. In time, ethnographers from Modernity can learn the moral language of the Corleones as Corleone children do—from the ground up. That option is always open when initial efforts at direct translation fail.[249]

The reference to learning the language in the same way as Corleone children mirrors MacIntyre's understanding of the process required to grasp an incommensurable conceptual system. Both Stout and MacIntyre acknowledge that there can be issues of incommensurability and untranslatability but suggest that a dialogue can take place between different traditions through individuals being socialized into the second tradition. The judgments made in an alien tradition may ultimately be made communicable to

---

248. For example, see Fowl, "Could Horace Talk with the Hebrews?"
249. Stout, *Ethics after Babel*, 64.

the adherents of another through the field reports of anthropologists providing a discursive account of the practices and forms of life that underpin the concepts used in the first tradition, and through the creation of new hermeneutic resources within the second tradition.[250] However, as Davidson's comment about interpreting disagreement as *either* incommensurability of concepts *or* disputes about truth suggests, what was initially a question of incommensurability may subsequently develop into a conflict of judgments of truth, because the process of conceptual development which overcomes incommensurability does not necessarily lead to agreement. Stout makes a similar point in the following way:

> It doesn't follow ... that understanding another culture's moral language necessitates adopting the moral beliefs held by its members ... If I can imitate Corleone moralizing ... predict what Corleones will say about new cases, make sense of their past behaviour by ascribing beliefs and desires that fit in nicely with my translations of their moral sentences ... then I understand their moral language. I might still refuse to join in when they moralize. I might vigorously dissent from their beliefs about women and strangers. Their claims about the necessity of vengeance might never influence my moral reasoning.[251]

What has occurred in the process of hermeneutic innovation necessary to facilitate understanding is a shift from conceptual incommensurability to a disagreement about the legitimacy of the concepts which have now been introduced into the first tradition. I conclude from these observations that MacIntyre's account of incommensurability and untranslatability is consistent with both Davidson and Stout. But while all three authors allow that conceptual innovation may ultimately facilitate communication between alien traditions, Stout's example shows that this does not imply that these traditions will adopt common processes for determining what is true or false. Each tradition may apply its own standards of justification to assessing the truth of assertions couched in these concepts and may make incompatible judgments of truth and falsity, legitimacy and illegitimacy even where (limited) conceptual incommensurability has been overcome by hermeneutic innovation. Each tradition will not be bound by the alternative rational processes used to construct such judgments that are applied by the alien tradition. Overcoming limited incommensurability would not lead to consensus on universally applicable standards of justification across different traditions. As a result, the conditions required for the revival of the

---

250. Ibid.
251. Ibid., 67.

Enlightenment project have not been met, and MacIntyre's critique of the Enlightenment can be sustained.

This discussion brings us back to another, unresolved, problem. The presuppositions which underpin the Modernist and Corleone traditions are too disparate to allow for consensus on moral judgment. Conceptual change may enable us to understand an alien view, but we may refuse to allow any legitimacy to such views. We may understand these views, but only as the strange and unjustified perspective of an alien tribe. But is this rejection of the alien view any more than an expression of our own specific tribal prejudices? Can we provide cogent reasons for declaring one ethical tradition to be superior to another? If we cannot do this, are we not once again left without a response to the challenge that MacIntyre's position is relativist? Is there a rational basis for committing to one tradition rather than another?

Relativism and Tradition-Constituted Rationality

The second strand of criticism that arises from the question of MacIntyre's relationship to the Enlightenment accepts that his denial of Enlightenment standards of justification is genuine, but claims that, as a result, he is committed to a form of relativism. Fuller, for example, argues that MacIntyre's claim that the success of a tradition has to be judged in accordance with the internal criteria of adequacy formulated by the tradition appears to lead to a form of fideism, in that the acceptance of these criteria is a matter of submission to the authority of the tradition, rather than a matter of rational justification.[252] Neil Ormerod also expresses anxiety at the apparent fideism implicit in Macintyre's position[253] while Norman Dahl criticizes MacIntyre for having no basis on which to choose between two equally successful traditions, thereby opening the door to a different form of relativism.[254] Christian Early welcomes this fideistic aspect of MacIntyre's work as warranting the acceptance of the primacy of authority in matters of religious belief.[255] However, Early's perspective leaves unresolved the question of how one is to decide between competing authorities.[256]

252. Fuller, *Making Sense of MacIntyre*, 28–29.
253. Ormerod, "Faith and Reason: Perspectives from MacIntyre and Lonergan."
254. Dahl, "Justice and Aristotelian Practical Reason," 157.
255. Early, "MacIntyre, Narrative Rationality and Faith."
256. Early's position also does not respond to the implications of MacIntyre's comment that in tradition-constituted rationality "The *weakest* form of argument, but none the less that which will prevail in the absence of any other, will be the appeal to the authority of established belief, merely as established" WJWR, 359; emphasis added.

John Milbank is perhaps the most interesting critic of MacIntyre's alleged relativism, particularly as he "does not find [MacIntyre] *sufficiently* relativistic or historicist."²⁵⁷ In *Theology and Social Theory* Milbank criticizes MacIntyre for his over-reliance on a philosophical and dialectical approach to understanding argument, justification, and reason, and argues for the superiority of a theological perspective. He contrasts MacIntyre's reliance on philosophical argument with the rhetorical and persuasive character of the warrants for the fundamental beliefs of Christianity.²⁵⁸ As a philosopher MacIntyre is committed to constructing a position which can be defended through logical argument, but Milbank suggests that MacIntyre's philosophical commitment leads him to ignore what can only be dealt with theologically in belief. As a consequence, this leaves him unable to address the basis for faith and Milbank comments that: "at the philosophic level an air of non-commitment hovers over MacIntyre's work, an implication even of the inevitable liberalism of philosophy itself."²⁵⁹ For Milbank philosophy cannot help with the fundamental business of belief and commitment. It can assist only with the business of working out the implications of a commitment once this has been made. Logical argument can only begin once one has accepted some basic presuppositions on different grounds.

Logical argument therefore applies only within and not between different discourses. Milbank "wants to insist against MacIntyre that at (the) level of 'objective' reasoning one is only talking about the inner consistency of a discourse or practice."²⁶⁰ Milbank's comments point to the belief that the core principles and assumptions of a tradition are *inherited* rather than proven, and their adoption is not therefore the consequence of a process of dialectical argument, but a prelude to it: our fundamental beliefs are convictions rather than conclusions. This observation raises issues about the nature of religious and philosophical conviction and commitment, and the relationship between the two. Milbank summarizes the contrast between the approaches as follows:

> A tension arises here between MacIntyre's "philosophic" perspective on Christianity on the one hand, which concedes the rhetorical, persuasive character of its fundamental texts, practices and credal beliefs, but then treats these only from the point of view of testing their validity by a universal method (dialectics), and, on the other hand, a theological perspective...which

257. Milbank, *Theology and Social Theory*, 327; emphasis original.
258. Ibid., 328.
259. Ibid., 329.
260. Ibid., 330.

speaks in modes beyond the point where dialectics leaves off, namely in terms of the imaginative explication of texts, practices and beliefs.[261]

Thomas Clark adopts a similar perspective to that of Milbank when he argues that "rationality operates within an already given system of assumptions and motives, and . . . even our conception of rationality itself is relative to a particular context. We will never be able, finally, to rationally justify our most basic values or fundamental beliefs about how the world is. These values and beliefs constitute the context within which our version of rationality works."[262] Clark suggests (following Rorty) that the collapse of correspondence theories of truth and the recognition that there is no theory neutral access to an independent world imply that we only ever represent reality from a particular perspective. He argues that "there is no point outside our view of the world from which to evaluate that view's truth; knowledge is always a representation of reality from within a particular perspective. Although we exist and participate in ultimate reality, we cannot know this reality objectively in the sense once hoped for. We cannot assume the detached vantage point of what philosopher Thomas Nagel calls 'the view from nowhere.'"[263]

MacIntyre would certainly reject the apparent perspectivism that underlies Clark's contentions, but he would do so without invoking a correspondence theory of truth and would argue as vehemently that there is no "detached vantage point" from which one can survey reality.[264] MacIntyre would also accept Milbank's assertion that the fundamental beliefs of a tradition are not accepted on the basis of demonstrative argument, and that rationality is internal to a tradition. I would suggest, however, that both those critics who claim that MacIntyre is (or, in Milbank's case, that he should be) a relativist, and those critics who assimilate his position to the Enlightenment project fail to fully acknowledge the extent to which MacIntyre is developing an alternative account of the nature of justification to the Enlightenment model. MacIntyre's hybrid model of rationality has both universal and tradition specific elements. The tradition-specific elements shape the conceptualization of reality and judgments of truth and falsity, and if these features are considered in isolation, they appear to point

---

261. Ibid., 328. Milbank's use of the word "credal" in this quotation is helpful in pointing to a set of beliefs to which one has to be committed if one is to be a member of a tradition.

262. Clark, "Relativism and the limits of rationality," 25.

263. Ibid., 30.

264. WJWR, 350.

in the direction of relativism. They are balanced, however, by the universal elements which act as potential tests of the overall coherence and viability of the system of thought represented by that tradition. Participation in a tradition of enquiry requires one to become convinced of its basic presuppositions through initial processes of socialization, persuasion, and rhetoric rather than through demonstrative proofs. But the beliefs so acquired may then be tested in terms of their logical coherence, their consistency with the standards of rationality that have emerged within that tradition, and by their ability to withstand the challenges generated by the tradition's epistemological openness. The ability of a tradition to maintain its coherence in response to these challenges is a measure of its superiority to traditions that are unable to overcome epistemological crises created by such challenges.

In chapter 4 I will argue that a tradition of enquiry can be identified with the type of comprehensive metaphysical viewpoint with which MacIntyre was concerned in his early publications. If this is the case, and MacIntyre has been successful in articulating an account of the superiority of one such tradition to another which clarifies how a person may become rationally justified in accepting the central tenets of a tradition, he has also provided a general account of the justification of a belief in a comprehensive metaphysical perspective, and will have addressed the issue of commitment to such a perspective that he had struggled to resolve in his early period. But before we can arrive at this point in the argument, it is necessary to become clearer about the nature of tradition-constituted rationality and epistemological crisis, and this means that I must also consider the question of the nature of a tradition.

In exploring these issues, I will also show that clarity with regards to the nature and identity of a tradition is the keystone to an effective evaluation of MacIntyre's mature position. In constructing an account of the nature of tradition I will draw on the work of the theologian George A. Lindbeck in his book *The Nature of Doctrine*. This account will also enable me to construct a more comprehensive account of tradition-constituted rationality and help to clarify the circumstances in which an epistemological crisis may arise. While Lindbeck's work helps to strengthen MacIntyre's position, my analysis will also help to clarify and strengthen Lindbeck's position, by incorporating MacIntyre's concept of tradition-constituted rationality into his account of superiority in matters of religion—a step which Lindbeck himself advocated in his afterword to the 25th anniversary edition of ND.[265] This process of cross-fertilization will also strengthen both Lindbeck's and MacIntyre's position against accusations of relativism or

---

265. Lindbeck, "Afterword," ND 2nd Edition, 125–40; 138.

fideism. The first step in addressing these issues is to sketch the background to Lindbeck's work and provide a summary of his cultural-linguistic (CL) model of religion and regulative account of the nature of doctrine. This is the focus of chapter 3.

3

LINDBECK AND THE IDENTITY OF THE CHRISTIAN TRADITION

3.1 Lindbeck, Ecumenism, and Doctrine

Lindbeck and Ecumenism

George Lindbeck is a Lutheran and Emeritus Professor of theology at Yale University. His life's work has been driven by a desire to overcome the differences between churches that have divided the Christian tradition. He was born in 1923 and his early years were spent in China,[1] which meant that he had contact with a range of religious and cultural groups. He has suggested that this early engagement with diversity helped to shape his theological development[2] and his later interest in ecumenism.[3] This interest was also stimulated by the fact that, despite his Protestant beliefs, his early teaching and research was "mostly related to the past and present of Roman Catholic thought."[4] His work on medieval philosophy meant that he was particularly well suited to act as an observer at the Second Vatican Council on behalf of the World Lutheran Federation, a role he undertook between 1962 and

    1. Adiprasetya, "George A. Lindbeck and Postliberal Theology."
    2. Lindbeck, "Confession and Community: An Israel-like view of the Church," 492.
    3. Lindbeck, "Paris, Rome, Jerusalem: An Ecumenical Journey," 389.
    4. Ibid., 395. Lindbeck also noted that his interest in Roman Catholicism was fostered by early contact with his Roman Catholic cousins: see Wright, ed., *Postliberal Theology and the Church Catholic,* 57.

1965, while living in Rome for much of this period.[5] He eventually became the Pitkin Professor of Historical Theology at Yale, retiring from this post in 1993.[6]

Lindbeck's experiences at Vatican II led him to see ecumenism in terms of the task of healing the divisions that separate the Roman Catholic Church from the Protestant churches in general and the Lutheran community in particular. He has pursued this aim by fostering an understanding of Protestantism as a reform movement *within* the wider Catholic Church:

> My ecumenical concerns have been tilted in a Catholic direction ... I came to think that Lutheranism should try to become what it started out to be, a reform movement within the Catholic Church of the West. By such a strategy it can best contribute to the goal of wider Christian unity. This goal and strategy have guided almost all my work since then.[7]

Lindbeck's ecumenical work can therefore be seen as a contribution to the reunification of a divided Christian tradition. The goal of ecumenism, as Lindbeck came to understand it during his studies in the Paris of 1950, "was a visibly united church" which would arise through the action of the Holy Spirit in enabling churches to move in the direction of a shared understanding of the faith. This deeper unity would allow each church to maintain its own distinctive identity. Unity would be achieved

> in God's own time by means largely hidden but [in ways] that can be pointed to by such words as *convergence, rapprochement* and *integration*. Each of the uniting bodies would have to change profoundly in order to enter into full communion, but they could do this, it was believed, without rejecting what is essential to their own identities.[8]

How long such a process would take and whether it "would be successful prior to the eschaton God only knew,"[9] but it would lead to a genuinely united church, albeit one rich in diversity. The precondition of the type of "convergence ecumenism"[10] that Lindbeck has advocated is a transdenominational unity that can develop around a common understanding

---

5. Weigel, "Re-viewing Vatican II," [Interview with Lindbeck]. See also Lindbeck, "Reminiscences of Vatican II," 10–18.

6. Adiprasetya, "George A. Lindbeck and Postliberal Theology."

7. Lindbeck, "Confession and Community," 494.

8. Lindbeck, "The Unity we Seek: Setting the Agenda for Ecumenism," 28.

9. Ibid., 28.

10. Ibid., 28.

of the principles of identity and authenticity within the Christian tradition: an "agreement on where and how the apostolic tradition is to be located and retrieved."[11] Ecumenism therefore requires a deepening of the way in which the identity of the Christian tradition is understood, and as a result Lindbeck's work provides an opportunity to examine an approach to the understanding of the nature and identity of tradition which complements the work of Alasdair MacIntyre.

The Criteriological Problem

Divisions within the Christian tradition can be seen to reflect a lack of shared and agreed criteria for determining what should count as authentic elements of that tradition. Lindbeck explored what might be required to overcome this barrier to unity in a lecture on "Infallibility" that he gave in 1972, and his account is an important precursor to the position he was to set out in ND some twelve years later. Lindbeck observes that the teaching office of the Catholic Church forms the source of authority which binds that Church into a single body. Lindbeck argues that one weakness of the protestant churches is that they lack such a "visible center of unity."[12] However, the authority of the teaching office is supported by the dogma of infallibility; and while the purpose of this dogma is to provide a criterion of authenticity that can secure the continued coherence and identity of the Christian tradition, in practice it has become a focus of disunity and a barrier to integration—as Pope Paul VI had recognized.[13] The dogma has, therefore, become a contested doctrine in its existing form, even within the Catholic Church itself.[14]

In "Infallibility" Lindbeck argues that the apparently contradictory positions adopted by Protestant and Roman Catholic churches with respect to this dogma may ultimately be reconcilable, because the terms used by each in the interpretation of this doctrine are almost certainly conceptualized differently within Protestant and Roman Catholic thought[15] (although he does not underestimate the difficulties associated with such a task). Moreover, the interpretation of the terms that constitute this doctrine may vary in different historical and religious contexts, so that positions that were clearly contradictory at one time in one environment may become recon-

11. Ibid., 31.
12. Lindbeck, Infallibility, 122.
13. Ibid., 123.
14. Ibid.
15. Ibid., 126.

cilable when that context has changed.[16] The issue of compatibility may therefore turn on the nature of the historical context in which doctrinal differences arise, and which shapes the interpretation of those doctrines at that point in time.[17]

In "Infallibility" Lindbeck contends that conflict between doctrinal formulations should not necessarily be identified with fundamental religious differences because doctrines are, in any case, always partial and incomplete attempts to express the fundamental religious truths that underpin the complexity of the life of faith:

> One must always remember that the faith affirmations, the real and primary dogmas of the community, are only very partially expressed in official definitions. The fundamental affirmations cannot be captured in isolated propositions because they are functioning parts of the organically unified language systems and correlated forms of life in which the faith of a religious community is basically articulated. Not even the most elaborate network of *de fide* formulae can begin to exhaust the rich complexities of the primary dogmas.[18]

A limited set of propositions cannot embody the potential for development encapsulated in "the primary dogmas," and it will always be possible to elaborate their significance further. Given this openness to development and interpretation, how are the authentic truths of Christianity to be recognized? In a review of a collection of papers edited by John Hick in 1979 (*The Myth of the God Incarnate*) Lindbeck describes this as the "criteriological problem," and proffers a solution in terms of the primacy of a process of interpretation that depends on the framework defined by biblical narrative:

> What is ignored [in Hick's book] . . . is the critical criteriological problem. From where does one get, not the concepts for describing, but the norms for identifying God, for defining the divine, for evaluating religious experience? Are these derived from within the world of biblical narrative (understood as culminating in the stories about Jesus), or from some other religious, intellectual, or cultural framework or language game? If the former, then some form of postmodern "orthodoxy" is the only alternative: the Christian God is defined by the Christian story. But this [Hick's] book takes the latter option. It tacitly seems to adopt the old liberal assumption that enlightened reason and

16. Ibid., 125–26.
17. Ibid., 131.
18. Ibid., 129.

conscience have access to independent or transcendent criteria which enable them to pick and choose what is of highest value from within the various religious traditions.[19]

This response to Hick reflects Lindbeck's fundamental epistemological perspective. Lindbeck, like MacIntyre, repudiates the modernist assumption that one can adjudicate between different comprehensive frameworks of belief through an appeal to some transcendent criterion of validity that is external to all frameworks.[20] But if one cannot do this, the criteria by which one determines the validity of religious perspectives will have to be found within the religious framework itself, and for Lindbeck the source of such criteria must rest within the scriptural canon. However, the meaning of these scriptural narratives needs to be interpreted, and there is, therefore, a need for a common hermeneutic approach which enables the meaning of these stories to be interpreted correctly. Lindbeck later argued that such a methodology is embodied in the principles which underpinned what he calls "classical biblical hermeneutics." In this approach "the Bible as interpreted within the Christian mainstream purports to provide a totally comprehensive framework, a universal perspective, within which everything can be properly construed and outside of which nothing can be equally well understood."[21]

The Bible provides the framework in which a community can understand its changing environment. The application of Scripture to the changing contexts in which communities find themselves is guided by the institutions, history, and practices of those communities. Text, history, and church form an inseparable whole which interpret each other and form the community's resources for interpreting the world. This interpretative capacity forms the basis for the sustained development of communities whose identity can be maintained over millennia.[22] Lindbeck's book, *The Nature of Doctrine* (ND), represents a sustained discussion of the nature of a religion as such an "interpretative medium."[23] In so far as *some* elements of a religion are comparable to a MacIntyrean tradition of enquiry (particularly its theological articulation), this discussion can also shed light on the identity of traditions; on the role played by doctrines (conceived as rules of assertion, expression, and practice) as constitutive elements in such traditions; on the

---

19. Lindbeck, Review of *The Myth of God Incarnate*, 249.

20. Battaglia notes the relationship between Lindbeck's thought and the erosion of Enlightenment foundationalism in "'Sect' or 'Denomination'?," 136.

21. Lindbeck, "The Gospel's Uniqueness: Election and Untranslatability," 429.

22. Lindbeck, "The Search for Habitable Texts," 155.

23. ND, 80.

Lindbeck and the Identity of the Christian Tradition

nature of tradition-constituted rationality; and on the nature of epistemological crisis.

3.2 The Nature of Doctrine

In ND Lindbeck suggests that doctrinal teachings differentiate churches from each other and define the boundaries between different communities of belief. Lindbeck asserts that "Church doctrines are communally authoritative teachings regarding beliefs and practices that are considered essential to the identity or welfare of the group in question. They may be formally stated or informally operative, but in any case they indicate what constitutes faithful adherence to a community."[24] A member who rejects the communally authoritative doctrines of a religious community will ultimately alienate herself from that community. Statements of doctrine therefore serve to articulate the identity of a religious community and its members, and articulate the community's most immediately important and defining commitments, both for the benefit of its adherents and in response to those who might challenge its views. In fulfilling this function doctrines identify a set of required beliefs and practices that should be shared by all members of the community. Lindbeck takes the existence of such a core set of distinctive beliefs or practices as a minimum requirement for the existence of a distinct religious community and asserts that "a religious body cannot exist as a recognizably distinctive collectivity unless it has some beliefs and/or practices by which it can be identified."[25]

Doctrinal statements may therefore serve to define the points of identity and difference between separate religious communities, at times when those differences need to be formally expressed. As a result of these identity-forming functions, differences in doctrine would appear to signal the existence of significant barriers to Christian unity, unless one community or another is prepared to abandon some of the doctrines which have served to define its identity as a distinct group. However, Lindbeck points out that the history of ecumenicism shows that differences between religious communities can sometimes be resolved, without either side having to abandon its beliefs and capitulate to the perspective of the other community.[26] There is, therefore, a dissonance between the theoretical presentation of doctrinal division and its allegedly church-dividing consequences, and the ecumenical reality with which Lindbeck had engaged. Lindbeck's governing assumption

24. ND, 74.
25. ND, 74.
26. ND, 15–16.

is that this dissonance has arisen because theology has embraced mistaken interpretations of the nature of doctrine, and that these interpretations have arisen in turn from the adoption of mistaken theories with respect to the nature of religion. These theories cannot account adequately for the strange intertwining of "variability and invariability in matters of faith"[27] that a study of ecumenical relationships reveals. Lindbeck therefore seeks to diagnose the faults of the dominant models of religion, and to construct a more effective model.

Lindbeck's Criticism of Contemporary Models of Religion

Lindbeck suggests that contemporary theories of religion predominantly take two main forms. Firstly, "cognitive-propositional" (CP) theories of religion contend that religious beliefs and statements of doctrine should be interpreted in primarily propositional terms, as assertions about the nature of a spiritual reality.[28] Secondly, "experiential-expressive" (EE) theories treat religious statements as primarily symbolic expressions of what would otherwise be inexpressible religious experiences.[29] He also identifies a third class of theories that seek to reconcile the opposition between cognitive-propositional and experiential-expressive interpretations by combining them into "two-dimensional" interpretations of the nature of religion,[30] thereby acknowledging that religious assertions have both propositional and expressive functions. However, Lindbeck devotes little attention to such theories, seeing them as combining the perspectives and the defects of both CP and EE accounts. It is therefore legitimate for this discussion to focus on his criticism of CP and EE models.[31]

Lindbeck argues that the CP theory has difficulty in explaining the possibility of ecumenical reconciliation where the doctrines of different communities conflict, because, if doctrinal statements express propositions about the nature of a spiritual reality, differences between doctrines must indicate fundamental disagreements about ontological commitments. And if this is the case, the resolution of doctrinal conflict would appear to require one community to abandon some of its identity-defining beliefs about reality, should it concede that the apparently contradictory doctrines

27. ND, 17.
28. ND, 16.
29. ND, 17.
30. ND, 17.

31. DeHart, *The Trial of the Witnesses*, 163, criticizes Lindbeck for unfairly dismissing such accounts.

of another community are true.³² He points out that "for a propositionalist, if a doctrine is once true, it is always true, and if it is once false, it is always false . . . Agreement can only be reached if one or both sides abandon their earlier positions."³³

Experiential-expressive interpretations of religious beliefs, on the other hand, treat religious statements as symbolic expressions of spiritual experiences that are common to all people. Religious doctrines act to symbolize, express or evoke such experiences. Variability in the terminology in which these common experiences are expressed should not act as a barrier to ecumenism, because such linguistic differences do not reflect fundamental differences in the nature of the religious experience that underpins all religious belief. If doctrinal statements act as symbols, differences in their formulation "are not crucial for religious agreement or disagreement, because these are constituted by harmony or conflict in the underlying feelings, attitudes, existential orientations or practices, rather than by what happens on the level of symbolic (including doctrinal) objectifications."³⁴ On this interpretation of the nature of religious language and doctrine, differences in religious belief are obliterated in the melting-pot of religious experience. Any degree of variation in doctrinal formulation appears to be consistent with an underlying unity of religious experience. On the EE model "there is . . . at least the logical possibility that a Buddhist and a Christian might have basically the same faith, although expressed very differently."³⁵

However, an experiential interpretation of the beliefs of religious communities would appear to be inconsistent with the way in which religious groups articulate their own identity. The differences between themselves and other communities are expressed in terms of (apparently) conflicting accounts of the nature of ultimate reality.³⁶ Lindbeck suggests that the consequences of the failure of both CP and EE models of religion to account for variability (on a CP interpretation) and identity (on an EE interpretation) may encourage a relativist or perspectivist interpretation of the claims to religious truth which characterize the identities of different religions.³⁷

---

32. ND, 16–17.
33. ND, 16.
34. ND, 17.
35. ND, 17.

36. Lindbeck's description of a debate between Buddhist and Christian students indicates that each groups conceptualized themselves as having a different understanding of the nature of reality that was entirely incommensurable with that of the "alien" religion. See Lindbeck, "Afterword," ND 2nd Edition 137–38.

37. ND, 78.

Ecumenical progress exhibits a combination of invariability (in that adherents of one religion continue to hold to the truth of their doctrines) and also variability (in that expressions of belief that at one time appeared irreconcilable can now be interpreted in ways that allow for their harmonization).[38] Lindbeck argues that the failure of the CP and EE models of religion to explain this type of phenomena reflects their underlying adherence to an Enlightenment epistemology. CP models of religion assume that religious language and religious assertions gain their meaning and truth by corresponding to aspects of some transcendent reality. However, such an interpretation of meaning was rendered problematic by Kant's philosophy, which identified the boundaries of propositional significance and knowability with the limits represented by the structure and contents of human experience. If religious assertions allegedly gain their significance by referring to some reality that transcends such experience their meaningfulness is brought into question. EE models of religion have sought to respond to this Kantian challenge by re-interpreting the function of religious discourse in terms of an expression of universal spiritual experiences.[39] Different religious doctrines, practices and languages are simply different ways of articulating the nature and implications of such experiences.[40] By linking religious discourse to human experience in this way the EE model ensures that its interpretation of the nature of religious assertion and language meets the Kantian criterion of significance. Despite their apparent opposition to each other, therefore, CP and EE models of religion can both be interpreted as responses to a single Enlightenment account of the nature and limits of meaning and truth.

3.3 Religion as an Interpretative Medium

In Lindbeck's schematic account, EE and CP interpretations of religion reduce the nature of religious belief to one particular aspect of religion—to propositional significance on the one hand or to the expression of religious experience on the other. Lindbeck argues that each model is based on an inadequate understanding of religious language and practice, and as a result

---

38. ND, 78–79; Lindbeck cites the resolution of conflict between Lutheran and Roman Catholic teachings on the Eucharist as an example of such reconciliation without capitulation (see Wright, ed., *Postliberal Theology and the Church Catholic*, 69).

39. ND, 20–21.

40. Lindbeck uses Bernard Lonergan's theory of religion as an example of an EE account (see ND, 31). However, the accuracy of Lindbeck's account has been challenged. See DeHart, *The Trial of the Witnesses*, 164.

the accounts of doctrine that have emerged from these perspectives are equally inadequate. Each theory lacks the conceptual resources required to solve their difficulties. From a MacIntyrean perspective what is required to overcome these problems is a creative process of conceptual innovation which will not only resolve the specific difficulties but also explain why these difficulties have arisen.[41]

Conceptual innovation is an explicit feature of Lindbeck's approach and his analysis of the nature of intractable intellectual problems could easily be expressed in the vocabulary of epistemological crisis. Lindbeck writes that in theology (as in other disciplines) "anomalies accumulate, old categories fail, and with luck or skill . . . new concepts are found that better serve to account for the data. If they are not found, the consequences can be intellectually and religiously traumatic."[42] In order to overcome the inadequacy of the existing conceptualizations of religion, Lindbeck seeks to construct concepts that explain how the propositional and experiential functions of religious language reified by the CP and EE models are rooted in the forms of life of religious communities. Lindbeck's approach treats the central features of a religion as akin to languages and their associated cultures and forms of life.[43] Lindbeck refers to this alternative model of religion as "cultural-linguistic," and labels the understanding of doctrine that emerges from this model as "a 'regulative' or 'rule' theory."[44] On the CL model, a religion is "an interpretative scheme"[45] that provides the community that embraces it with a set of resources for interpreting and understanding both the external world and the world of inner experience, and defines a set of practices associated with the conduct of the religion. It also provides a cultural framework for shaping the personal qualities and behavior of members of the community in approved ways. It therefore provides a

---

41. DeHart *The Trial of the Witnesses*, 163, criticizes the way in which Lindbeck describes such accounts as setting up straw men for him to demolish, and this may well be legitimate. However, this criticism of itself does not undermine the positive value of Lindbeck's cultural-linguistic account as a model for understanding the nature of comprehensive belief systems.

42. ND, 8–9. Lindbeck's reference to theological trauma is redolent of MacIntyre's description of epistemological crisis.

43. Like MacIntyre, Lindbeck's position is influenced by the later philosophy of Wittgenstein, (See ND, 33 and 38–39 for example). Wittgenstein introduced the concept of a "form of life" in his *Philosophical Investigations* to emphasise the primacy of shared practices in underpinning communication and the interpretation of judgments (see *Philosophical Investigations*, paras. 241–42 for example).

44. ND, 18.

45. ND, 33.

total framework for the interpretation, understanding and governance of all aspects of the life of a community:

> a religion may be viewed as a kind of cultural and/or linguistic framework or medium that shapes the entirety of life and thought. It functions somewhat like a Kantian a priori, although in this case the a priori is a set of required skills that could be different. It is not primarily an array of beliefs about the true and the good (although it may involve these), or a symbolism expressive of basic attitudes, feelings, or sentiments (though these will be generated). Rather, it is similar to an idiom that makes possible the description of realities, the formulation of beliefs, and the experiencing of inner attitudes, feelings, and sentiments. Like a culture or language, it is a communal phenomenon that shapes the subjectivities of individuals rather than being primarily a manifestation of those subjectivities.[46]

As such a "Kantian a priori" a religion provides both the resources through which propositions about the nature of spiritual reality can be asserted, and also the means through which spiritual and other experiences can be articulated. Lindbeck argues that the relationship between religion and experience is not "unilateral but dialectical." In this interaction, however, it is "religious and cultural factors . . . that can be viewed as the leading partners."[47] The CL model "reverses the relation of the inner and the outer. Instead of deriving external features of religion from inner experience, it is the inner experiences which are viewed as derivative."[48] Religious experience is constituted through the cultural and linguistic forms of the religion.[49] Because experience can only be classified through the medium of language, the source of religious concepts cannot be prior experience.[50] Lindbeck therefore challenges the notion that there is an inner experience of God common to all human beings which provides the fundamental basis for the development of religions.[51] Rather, he views religions as idioms for dealing with whatever is most important in human life.[52]

---

46. ND, 33.

47. ND, 33–34.

48. ND, 34.

49. This point is reinforced by Lindbeck's view (derived from Wittgenstein among others) that all thought and feeling is language dependent (34, see also 37–39).

50. ND, 37–39.

51. ND, 39–40.

52. ND, 40.

Lindbeck's CL model suggests that becoming socialized into a religion involves a process of assimilation to a new culture in which one must learn a new language and forms of behavior, and become initiated into social practices whose purpose may not be apparent at the beginning of the process. Through this process of socialization, the initiate develops the conceptual resources and practice skills necessary to reinterpret the world within the semiotic framework provided by the religion, and to conceptualize their inner experience in spiritual terms.

> In thus inverting the relation of the internal and external dimensions of religion, linguistic and cultural approaches resemble cognitivist theories for which external (i.e., propositionally stable) beliefs are primary, but without the intellectualism of the latter. A comprehensive scheme or story used to structure all dimensions of existence is not primarily a set of propositions to be believed, but is rather the medium in which one moves, a set of skills that one employs in living one's life.[53]

Although Lindbeck does not make this point explicitly, his theory does not simply replace CP, EE or two-dimensional theories of religion by showing that they are false and should be discarded. Rather, it explains how the propositional and experiential functions that they identify with the essence of religion have arisen through the way in which a religion functions as an interpretative medium.[54] EE and CP accounts of religion mistakenly privilege the ways in which the interpretative framework formed by a religion can both determine the way in which reality is described and the way in which experience is expressed, and mistakenly identify the essence of the religion with these subsidiary functions.

Lindbeck argues that CP and EE models also lead to mistaken emphases in the interpretation of Scripture, treating these texts as either attempts to formulate philosophical propositions about the nature of ultimate reality, or as attempts to exemplify or give symbolic expression to universal spiritual experiences. On a CL account of religion, in contrast, the originating narratives of the religion are conceptualized as a set of stories which provide the initiating and continuing resources through which a community can interpret the meaning of its forms of life and its history in terms of moral and religious truths.[55] The CL model therefore not only provides a means of overcoming the limitations of these alternative models, but also explains

---

53. ND, 35.

54. Murphy and McClendon Jr. make a similar point in their paper "Distinguishing Modern and Postmodern Theologies," 206.

55. See ND, 84.

why the difficulties associated with the alternative models have arisen. Lindbeck's conceptual innovation therefore exemplifies MacIntyre's account of what is needed in order to resolve an epistemological crisis.[56]

As an IM, religions must engage with the wider cultural and social environments in which the community's religious social life is embedded. Members of the community must make sense of this environment in ways that are consistent with the narratives that form the abiding core of the religion.[57] These narratives provide the appropriately skilled adherent with a set of resources for interpreting their beliefs and experiences, constituted by a framework of ontological and ethical presuppositions—and, (within the Abrahamic religions at least), an overall narrative of the trajectory of the creation and the trajectory of a human life. As a result, Lindbeck argues that changes in religious belief do not proceed from new spiritual experiences or from the epistemological evaluation of religious truth claims, but from the interaction of a community and its religious convictions with their changing social and intellectual environment. As a consequence, the nature of the propositional truth-claims which are legitimately made within the religious framework will also change:

> The first-order truth claims of a religion change in so far as these arise from the application of the interpretive scheme to the shifting worlds that human beings inhabit. What is taken to be reality is in large part socially constructed and consequently alters in the course of time. The universe of the ancient Near East was very different from that of Greek philosophy, and both are dissimilar from the modern cosmos. Inevitably, the Christianized versions of these various world pictures are far from identical. When different worlds with their distinct definitions of the good and the real, the divine and human, are re-described within one and the same framework of Biblical narrative, they continue to remain different worlds.[58]

On the basis of this model, religious propositions are constructed through the application of the central narratives of the religion to the varying cultural materials available to a community at different times in its history, and as a result of this interaction, new propositions may be formulated and earlier formulations may come to be held as false because of changes in the intellectual and cultural context. For example, doctrines that assert the immortality of the soul may be considered implausible today because

---

56. See section 2.5 above.
57. ND, 80.
58. ND, 82.

Lindbeck and the Identity of the Christian Tradition 153

mind-body dualism is now seen as logically incoherent.[59] Propositional theories of religion struggle to accommodate such changes in what can be held to be true (although Lindbeck points out that more sophisticated versions of propositionalism can deal with such changes by distinguishing between the central proposition asserted and the form of words which are used to convey that assertion[60]). However, on a cultural-linguistic model what remains constant and invariable in the religion is not some immutable set of propositions, but the underlying rules to which different formulations of the same core beliefs conform. To assert the immortality of the soul is one way of asserting the promise of eternal life that is central to the Christian religion. Other ways of formulating propositions may still embody this central promise, without relying on a doubtful metaphysical dualism. Faithfulness requires adherence to the rule through which such propositions are generated, rather than through a conviction of the truth of any particular formulation.

3.4 Doctrine, Rules, and Identity

Lindbeck argues that the interaction between a religious community and its environment is governed by processes of interpretation that are embodied in the community's beliefs and practices. The interpretative practices, capacities, and skills that guide this interaction are rule governed, even where these rules are not explicitly formulated.[61] Lindbeck argues that religious doctrines embody some of the rules that govern these practices. The formation of explicit doctrines is driven by the need for a community to define its core beliefs and maintain its continued identity against external or internal challenge, and such doctrines are therefore occasioned responses to conflict.[62] These origins in internecine and external controversy shape what formal doctrines do and do not embody:

> insofar as official doctrines are the products of conflict, there are two important consequences: first, they must be understood in terms of what they oppose (it is usually much easier to specify

---

59. ND, 107.
60. ND, 105.

61. This point is made clear if one considers the question of whether there can be correct or incorrect performance of a particular activity. If it is possible for the skilled members of the community to make judgments about the quality of a performance that are accepted by others there is some underlying rules that are being applied, even if these are not written down.

62. ND, 75.

what they deny than what they affirm); and, second, the official doctrines of a community may poorly reflect the most important and abiding orientations or beliefs, either because some of the latter may never have been seriously challenged (and therefore never officially defined) or because points that are under most circumstances trivial may on occasion become matters of life and death.[63]

The occasioned nature of official doctrines means that only some of the rules that govern the practices of the religious community will be explicitly formulated. Formal doctrines will be defined only at those points where challenge has so threatened the cohesion and identity of the community that a definitive ruling has had to be given on particular aspects of the community's faith. Many other rules will not be formally articulated, but will be implicit in the accepted practices of the community, and the standards of performance associated with those practices. Both formal and informal doctrines will act as the source of authority and identity within a religious community. Together they will define the requirements that have to be met if someone is to be considered a member of that community in good standing. Such rules define what is required or permissible within that community and therefore define what it is for that community to exist as a collectivity distinct from other religious (and indeed non-religious) collectivities.[64]

Doctrines, therefore, encapsulate the standards of assertion, expressions of experience and practice that should be observed by members of the religious community. However, the rule qua rule is not a proposition asserting the existence of some spiritual reality, nor does it express some religious experience or embody a practice. Rather, the role of doctrines is regulatory. In assertion, for example, "doctrines regulate truth claims by excluding some and permitting others, the logic of their communally authoritative use hinders or prevents them from specifying positively what is to be affirmed."[65] Thus on Lindbeck's account doctrines are primarily "communally authoritative rules of discourse, attitude and action."[66] The truth of the statements which describe such doctrines has to be determined by ref-

---

63. ND, 75; Lindbeck's position here is strongly influenced by Newman's *An Essay on the Development of Christian Doctrine*. Similarly MacIntyre acknowledges the influence of Newman's work on doctrine on his account of tradition in WJWR, see 353–4. The synergy between Lindbeck's position and that of MacIntyre may reflect this mutual influence, among other factors.

64. ND, 74.

65. ND, 19.

66. ND, 18.

erence to human cultural institutions, rather than to religious experiences or spiritual realities. Interpreted in this way, such rules are not first order propositions making ontological or knowledge claims, but second order assertions which make intra-systematic truth claims, as Lindbeck asserts.[67] On this regulative model, doctrines can be conceived as conditional statements of the form "if you wish to be a (good) member of this community then you must assert a, b, and c, and/or engage in practices such as x, y and z, and refrain from asserting/practicing [and so on]." Such rules would not assert propositions a, b. and c directly (and therefore would not assert these propositions "positively," to use Lindbeck's word), nor would they provide a theological interpretation of the terms used in constructing the statement of doctrine. Such rules of assertion *specify* rather than *interpret* those propositions that can be asserted as true if an individual or group is to meet requirements for community membership. As descriptions of standards that apply to particular human communities in particular environments, doctrines may be binding at one time and in some circumstances, but in other times and in different circumstances they may not be binding.

Lindbeck does not claim that statements of doctrine cannot be used propositionally or expressively, but holds that where doctrines are used as first order propositions or symbols they are not functioning as doctrines per se: "what is innovative about the present proposal is that this [regulative function] becomes the only job that doctrines do in their role as church teachings."[68] Thus if we adopt an anthropological perspective with respect to a religious community we would find occasions on which a statement of doctrine is used regulatively, and occasions when it is used propositionally or expressively, but it is the regulative role alone that represents its doctrinal function for Lindbeck.[69] This is not only because this function is logically prior to the application of the rule to make specific assertions or symbolize experience, but also because treating the assertive function as

---

67. ND, 80.
68. ND, 19.
69. Barrett criticizes Lindbeck's position on the basis that it is not possible to make a distinction between a rule and its application in the way that Lindbeck seeks to do, because a rule can only be learned by the production of paradigm instantiations. See Barrett, "Theology as Grammar," 169. One rejoinder to this criticism is that while providing examples of following a rule may be a precondition of learning its application, this does not imply that the rule itself cannot be logically distinguished from such applications. In principle a description of the rule can be formulated that explains why *these* examples act as instantiations of the particular rule. The rule explains the nature of the identity of the instantiations in the same way as reference to context and intentions interprets a behavior as an action of a particular sort.

primary would fail to clarify and resolve the conflicts that act as a barrier to ecumenism.

Treating the regulative function of doctrine as central helps to explain why propositional variability should not automatically be a major barrier to Christian unity. Such variability would not necessarily affect the underlying identity of the religious community for Lindbeck, because a religion should not be identified with any particular set of propositions. It is an interpretative framework built upon the narrative resources defined by the Biblical stories.[70] The doctrines defined by a community shape the vocabulary and rules of grammar that can be applied to this narrative core and to the practices that govern other aspects of its life at any one time. As a result of the interaction between the secular and the sacred, the language within which the divine is described will change as worldviews change but in Christianity the underlying story of passion and resurrection and the basic rules for the application of this story remain the same.[71] "Theological and religious transformations that lead to relativistic denials of an abiding identity (when one assumes constancy must be propositional, or symbolic, or experiential) can be seen, if one adopts rule theory, as the fusion of a self-identical story with the new worlds within which it is told and retold."[72]

Lindbeck points out that this type of constancy is characteristic of different natural languages, cultures, and other religions, and does not require any supernatural explanation. He argues that attempting to identify what is constant in a religion with either propositions or experiences is doomed to failure because how both experiences and propositions are expressed will vary, depending on the cultural world in which they are formulated, and the different articulations of knowledge within which they may be presented.

> The experiences generated by religion are on this view just as variable as its propositionally stable descriptions of the world and of God. This contrasts with an expressivist model, which locates what is religiously normative and abiding in the depths of the inner self. Such a model may suggest that the experience of love, for example, identifies what is truly Christian, but for rule theory, it is the Christian story which alone is able to identify what for Christians is true love.[73]

---

70. ND, 80.
71. ND, 82–83.
72. ND, 83.
73. ND, 83.

What is invariable as far as Lindbeck is concerned is "the framework and the medium within which Christians know and experience."[74]

> When put this way, it seems almost self-evident that the permanence and unity of doctrines, despite changing and diverse formulation, is more easily accounted for if they are taken to resemble grammatical rules rather than propositions or expressive symbols (though, as we have noted, the same sentences in which the rules are stated may function in these other ways also).[75]

3.5 The Permanence of Belief

One challenge that needs to be considered in relation to Lindbeck's theory of religion is whether his account of the nature of doctrine gives such scope to variability as to erode any significant degree of permanence from religious belief, because it identifies religion with a set of variably interpreted narratives and a (changing) interpretative framework. The stability of the faith would require that not only the narratives but also some elements of the interpretative framework should be fixed and unchanging. On Lindbeck's account the interpretative framework is defined by doctrinal rules, in part at least. There must, therefore, be some doctrines that identify and express these invariant components of that framework. Lindbeck acknowledges that, while some doctrines may be temporary and reversible, others must be considered to be permanent and irreversible rules that are essential components of the Christian faith.[76] But what then is the criterion for distinguishing between the permanent and the impermanent? This is, of course, a version of the criteriological question I described at the beginning of this chapter.

Some doctrines are clearly behavioral and ethical directives, and their status as rules is, therefore, non-controversial. Lindbeck refers to these as "practical doctrines." Some practical doctrines, such as the "law of love" are, he suggests, "unconditionally necessary" elements of the faith, "as [for example] there are no circumstances in which Christians are not commanded to love God or neighbor." Such injunctions apply irrespective of changes in circumstances. Other rules are "conditionally essential" and may no longer apply in changed circumstances, and into this category Lindbeck places

---

74. ND, 84.
75. ND, 84.
76. ND, 84–88.

the injunction that Christians should not participate in war (for example). All unconditionally necessary rules are permanent, but some conditionally necessary rules may also become permanent, because they will remain in force while the conditions which require them remain, and if these conditions are permanent features of the environment then the doctrine will equally be permanent.[77] Lindbeck places the church's modern opposition to slavery into this category.[78]

This taxonomy allows for the development of practical doctrines (since a new conditional doctrine may emerge when changing circumstances demand it), and equally allows for debate as to whether any particular doctrine is necessary and permanent. Agreement that a practical doctrine is conditionally necessary allows for the possibility of changed circumstances rendering such a doctrine redundant, and therefore allows for the prospect of conciliation between churches who (because of different circumstances) espouse apparently conflicting conditional practical doctrines. Does this taxonomy apply to doctrines that govern the formulation of assertoric propositions with ontological import? Lindbeck suggests that it does:

> [assertoric doctrines] also can be viewed as unconditionally or irreversibly necessary, as permanent or temporary, as reversible or irreversible. Historically the Apostle's creed and the ancient Trinitarian and Christological confessions of faith of Nicaea and Chalcedon have been treated as unconditionally and permanently essential. A doctrine such as the immortality of the soul, in contrast, could perhaps be classified as conditional, temporary, and reversible.[79]

As we have seen, the immortality of the soul is a conditional doctrine because it expresses the promise of eternal life in terms of a Hellenistic division of body and soul. It may, therefore be necessary to assert this proposition as a truth whenever such concepts are used in order to express Christian truths, but not when such dualism is rejected and an alternative vocabulary is employed. The regulative element of such a doctrine arises because it requires certain forms of assertion in one particular conceptual context. However, this regulative aspect reflects the requirements of another doctrine which *is* unconditionally necessary: the promise of eternal life. The doctrine of the immortality of the soul may be a specific, conditional, and temporary formulation of this more fundamental and permanent doctrine.

---

77. ND, 85.
78. ND, 86.
79. ND, 86.

Lindbeck and the Identity of the Christian Tradition

However, the unconditionally necessary doctrine of eternal life appears to express a rule of assertion that could also be expressed in propositional terms. Doctrines that enjoin such beliefs arguably have a dual function as model or exemplar propositions which act both as assertions of the truth of a particular belief and specify some of the boundaries of legitimate forms of expression. If a doctrine is considered as an exemplar proposition then it is either true and irreversible or false.[80] Lindbeck's assertion, that theoretical doctrines can "perhaps be classified" in the same way as a practical doctrine, begs the question as to whether theoretical doctrines embody an irreducible propositional function, as well as regulating assertion. Lindbeck does not offer any conclusive arguments to establish their status as rules, other than a historical one (in terms of the alleged priority of the regulative function when these doctrinal statements were first formulated).[81]

In proposing the regulative theory, Lindbeck is proffering a choice with respect to the interpretation of the status of theoretical doctrines: one can either treat theoretical doctrines as rules or one can choose to interpret them as propositions. He acknowledges that "a sophisticated propositionalism" can distinguish between a particular formulation of a proposition (which may be recognized as in error) and the underlying meaning (which may be permanent and unchanging, and indeed of such profundity so that the full meaning of a doctrine remains inexpressible). But if one adopts a propositional interpretation of a doctrine one is presumably accepting that the assertion of the doctrine implies a specific ontological commitment, and one is then in danger of reaching the impasse he identified in relation to CP models in general: conflict over the formulation of doctrines represents conflict over ontological commitments. The attraction of the regulative model is that it does not *require*, as a condition of faithfulness, a commitment to particular (and potentially ecumenically unhelpful) interpretations of the assertions that flow from these rules.

> The issue [of the distinction between regulative and propositional interpretations of doctrine] is a narrow one. Rule theory does not prohibit speculation on the possible correspondence of the Trinitarian pattern of Christian language to the metaphysical structure of the Godhead, but simply says that these are not doctrinally necessary and cannot be binding . . . ontological interpretations of the Trinity *do not, or should not*, be made

---

80. This is the valid point made by Barrett's paper cited earlier in this section; "Theology as Grammar," 171.

81. ND, 105.

communally normative for the way in which Christians live and think.[82]

Lindbeck's conceptual innovation, therefore, can be seen as requiring an interpretation of conformity to the Christian faith as conformity to the requirements of all unconditionally and conditionally necessary doctrines, interpreted as rules of behavior, expression, and assertion. It does not require an acceptance of particular interpretations of the ontological truth of the propositions that flow from these requirements as a condition of orthodoxy and community membership. As a result, disagreement about the ontological implications of the doctrine of eternal life (for example) would not act as a barrier to a deeper unity embodied in the regulative functions of the rules (or propositions) that form the permanent elements of the Christian faith.

The weakness of Lindbeck's position here is twofold. Firstly, it does not offer a clear criterion for distinguishing between temporary, unconditionally necessary, and conditionally necessary doctrines, or between permanent and reversible doctrines. In section 4.3 I suggest that the emergence of an epistemological crisis may provide an empirical test as to which doctrines might be considered permanent and irreversible, but there appears to be no *a priori* basis on which one might distinguish such decisions in advance of an anthropological investigation of their role within a particular community. Secondly, the cultural-linguistic interpretation of religion is offered as a model which offers certain benefits if it is adopted, but which is not ontologically true in all respects. Practical doctrines are clearly rules, but theoretical doctrines are at best hybrid formulations which embody both regulative and propositional elements. Lindbeck's model is pragmatically helpful in fostering ecumenism[83] but it cannot be defended as a definitively correct account of the nature of religion, doctrine and Christian identity.

This deficit is an inevitable consequence of the fact that Lindbeck is seeking to construct a model. Models are modes of interpretation, ways of identifying and constructing patterns that make sense of disparate phenomena. Indeed, William Placher claims that Christian theology is always engaged in constructing such interpretative patterns.[84] However, the creation of one particular interpretation does not exclude the possibility of other plausible patterns being constructed from the same set of phenomena. A model is an interpretation which selects out and favors some limited set of

---

82. ND, 106, emphasis added.

83. Lindbeck's implicit pragmatism has been highlighted by Pecknold, *Transforming Postliberal Theology*. See 17–19 for the pragmatic links between Lindbeck's ecumenical objectives and the development of his model.

84. Placher, *Unapologetic Theology*, 126.

elements of a complex whole. Such a model may embody elements of truth, but it will not fully encapsulate the nature of the complex reality from which it is drawn, and at times an interpretation must be discarded and replaced by different models that embody other elements of the truth. MacIntyre's notion of a tradition is also a model, a way of constructing an explanatory pattern in a highly complex social and intellectual history. Neither Lindbeck's cultural linguistic model of religion nor MacIntyre's account of a tradition of enquiry is able to claim to represent some unchallengeable truth about the nature of a religion or a tradition, because each represents the outcome of a selective process of interpretation. But bringing the CL model of religion and the MacIntyrean model of a tradition of enquiry into dialogue will enable me to strengthen the coherence of these models in particular ways. My intention is to use Lindbeck's notion of religion as an interpretative medium as a way of illuminating the nature of a MacIntyrean tradition of enquiry. But before doing this it is necessary to issue some notes of caution with respect to the limitations of Lindbeck's model. These cautionary notes relate to the metaphorical nature of Lindbeck's account of religion and doctrine, his assumptions about the nature of culture, and the applicability of his model to MacIntyre's position.

3.6 Some Limitations of Lindbeck's Model

Lindbeck's account of the nature of religion is constructed through metaphor, and metaphors can distort as well as illuminate.[85] Two sets of metaphors are particularly important in Lindbeck's account, each corresponding to one of the terms "linguistic" and "cultural." Firstly, a set of metaphors grow from the idea that a religion is like a language, both because it provides the conceptual resources that underpin interpretation, and because participation in the religion involves adherence to an underlying set of syntactic and semantic rules defined and exemplified in religious doctrines. The second set of images grows from the idea that a religion is like a culture into which adherents are socialized.

Both sets of images present a picture of an adherent's understanding and interpretation of the world as shaped by the cultural and linguistic resources provided by the religion. This process is described as essentially unidirectional, flowing from the religion to the adherent and the world,

---

85. Lindbeck's dependence on metaphor does not contradict my claim that he is constructing a model of the nature of religion. Janet Soskice argues that the use of metaphor is central to the construction and interpretation of models in both science and religion. See Soskice, *Metaphor and Religious Language*, 49–51.

rather than from the adherent or the world to the religion. It is not that religious beliefs change as secular worldviews develop and change. Rather "changing worldviews are reinterpreted by one and the same religion."[86] For Lindbeck, what is core to the identity of the religion are the rules that govern these interpretative processes, so that each Christian interpretation of new and alien worlds reflects the same underlying principles.[87] And this analogy with a language provides Lindbeck with an account of the continuing identity of a religion, because the syntactic and semantic rules which embody these underlying principles provide the continuity that enables it to remain essentially unchanged despite successive changes in the environment with which it engages. Thus, the religion will retain its underlying identity even if the content of the propositions that are asserted by the community change or the way in which that community conceptualizes religious experience becomes radically different. "To the degree that religions are like languages they can obviously remain the same amid vast transformations of affirmation and experience."[88]

But, one has to ask, to what degree are religions like languages in this respect? Here Lindbeck is pushing his analogy beyond reasonable limits. A natural language can be used to create fictions and scientific prose, philosophy and nonsense verse, the theory of relativity and *Finnegan's Wake*. There are no built in rules which define the semantic limits of such innovation and experimentation. As an interpretative medium a language can respond with unlimited flexibility to new and contradictory thoughts and experiences. The principle of identity of a language is not, therefore, linked to anything that limits what can be legitimately asserted. But not all assertions or ways of characterizing experience will be legitimate if one wishes to remain faithful to the narrative core of a religion. The linguistic analogy exhibits one function of the nature of a religion, but this analogy should not blind us to the differences. The rules which constitute the religion frame what can be legitimately asserted, frame how experiences can be described and define what practices should be pursued. It therefore shapes what counts as legitimate interpretation and behavior in a religious community far more thoroughly than a natural language shapes what counts as legitimate interpretation and behavior among users of that language.

The differences between a religion and a language are addressed in Lindbeck's second metaphor, which compares a religion to a culture that shapes its adherents in particular ways. But here again the comparison

---

86. ND, 82.
87. ND, 83.
88. ND, 84.

can be misleading. The norms that shape the behavior of the faithful can be interpreted in terms of cultural rules, but such rules do not determine the behavior of members of the community in a linear fashion. Within the religious community there will be debate and conflict around the content and legitimacy of the quasi-syntactic and quasi-semantic rules that govern the religious form of life, and these debates will shape the nature and interpretation of these cultural rules. But although Lindbeck acknowledges that the relationship between religion and experience is dialectical, in practice he tends to write as if the direction is unilateral. A religion "shapes the subjectivities of individuals rather than being primarily a manifestation of those subjectivities."[89] He acknowledges the looseness of this mode of expression,[90] but suggests that the most appropriate way of understanding the CL model is in terms of a reversal of the relationship between inner and outer. This emphasis reinforces an image of culture as the static determinant of experience,[91] and this provides evidence for those critics such as Kathryn Tanner, who see Lindbeck as failing to fully acknowledge the internal dynamism of a culture, and the complementarity of its relationship to the external environment.[92] In this respect Lindbeck's cultural-linguistic account of religion shares some of the limitations of classical anthropological theory.

Tanner points out that the classical anthropological notion of culture assumes a form of social determinism which regulates human nature and shapes the actions of the members of particular cultural groups.[93] On this model the ideal type of a culture is an autonomous community which has a clearly defined boundary and is insulated from external influences. Differences are suppressed within each culture by rules which define the appropriate behavior of members, and the anthropologist assumes that consensus is the norm when she describes the culture.[94] The norms that govern the behavior of participants are interpreted as the constitutive rules of the culture.

Tanner criticizes this model for failing to recognize the diversity present within any culture. The model identifies the constitutive rules by

---

89. ND, 33.

90. See ND, 33–34.

91. Vidu, *Postliberal Theological Method*, 24, notes the dominance of spatial metaphor in postliberal accounts of culture as opposed to temporal metaphor. The spatial image results in a visualization of culture as a fixed framework to which individuals conform. A temporal image emphasizes the processes of debate and evolution that are characteristic of cultures at all times. It is this dynamic dimension that Lindbeck's account tends to neglect.

92. Tanner, *Theories of Culture*, 105.

93. Ibid., 28.

94. Ibid., 27.

privileging the discourse of some influential individuals in the community who are accepted as authoritative sources of information with respect to these rules, thereby confusing the acceptance of authority and power with the empirical description of norms that underpin the behavioral regularities of the group. Anthropology reifies these rules into the constitutive principles of a culture, and conveys an idealized impression of a community which is conflict free. But any culture will contain conflicts and debates over what count as legitimate and illegitimate expressions of the rules—and, indeed, will be the forum of conflict over what these rules are or should be. As a result these norms will be subject to challenge, debate, and change within a culture without that culture ceasing to exist.[95] Successful communities develop processes for managing these conflicts and maintaining a stable consensus within which conflict can be identified and addressed. But this implies that the elements which form the self-identity of the culture may also evolve through these processes of conflict. Hence cultures are not fixed and unchanging: the historical process of debate, conflict and negotiation that has given rise to the current uneasy consensus will continue, and as a result the components of that consensus may change in the future.[96]

Tanner's arguments suggest that caution should be exercised in using the concept of culture in either philosophy or theology. The "culture" of a community is a social construction that is defined through its description in anthropological discourse, rather than the name of a fixed object that quietly awaits our discovery. The descriptions of cultures which are the outcome of ethnographic research should, therefore, be seen as products of processes of interpretation which are contestable and subjective, rather than objective and factual. Nonetheless, the concepts of culture and cultural rules are helpful ways of understanding the interactions between people and who identify themselves as members of a single community. In seeking to apply Lindbeck's account of the nature of religion and doctrine to MacIntyre's account of tradition, I will seek to balance an understanding of culture as a force which shapes individuals and their perceptions, with an account of the way in which that culture is shaped by processes of internal debate and conflict over its purpose and identity. I will be assisted in this by the fact that MacIntyre's account of tradition is very sensitive to the delicate balance between consensus and conflict in a tradition,[97] and this element of his work will also help me strengthen Lindbeck's account.

95. Ibid., 57.
96. Ibid., 45–53.
97. See, for example AV, 163–64, where MacIntyre emphasizes the central importance of conflict in all human institutions, following the views of the Australian philosopher John Anderson.

Lindbeck and the Identity of the Christian Tradition

A religion and a tradition of enquiry are not identical and a further challenge to my approach is the claim that faith communities and traditions of enquiry are too dissimilar for the application of Lindbeck's model to MacIntyre to bear fruit. However, Lindbeck offers a definition of religion which is so broad as to embrace forms of belief that would not normally be identified as examples of religious faith. Thus in the afterword to ND Lindbeck notes that his definition of religion as "comprehensive interpretive schemes" means that

> Much that is religious in ordinary usage is excluded by this definition, and much that is not religious is included. Belief in supernatural beings . . . is not religious unless one seeks to organize all of life, all beliefs and behaviour, around one or more of these entities. Analogously, denial of the supernatural, what is usually called secularism, is religious when this denial is of all-embracing importance.[98]

On this definition the nature of a religion lies in its capacity to form the interpretative center of a life so that all aspects of reality, experience and action can be accommodated within its framework. A belief in the truth of any particular spiritual or ontological commitments is not its defining characteristic, although its *use* within a community may require such ontological commitments by members of that community. In acting as such an interpretative or hermeneutic framework a religion, like a tradition of enquiry into the nature of the good, may succeed or fail to interpret external concepts and events effectively, and may be successful or unsuccessful in shaping the lives of its adherents in ways that embody a plausible understanding of the good life. There is therefore, a prima facie basis for comparing Lindbeck's account of religion to MacIntyre's account of a tradition of enquiry. But can this process strengthen Lindbeck's model?

3. 7 MacIntyre's Relevance to Lindbeck

As we saw in section 3.2, Lindbeck's cultural-linguistic model of religion has been developed in response to the need to explain the coexistence of variability and invariability of belief in the history of the Christian faith. Lindbeck's answer to this question of variability and invariability is twofold. Firstly, for Lindbeck there is an unchanging core to the religion in

---

98. Lindbeck, "Afterword," ND 2nd Edition, 132. On this definition Richard Dawkins might well be regarded as a religious man, as would be the committed, though atheist, Marxist.

the original narratives which led to the establishment and evolution of the belief system. Secondly, the evolution of that system involves a response to internal and external challenges which leads to the construction of formal statements of doctrine, which specify what it is legitimate to assert and what practices it is appropriate to pursue.[99] Many of the community's beliefs will however never be formalized and the formal doctrines will form only part of the regulative system of the community, which will also include many informal doctrines. Lindbeck argues that some of these formal and informal doctrines are unconditionally permanent. These doctrines can be seen as forming the non-negotiable core of the Christian religion, although there will be considerable debate around *which* doctrines might form that core, and, indeed, about the interpretation of the significance of these doctrines.

The resolution of such debates depends on the ability to establish and agree some criteria which can be used to establish the superiority or truth of one perspective over another. Lindbeck's "nontheological"[100] account of religion relies on a quasi-sociological and uncommitted perspective which does not need to resolve such questions of truth or superiority. But as a Christian and a theologian, Lindbeck's book is not simply a contribution to religious studies; it is the prolegomena to his attempt to establish a new postliberal method for theology, a topic to which he turns in the final chapter of ND. To be of interest and use to believers, Lindbeck recognizes that his account must also be consistent with the way in which believers conceptualize their religion, and here the analogy with a language places his account at a disadvantage. While one language or culture does not seem to be superior to another, some religions claim such superiority over other faiths, and, indeed, may claim to be unsurpassably true. As Lindbeck points out, a nontheological theory does not need to *demonstrate* the superiority of one religion over another—but it at least needs to explain the meaning of such claims and show that such claims are coherent.[101]

This requirement is particularly problematic for a cultural–linguistic account of religion, as according to the theory, religions qua interpretative mediums can interpret any set of events, challenges or theories within their framework. As Lindbeck says with respect to Christianity, "a scriptural world is . . . able to absorb the universe. It supplies the interpretive

99. One of the outcomes of the history of controversy is to determine who will be accepted by a community as an authority. There is therefore a complex process of negotiation that takes place in determining what counts as the relevant community, what counts as an authority and what counts as the belief system. This is a point that Lindbeck emphasizes in his later work. See Lindbeck, "Scripture, Consensus and Community."

100. ND, 46.

101. ND, 46.

Lindbeck and the Identity of the Christian Tradition 167

framework within which believers seek to live their lives and understand reality."[102] But if any religion can accommodate any set of events then it would appear to be immune from falsification. A corollary of this is that it will also be unable to demonstrate its claims to superiority with respect to other religions, because rival religions will be equally able to absorb apparently contrary events into their own frameworks. Lindbeck's general epistemological perspective is one that he shares with MacIntyre, and for both thinkers it appears to militate against constructing any immediately clear and straightforward answer to the question of superiority because "there is no higher neutral standpoint from which to adjudicate [each religion's] . . . competing perceptions of what is factual and/or anomalous. Comprehensive outlooks on religion, not to mention religions themselves, are not susceptible to decisive confirmation or disconfirmation."[103]

Each interpretative medium is unique to a particular religion and helps to define the characteristics of a particular cultural group. Each interpretative medium may develop different notions of truth and justification. Mutual incommensurability means that there may be no basis for judging between their competing claims. Indeed Lindbeck suggests that attempts to incorporate elements of one religion into the conceptual framework of another religion will result in nonsense, frustrating the attempt to evaluate one religion from the perspective of another:

> In short, the cultural-linguistic approach is open to the possibility that different religions and/or philosophies may have incommensurable notions of truth, of experience, and of categorial adequacy, and therefore also of what it would mean for something to be most important (i.e., "God"). Unlike other perspectives, this approach proposes no common framework such as that supplied by the propositionalist concept of truth or the expressivist concept of experience within which to compare religions. Thus when affirmations or ideas from categorially different religious or philosophical frameworks are introduced into a given religious outlook, these are either simply babbling or else, like mathematical formulas employed in a poetic text, they have vastly different functions and meanings than they had in their original settings.[104]

Despite these difficulties, Lindbeck attempts to provide an account of superiority in religious contexts, developing his account in terms of the

102. ND, 117.
103. ND, 11.
104. ND, 49.

notions of categorial adequacy and performative truth. The problem which Lindbeck is addressing in developing these concepts is similar to the issues that MacIntyre addresses in attempting to construct an account of the superiority of one tradition of enquiry to another, and their accounts can help to support and clarify each other, as I will show in the following chapter.

There are important parallels between the question of *inter*-religious superiority and *intra*-religious superiority. Lindbeck also seeks to clarify criteria for determining whether one position is superior to another when differences arise within the Christian community. He constructs the notion of intratextuality in order to provide such a criterion and I will discuss this in more detail in section 4.6. The concept of "intratextuality" is defined in contrast to the "extratextual" resources that CP and EE theories rely upon for the validation of religious belief.

> [Extratextual method] locates religious meaning outside the text or semiotic system either in the objective realities to which it refers or in the experiences it symbolizes, whereas for cultural-linguists the meaning is immanent . . . Thus the proper way to determine what God signifies, for example, is by examining how the word operates within a religion and thereby shapes reality and experience . . . It is in this sense that theological description in the cultural-linguistic mode is intrasemiotic or intratextual.[105]

The difficulty that Lindbeck is attempting to resolve with the notion of intratextuality as a theological method is a further version of the criteriological problem I described earlier. If a religion is able to "absorb the universe" it cannot rely on external, extratextual, resources to adjudicate between competing perspectives within the community. It must rely on the internal semiotic resources available to that community, through the interpretation of its seminal texts and narratives. But how is it possible to decide between conflicting interpretations of these texts? Here again, MacIntyre's work will prove helpful in clarifying and extending Lindbeck's account of intratextuality as a criterion for the resolution of disputes. Moreover, precisely the same issue of a lack of extra-textual resources relevant to determining the question of superiority arises in inter-religious and inter-denominational contexts. If each religion is capable of absorbing the universe within its framework then external evidence of confirmation or disconfirmation will not be available. My argument is that the resolution or non-resolution of the tensions which arise within the internal processes of absorption and interpretation form the basis for judgments of superiority in both intra- and

---

105. ND, 114.

Lindbeck and the Identity of the Christian Tradition

inter-religious contexts, and that MacIntyre's notions of tradition-constituted rationality and epistemological crisis will be relevant to clarifying the nature of such processes.

A third issue in relation to superiority arises in relation to theory choice in theology and within other disciplines. Lindbeck's advocacy of a regulative account of doctrine appears to involve a process of persuasive definition, in which the propositional and expressive functions of doctrine are relegated to non-doctrinal status, at least in part for ecumenical reasons. However, such an approach is not simply pragmatic: it also reflects Lindbeck's interpretation of the nature of theory and epistemic progress. The construction of knowledge depends less on the deployment of successful argument and demonstrative proof or disproof than on a question of the pragmatic adoption and abandonment of particular perspectives, because they do or do not prove fruitful in tackling particular problems: "theories are abandoned not so much because they are refuted . . . but because they are unfruitful for new or different questions."[106] If theories are abandoned when they are no longer fruitful, does that mean that theories should also be adopted for such pragmatic reasons?[107] This may be inevitable if there is no theory-transcendent criterion of justification, and, indeed, Lindbeck argues that different theological approaches, like interpretative media, define their own criteria of legitimacy and justification: "the problem . . . is that each type of theology is embedded in a conceptual framework so comprehensive that it shapes its own criteria of adequacy."[108] If this is the case, there will be an element of pragmatism in any theory selection. It is however, important to give an account of how such theory selection would be legitimate if the position is not to be seen as inviting the challenge that it is relativist or fideist.

Lindbeck recognizes and is concerned to repudiate such challenges, and he is particularly conscious of the way in which intratextuality appears to portray belief systems as hermetically sealed self-justifying universes: "First, intratextuality seems wholly relativistic: it turns religions, so one can argue, into self-enclosed and incommensurable intellectual ghettoes. Associated with this, in the second place, is the fideistic dilemma: it appears that choice between religions is purely arbitrary, a matter of blind faith."[109] And again: "if intratextuality implies relativism and fideism the cost for

---

106. ND, 42.

107. See Pecknold, *Transforming Postliberal Theology*, 96, for the view that "Lindbeck is best read as a Christian scriptural pragmatist."

108. ND, 113.

109. ND, 128.

most religious traditions is much too high . . . [because] this conclusion . . . is antithetical to what most religions, whether interpreted in liberal, preliberal, or postliberal fashion, have affirmed."[110] What underlies this challenge is the claim that once one has abandoned Enlightenment models of justification the choice of any belief system must be arbitrary, because the only alternative to rational proof is fideism. As a result the rejection of such Enlightenment standards will, it is claimed, lead to an inexorable slide into relativism. Lindbeck's response to this viewpoint is brief, but points towards the need for an alternative account of rationality if the challenge is to be overcome. Lindbeck argues that

> The issue is not whether there are universal norms of reasonableness, but whether these can be formulated in some neutral, framework independent language. Increasing awareness of how standards of rationality vary from field to field and age to age makes the discovery of such a language more and more unlikely and the possibility of foundational disciplines doubtful. Yet this does not reduce the choice between different frameworks to whim or chance.[111]

Lindbeck suggests, in terms that echo MacIntyre's position, that, although "definitive refutation" may be impossible, there are still rational constraints on what can be held to be true, even though "these constraints are too flexible and informal to be spelled out."[112] Lindbeck argues that while religious and theological positions cannot be decisively refuted or confirmed "[they] can nevertheless be tested and argued about in various ways, and these tests and arguments in the long run make the difference."[113] MacIntyre's account of tradition-constituted rationality can flesh out the brief account given by Lindbeck and help to clarify how religious and theological positions can be subject to such testing. In the next chapter I am going to bring Lindbeck's and MacIntyre's work into dialogue in order to show that Lindbeck's position can be developed into a more robust form if it is expressed in MacIntyrean terms. And like the relationship between a religion and the world that it interprets, this will be a two-way process: Lindbeck's notions of religion as an interpretative medium and his regulative account of doctrine will also amplify and strengthen MacIntyre's accounts of rationality and tradition.

110. ND, 130.
111. ND, 130.
112. ND, 131.
113. ND, 131.

4

LINDBECK AND MACINTYRE AS COMPLEMENTARY THINKERS

4.1 Introduction

This chapter draws on the previous discussion to show that MacIntyre's and Lindbeck's positions are complementary, and that combining their positions can deepen an understanding of the nature of knowledge, of rationality, and of the superiority of one tradition to its rivals. This overall objective will be addressed by arguing a number of interconnected points. I will argue:

1. That the common elements of Lindbeck's and MacIntyre's theories can be described in terms of what I call a "hermeneutic framework" (section 4.2).

2. That MacIntyre's central concept of tradition can be given greater specificity and empirical application by interpreting the "fundamental agreements" that MacIntyre claims constitute such a tradition in terms of Lindbeck's concept of operative doctrines (section 4.3)

3. That this interpretation of the nature of a tradition illuminates the concepts of incommensurability and tradition-constituted rationality, and that it enables one to define more precisely the circumstances in which an epistemological crisis may arise (section 4.4).

4. That Lindbeck's account of the CL model does not provide a coherent basis for judgments with respect to the superiority of one religious

position to another, either in relation to inter- or intra-religious disagreements (sections 4.5–4.6), and that this failure leaves his position vulnerable to the challenge that it is relativist (section 4.6).

5. That Lindbeck's position can be strengthened by the incorporation of MacIntyre's accounts of tradition-constituted rationality and epistemological crisis (section 4.7).

The final section of this chapter concludes the book. It briefly summarizes what has been achieved and then turns to the question of whether MacIntyre's and Lindbeck's positions are correctly described as relativist. It explicitly addresses the question that has been under consideration throughout this book, as to whether MacIntyre's theory provides an adequate account of the justification of belief in a comprehensive metaphysical system, and considers the extent to which MacIntyre's account is of practical relevance to the individual who is considering whether to commit themselves to a particular tradition (section 4.8).

4.2 Lindbeck, MacIntyre, and the Notion of a Hermeneutic Framework

The Relationship between MacIntyre's and Lindbeck's Thought

The relationship between Lindbeck's and MacIntyre's thought has been acknowledged in the secondary literature. Both men are seen as complementary figures in a broader philosophical and theological reaction to the principles of modernity,[1] and some parallels between their perspectives have been noted. For example, Dennis Doyle has commented on the degree to which MacIntyre's account of community and tradition resonates with Lindbeck's ecclesiology and with the latter's emphasis on the maintenance of a Christian culture in a pluralistic society.[2] Victoria Harrison has drawn on both MacIntyre and Lindbeck to explore the issues arising from the decline of scriptural knowledge within Christian communities,[3] while Nicholas Healy has examined Lindbeck's and MacIntyre's use of the concept of practices in order to criticize and strengthen the use of this notion in the

---

1. See, for example, Milbank, *Theology and Social Theory*; Badham and Sigurdson, "The De-Centered Post-Constantinian Church"; Clayton, "On Holisms"; Dueck and Parsons, "Integration Discourse"; Battaglia, "'Sect' or 'Denomination'?"

2. Doyle, "The Contribution of a Lifetime: *George Lindbeck's The Church in a Postliberal Age*," 160.

3. Harrison, "Narrative, Postmodernity and the Problem of 'Religious Illiteracy.'"

construction of what he calls the "new ecclesiology."[4] Dean Smith has used MacIntyre's work to argue that Evangelical and Liberal Christians occupy incommensurable traditions, and has used Lindbeck's account of CP and EE models of religion to suggest that each group have embraced incompatible epistemological assumptions.[5]

There are, however, deeper synergies in their positions than has been generally recognized. This lack of recognition may be a consequence of the fact that Lindbeck and Macintyre have pursued separate academic disciplines and areas of enquiry during their distinguished careers. As I have argued, the underlying unity of MacIntyre's investigations can be understood in terms of the question of the justification of belief in a comprehensive metaphysical position. In contrast, Lindbeck has been primarily concerned with the apparently unrelated question of the unity of the Christian faith. But each of them has become profoundly dissatisfied with the contemporary self-perception and theoretical approaches of their disciplines and both have come to see these disciplines as incapable of resolving the concerns they had identified. As a result both authors have constructed an alternative theoretical viewpoint which has enabled them to re-conceptualize their respective problem areas, and this process of reconstruction has generated significant similarities in their positions.

Some of these similarities have arisen because each has worked in the same cultural milieu and have been exposed to similar influences. Both have been influenced by philosophers such as Wittgenstein[6] and each has been engaged by ideas drawn from social anthropology and sociological research.[7] However, there is a deeper unity to their positions than the accidental similarities that can arise from engagement in a shared cultural environment. Both see their perspectives as deeply influenced by the theology and philosophy of Thomas Aquinas.[8] Both reject the Enlightenment assumption that there must be some universal criterion by which genuine knowledge and truth can be distinguished from fool's gold,[9] and both have sought to construct accounts of the nature of knowledge and belief which places emphasis on communal processes of interpretation underpinned by the conceptual resources of a tradition.

---

4. Healy, "Practices and the New Ecclesiology."
5. Smith, "Are Liberals and Evangelicals Singing from the Same Song Sheet?"
6. There are multiple references to the later Wittgenstein in ND; and more sporadic references throughout MacIntyre's works.
7. ND, 20; AV chapters 3 and 9.
8. See Lindbeck "Response to Bruce Marshall," 405; WJWR, 402–3.
9. ND, 11 and 132; AV 2nd Edition Postscript, 266–67.

MacIntyre's account of a tradition of enquiry shifts the question of justification away from a notion of knowledge, conceived as the possession of a fixed stock of demonstrably true propositions, to a focus on the legitimacy of the processes of enquiry which underpin the development of the theoretical perspective that constitutes the telos of that tradition. The legitimacy of the tradition's claims to knowledge rests on its sustained capacity to resolve the successive challenges to its coherence as a system of belief that arise throughout its history. Successful attempts to address these difficulties through the process of enquiry will generate closer (but never perfect) expressions of the culture's underlying beliefs, but there is no guarantee that the tradition will be able to resolve all the problems that emerge during its history.

Lindbeck also rejects the identification of the legitimacy of belief with the possession of a fixed stock of demonstrably true propositions. For Lindbeck, what makes a religion a potential source of truth is its construction of semiotic categories which can be made to correspond to aspects of reality. The construction of these categories, together with rules for their application to the world and to experience, creates a community's capacity to assert both true and false propositions.[10] The way in which these concepts are applied will vary over time as a consequence of changes in the conceptual resources available to a particular culture. As a result of changes to this external conceptual environment, assertions that can be held to be propositionally true at time A may no longer be sustainable as true at a later time B. But such variability does not affect the underlying continuity and legitimacy of the fundamental presuppositions of the belief system and the rules for their application to the world. What is permanent in MacIntyre's notion of tradition and Lindbeck's cultural-linguistic model of religion is the nature of the underlying concepts which embody the fundamental (albeit initially unelaborated) ontological presuppositions of the tradition/Interpretative medium, and the rules for their application to the interpretation of the world. It is these rules that form the center of identity of the tradition/interpretative medium.

Lindbeck acknowledges the links between his cultural-linguistic model and MacIntyre's notion of tradition of enquiry,[11] and has suggested that his position might be strengthened if MacIntyre's account of tradition-constituted rationality were to be incorporated into his account of superiority.[12] One can illustrate the benefits of integrating elements of Lindbeck's and

---

10. ND, 48.
11. Lindbeck, "Foreword to the German edition of *The Nature of Doctrine*," 199.
12. Lindbeck, "Afterword" ND 25th Anniversary Edition, 138.

MacIntyre's work by considering Adonis Vidu's criticisms of both thinkers. Vidu is concerned that the priority given to the conceptual scheme in shaping belief in postliberal accounts of religion results in a failure to give any clear account of the relationship of that conceptual scheme to a reality that exists independently of the community.[13] As a result Vidu suggests that postliberal theology has undermined theological realism,[14] and criticizes Lindbeck for what he describes as his inability to reconcile the ontological priority of God with the epistemological priority of language and culture.[15] In contrast, Vidu challenges MacIntyre because of his alleged over-reliance on rational dialectics and philosophical demonstration, and a consequent failure to acknowledge the centrality of rhetoric in determining commitment to a particular belief system, whether religious or secular.[16] Vidu's objective in criticizing Lindbeck is to strengthen ontological commitments in postliberal theology, but he does not recognize the extent to which this objective is shared by Lindbeck, nor does he recognize the extent to which MacIntyre's philosophy can provide the resources required to address his concerns about the anti-realist implications of Lindbeck's position.

Achieving Vidu's realist objective requires the establishment of a robust basis for identifying whether one conceptual scheme is superior or inferior to its rivals with respect to the ability to encapsulate what is real. I will demonstrate that by integrating some elements of Lindbeck's and MacIntyre's accounts it is possible to develop a plausible critical realist perspective which allows for judgments of superiority, although an implication of this position is that final knowledge of ontological truth has still to be determined eschatologically. This approach builds on a point made by David Fergusson, who observed that postliberal theology might benefit from the addition of some MacIntyrean insights, because "The greater emphasis on realism, conversation, and partial translatability in MacIntyre may . . . enhance aspects of Lindbeckian postliberalism."[17] My contention is that MacIntyrean philosophy can equally benefit from the application of some insights drawn from postliberal theology, and that this process may also help to address some of Vidu's and Milbank's criticisms of MacIntyre.

---

13. Vidu, *Postliberal Theological Method*, 241–45; the problem that Vidu addresses also arises in with respect to the position that MacIntyre had sketched in LS, a position that he had subsequently repudiated in his preface to the 1970 edition of that work, as we saw in section 1.4 above.

14. Vidu, *Postliberal Theological Method*, 95 and 99.

15. Ibid., xiii.

16. Ibid., 139ff. In this Vidu follows the criticisms of MacIntyre in Milbank, *Theology and Social Theory*, chapter 11.

17. David Fergusson, *Community, Liberalism and Christian Ethics*, 132.

Hermeneutic Frameworks

I am going to refer to the common elements of Lindbeck's account of the nature of religion and MacIntyre's notion of a tradition of enquiry as defining what I will call a "hermeneutic framework" (HF). I will define a HF as a set of resources for interpreting aspects of experience and the world and for guiding action, so that both the interpretation of the world and individual and communal activities are rendered intelligible and consistent with the fundamental presuppositions of the tradition (or interpretative medium). These resources consist of four elements, although not all traditions or IMs will exhibit all of these characteristics:

1. A set of conceptual categories which are taken to reflect aspects of reality and whose abandonment would constitute a rejection of the tradition's fundamental presuppositions.

2. A set of rules of assertion which determine (in part) what it is legitimate and illegitimate to assert with respect to those categories if one is a participant in the tradition.

3. These conceptual categories and rules of assertion will underpin interpretative processes which seek to ensure that dissonant events and alien perspectives are rendered consistent with the fundamental assumptions of the tradition. Attempts to explain apparent inconsistencies will drive processes of theoretical (or doctrinal) development in order to reconcile belief and experience. Where such reconciliation is not possible, such inconsistencies may generate an epistemological crisis.

4. In so far as a tradition or interpretative medium underpins a mode of life, it will also generate a set of rules that require or guide action, both by directing participation in specific practices and by expressing general rules of conduct to shape practical reasoning. These rules will be implicit in the conduct of members of the tradition and may not be explicitly formulated. They can be recognized as rules because when they are specified they will render intelligible the behavior of those people who participate in (some specific aspects of) the tradition/IM.

Point one above follows from the fact that any religion or tradition begins from some particular set of narratives or beliefs about the nature of the world and the nature of humanity, and these beliefs form an element of the identity of the tradition. These narratives or beliefs are taken to express or embody some fundamental aspects of reality which cannot be denied if one is to remain a member of the believing community. No one can remain an Aristotelian if they reject the notion that there is a telos towards which human life should be directed. Nor could a person remain a Christian if they rejected the significance of Christ and his redemptive role in the world. But what it means to believe these things may be subject to intense debate.[18] This process of debate and the consequent elaboration of the fundamental beliefs generated through this process may generate rules of assertion. These rules may determine what it is legitimate to assert, by specifying certain formulations that are held to be consistent with the key presuppositions of the tradition; and they may also identify what cannot be asserted, by specifying assertions that are held to be inconsistent with the fundamental assumptions of that tradition (Point 2 above). In retaining and elaborating these beliefs, adherents must also respond to the challenge of interpreting events that are apparently inconsistent with the assumptions of the tradition in ways which sustain the logical coherence of that tradition. The critical task is to render the dissonant event intelligible within the framework of beliefs that constitute enduring elements of the tradition.[19] Some of these challenges may be resolved through processes of interpretation (Point 3). Such processes can be illustrated by MacIntyre's treatment of the problem of evil in *Difficulties in Christian Belief* (DCB).

In DCB MacIntyre argues that there is an apparent inconsistency between the set of beliefs about God that are taken to constitute Christian faith, and the reality of pain and suffering, and asserts that this inconsistency threatens the intelligibility of Christian belief.[20] MacIntyre attempts to resolve this tension by arguing that there is no contradiction between asserting "everything happens by the will of God" and "evil does not happen by the will of God."[21] MacIntyre points out that the first proposition can be interpreted as incorporating the belief that God created people free and able to act in accordance with their own will. He cannot, therefore, be held to be the author of the pain and suffering arising from their actions. Whatever the merits of MacIntyre's argument[22] his strategy can be described as the construction of an interpretation of the nature and origin of evil which enables

18. Such debate may, of course, challenge the limits within which one can be held to share such beliefs. One example would be the "Honest to God" controversy which arose in the 1960's following the publication of a book by John Robinson (Bishop of Woolwich), *Honest to God*, in which he was interpreted as challenging the reality of God. MacIntyre discussed this book in a paper called "God and the Theologians" in which he described Robinson's position as "atheist" (see page 13).

19. These beliefs may be expressed in theories, but they may also be embedded in stories or practices.

20. DCB, 17.

21. DCB, 34.

22. *As it stands* it simply fails to render the reality of the pain and suffering that arises from natural events consistent with the notion of an omnipotent, omniscient and good God, for example. This is a point that MacIntyre addresses later in his discussion.

one to explain evil events in a way that is consistent with God's goodness and omnipotence. His argument seeks to specify that a particular type of interpretation should be applied to particular events, so that the mutual consistency of different (and apparently incompatible) assertions can be secured. This is a specific example of a general process of argument and debate which may take place in any tradition, and which may therefore progressively generate more and more elaborate rules for interpretation and assertion which are designed to secure the coherence of the system. These processes of interpretation enable the tradition or interpretative medium to incorporate apparently contradictory elements within its framework and thereby protect itself from falsification. But there are limits to such processes, and when these limits are reached a crisis may emerge. This process is discussed further in section 4.4.

The fourth element of a hermeneutic framework consists of rules of conduct. As we saw in chapter 3, Aristotle's account of practical reasoning emphasizes that there is a process of interpretation involved in selecting any action. We have to be able to recognize those goods that we should seek; identify the means by which those goods can be achieved; and select a course of action which is likely to secure those preferred goods. Learning to identify appropriate goods may require engagement with the different practices required by the tradition, (which may embody goods in their own right); and will also involve internalizing rules that guide practical reasoning so that we may choose the appropriate action to secure the required goods. Where an action is undertaken in accordance with a rule, it can be rendered intelligible partly by specifying the rule that is being applied, But to fully understand the action involves showing how both the action and the rules that govern it are related to the pattern of beliefs, social roles, and practices that constitute the community, as MacIntyre's analysis of the philosophy of action has shown (see section 2.3). To render activities such as prayer fully intelligible is to link them to a widening framework of other practices and beliefs with which they are interdependent. The attempt to articulate the significance and justification of this interdependent network of beliefs, rules of assertion, and practice, and processes of interpretation, drives the development of the hermeneutic framework.

The characteristics I have specified as constituting a hermeneutic framework are not only intended to identify some of the common elements shared by Lindbeck's notion of a religion as an interpretative medium and MacIntyre's concept of a tradition of enquiry, they are also intended to characterize what I referred to as a comprehensive metaphysical position in section 1.1. I defined such a position as "a set of ontological and ethical presuppositions which are taken to encompass and explain the nature of the

Lindbeck and MacIntyre as Complementary Thinkers

universe of which our species is a part, and which provide a framework for human practical reasoning and action." The four elements of hermeneutic framework identified above are consistent with this definition, and the concept therefore enables me to draw on different elements of MacIntyre's and Lindbeck's theories in order to identify and address a number of areas that require clarification in their work.

Interaction between Hermeneutic Frameworks

The notion of a hermeneutic framework can be used in order to illuminate some of the points MacIntyre makes when discussing the interaction between different traditions. A hermeneutic framework consists of a set of conceptual categories which are taken to reflect or express aspects of reality. Questions of justification and interpretation will be addressed in the evolution of the framework and will establish precedents for what can and cannot be asserted. Through this process of evolution, a hermeneutic framework will establish its own standards of validity and argumentative adequacy. As a result, there will be no basis on which a person who has not become immersed in such a framework can assess the grounds of belief in that framework. Becoming convinced of the truth of a religion (for example), considered as a hermeneutic framework, cannot, therefore, be a matter of rational persuasion by universally acceptable arguments, because the force of an argument depends on the acceptance of shared presuppositions that can only be acquired through socialization into the culture of that religion. As Lindbeck says, "the logic of coming to believe, because it is like that of learning a language, has little room for argument, but once one has learnt to speak the language of faith, argument becomes possible."[23]

For both Lindbeck and MacIntyre, therefore, a tradition or religion represent potentially independent intellectual universes that may be separated from each other by incommensurable and untranslatable concepts, and exhibit distinct standards of justification and argument. But as we saw in section 2.6, the partial incommensurability of alien traditions can be overcome by processes of immersion and enculturation. MacIntyre holds that it is possible to describe the presuppositions of at least some alien traditions from the perspective of one's own tradition. This involves adopting a perspective comparable to that of an anthropologist who engages with an alien culture as best she can by immersing herself in that culture (learning it as a second first language) but then reconstructs its insights as far as this is possible within the language and perspectives of her own culture. Such

---

23. ND, 132.

a process may require hermeneutic innovation, as Stout has pointed out.[24] Lindbeck also adopts such an anthropological perspective to explain how it is possible to articulate an understanding of an alien religion. For Lindbeck, understanding a religion involves mapping the way in which a community interprets and renders intelligible the world in which it finds itself, a process he describes as "thick description," following Ryle and Geertz.[25] There are limits to the extent that such translation is possible and these limits are set by conceptual incommensurability. However, the possibility of at least partial translatability means that a hermeneutic framework is not impermeable: it will interact with the wider cultural and intellectual environment in which it is set.

The Problem of Superiority

While an anthropological approach can be used to illustrate the relationships between different traditions and IMs, it treats them as cultural products and is not concerned with the evaluation of their claims to superiority over other hermeneutic frameworks. However, when the anthropological perspective shifts to a theological or philosophical viewpoint it is the question of which framework is superior or inferior that comes to the fore. One natural way to conceptualize the superiority of one HF to another is in terms of the claim that one position is rationally justified while rival positions are not. However, both MacIntyre and Lindbeck argue that standards of justification are internal to an HF, and if the standards of different HFs are incommensurable there will be no generally accepted set of standards to enable one to determine which of their claims to justification is correct. Once again this raises our central question: how can one judge one tradition, one religion, one interpretative medium to be superior to another?

Both MacIntyre and Lindbeck balance the view that traditions/IMs set their own standards of consistency and justification (and therefore of

---

24. Stout, *Ethics after Babel*, 64.

25. ND, 115; "Thick description" is a term which Ryle uses to distinguish between the most basic level of description of a movement in physical terms ("thin description") and the "thick description" of an action in terms which relate it to the multiple levels of cultural context which are required to fully characterize the action in its various levels of meaning (see Ryle, "The Thinking of Thoughts." Geertz extends this notion of thick description to the comprehensive characterization of the semiotic elements of a culture which render the activities of its participants intelligible. See Geertz, "Thick description" in his collection of papers, *The Interpretation of Culture*, 6–7.He suggests that understanding a culture involves interpreting the "webs of significance which [humanity] has spun" (ibid., 5). Ethnography is therefore a hermeneutic process.

rationality) with what I called a "principle of epistemological openness" (PEO).[26] This principle is a manifestation of the fact that both a religion and a tradition of enquiry qua hermeneutic frameworks have to engage with and interpret other perspectives and events in accordance with their own presuppositions. HFs are distinct from their environment, but have to engage with that environment in ways that challenge the HF and drive its development. As a result, HFs may interact with each other, and this openness to the cultural environment provides some basis for the development of a concept of superiority that transcends the boundaries of one particular tradition. In the final section I argue that this account of superiority and inferiority can provide an effective defense against accusations of fideism or relativism.

However, in order to create such a robust defense it is necessary to address some deficits in each of MacIntyre and Lindbeck's positions. MacIntyre's central concept is "tradition," but his account of this concept lacks precision. In the following section I argue that the notion of a hermeneutic framework can be used to give greater empirical specificity to the concept of a tradition. One test of the adequacy of a tradition or interpretative framework is its ability to overcome epistemological crises. This clarification of the concept will also enable me to explore the circumstances in which an epistemological crisis may arise, and this will also help me to address the question of superiority.

4.3 Operative Doctrines and the Identity of a Tradition

A number of writers have argued that MacIntyre fails to offer a satisfactory account of the concept of a tradition,[27] while others have questioned whether MacIntyre uses the concept in a consistent fashion. Allen comments that "it is not entirely clear what he [MacIntyre] even means by this crucial concept, since he never gives a unified account of it; instead, his conception of a tradition must be pieced together from remarks and arguments which are scattered throughout his three books on moral and political theory."[28] Allen goes on to argue that MacIntyre's account of the relationship between tradition and rationality is inconsistent and confused.

The view that MacIntyre's account is inconsistent is reinforced by Jean Porter, who observes that the concept of a tradition in TRV and WJWR is

26. See section 2.6 above.

27. See (for example) Allen, "MacIntyre's Traditionalism"; Porter, "Tradition in the Recent Works of Alasdair MacIntyre," 38; Annas, "MacIntyre on Traditions," 389.

28. Allen, "MacIntyre's Traditionalism," 511.

significantly different from the concept described in AV.[29] These comments suggest that "tradition" in MacIntyre's writing is a fluid and potentially ambiguous concept which does not easily lend itself to definition. This lack of clear definition is partly methodological in origin, as Julia Annas points out. She notes that MacIntyre does not seek to define the nature of a tradition in WJWR but rather attempts to show that nature through his examples.[30] Annas' observation is supported by MacIntyre's own comment about definition in WJWR: "finally, it is crucial that the concept of tradition-constituted and tradition-constitutive rational enquiry cannot be elucidated apart from its exemplifications, something which I take to be true of all concepts."[31]

MacIntyre's comment suggests that I might be making an illegitimate move in seeking to provide a more general theoretical account of the nature of a tradition. But without a satisfactory definition of a tradition one cannot unambiguously identify discrete traditions. Is Aristotelian ethics a discrete philosophical tradition, for example, or should it be seen as one element in a broader Western tradition of moral philosophy? Are Augustine and Aquinas founders of discrete traditions in philosophical theology or do they each represent different facets of a single developing tradition represented by Christian theology as a whole? And if one cannot adequately identify distinct traditions, how can one answer such questions as whether different traditions are or are not mutually incommensurable and untranslatable?

As these questions illustrate, the term "tradition" has extremely fuzzy boundaries in general discourse, and it is largely a matter of choice (and argumentative convenience) whether I treat Thomist and Augustinian theologies (for example) as independent traditions or as related elements in a broader tradition. But in Macintyre's philosophy the word "tradition" takes on a more limited and technical meaning. Different traditions are (we are told) independent, incommensurable and untranslatable and driven by their own characteristic rationality. Challenges to the fundamental presuppositions of these traditions may result in epistemological crises in which the identity of the tradition and the identity of its adherents are threatened. The concept of tradition is, therefore, at the heart of MacIntyre's account of rational justification. However, unless one can clearly identify different traditions it will not be possible to apply MacIntyre's theory to the real world nor to test out whether different traditions possess the characteristics he describes.

---

29. Porter, "Tradition in the Recent Works of Alasdair MacIntyre," 43.
30. Annas, "MacIntyre on Traditions," 389.
31. WJWR, 10.

It is therefore necessary to try to give some general account of the nature of a MacIntyrean tradition. This approach is supported by MacIntyre's own practice. Notwithstanding his claim that concepts can only be exemplified, MacIntyre himself makes some general observations about the nature and origins of tradition in his writings, as Adonis Vidu has pointed out.[32] While these comments are not sufficiently specific to enable one to unambiguously distinguish one tradition from another, they do provide a legitimate starting point for an attempt to provide a general account of the nature of a tradition. In AV MacIntyre characterizes a tradition in the following way:

> A living tradition then is an historically extended, socially embodied argument and an argument precisely in part about the goods which constitute that tradition. Within a tradition the pursuit of goods extends through generations, sometimes through many generations. Here the individual's search for his or her good is generally and characteristically conducted within a context defined by those traditions of which the individual's life is a part.[33]

This definition is expanded in WJWR into the following statement:

> A tradition is an argument extended through time in which certain fundamental agreements are defined and redefined in terms of two kinds of conflict: those with critics and enemies external to the tradition who reject all or at least key parts of those fundamental agreements, and those internal, interpretative debates through which the meaning and rationale of the fundamental agreements come to be expressed and by whose progress tradition is constituted. Such internal debates may on occasion destroy what had been the basis of common fundamental agreement, so that either a tradition divides into two or more warring components, whose adherents are transformed into external critics of each other's positions, or else the tradition loses all coherence and fails to survive. It can also happen that two traditions, hitherto independent and even antagonistic, can come to recognize certain possibilities of fundamental agreement and reconstitute themselves as a single, more complex debate.[34]

Taking these two attempts at definition together we can identify five key features of MacIntyre's account of a tradition.

---

32. Vidu, *Postliberal Theological Method*, 22.
33. AV, 222.
34. WJWR, 12.

1. A tradition is a form of social life that is characterized by a single extended argument which maintains its identity throughout the life of the tradition. It is a debate around the meaning, practical relevance and truth of a set of inter-related theses. This debate requires continued engagement over time by successive participants who recognize that they are engaged in a discussion which has a certain history and which remains the *same* debate at different times, notwithstanding changes in language and the development or abandonment of certain subsidiary elements of the central contentions of the tradition.

2. A tradition is, therefore, an argument that is "historically extended," and (as the second definition indicates) the argument is constituted and bounded by "certain fundamental agreements" which the parties do not (normally) bring into question.

3. The focus of this historically extended argument is twofold: firstly it relates to the "goods which constitute the tradition"; secondly it relates to the participants' individual and communal search for the good of their own life in the context of the traditions (plural in the AV definition) in which they participate.

4. The development of the tradition is driven by internal and external conflict and leads to a continuing process of definition and redefinition of the fundamental agreements about goods that characterize the tradition.

5. Internal debate can result in a the adherents of a tradition dividing into antagonistic groups (potentially creating a number of competing traditions); equally it is possible for different traditions to recognize sufficient common ground for them to reconstitute themselves as a single integrated debate and therefore become an amalgamated tradition.

The WJWR definition in particular places an emphasis on the intellectual dimensions of participation within a tradition. But most people would not conceive of themselves as engaging in a "historically extended argument," and this intellectualization of the identity of a tradition raises a problem in understanding a tradition as a mode of living in which all people can participate. MacIntyre's account sometimes appears to point towards an understanding of traditions as intellectual perspectives which are most at home in the environment of the departmental seminar. Indeed MacIntyre's discussion of the importance of the structure and curriculum of the University[35] may also reinforce a perception of a tradition as primarily an academic perspective. However, neither a religion nor an ethical system

---

35. TRV, chapter X.

is intrinsically a topic of intellectual debate or academic study. As the AV definition emphasizes, they are modes of living which are embraced by successive generations, and which are underpinned by faith in the case of a religion and by a particular understanding of the nature of the moral life in the case of an ethical tradition.

There is, therefore, a potential tension between MacIntyre's accounts of a tradition as a theoretical inquiry into the nature of the good (for example), and his understanding of ethics as embodied in practice rather than theory. While it would take detailed exegesis to demonstrate this, I suspect that Allen's and Porter's comments with respect to the apparent inconsistency of MacIntyre's account of tradition relate to the fact that the term is used to refer to two closely related but distinct cultural phenomena. The differences between the accounts of tradition in AV and WJWR/TRV noted by Porter can be explained by the fact that in AV MacIntyre is writing of tradition as a form of life characterized by engagement in social practices, while in the later books it is tradition conceived as the second order articulation of the theoretical rationale of such forms of life that is his focus. MacIntyre's theoretical account of tradition-as-enquiry in WJWR and TRV bears the same relationship to his account of tradition-as-a-mode-of-living in AV as the second-order activity of theology bears to a religion.

The recognition of the dual functions of the word "tradition" in MacIntyre's work provides a partial explanation of the apparent inconsistency of his accounts, but MacIntyre's exposition still leaves a lack of definition about three further elements of the concept. Firstly, it is unclear what constitutes the "fundamental agreements" that characterize a tradition. Secondly, there is a consequent lack of clarity about what it means for someone to enter into such agreements to become a member of a tradition. For many people membership of a tradition will be characterized by participation in its characteristic social structures rather than engagement in its intellectual debates. Indeed as MacIntyre acknowledges, many people who are engaged in a tradition may have no awareness of their intellectual environment as a distinct tradition at all.[36] There is therefore a need to clarify how such a person can be counted as a member of a tradition. Thirdly, without a more precise understanding of the nature of the agreements that constitute a tradition, it is difficult to define the circumstances in which a tradition may subdivide into warring factions, or to specify the conditions in which two independent traditions can come to coalesce into new united tradition.

---

36. MacIntyre, "Reply to Dahl, Baier and Schneewind," 175.

Doctrine, Tradition, and Identity

Lindbeck identifies the source of identity of a religious community with the set of beliefs and practices that constitute the doctrines of that religious community and these doctrines also play a constitutive role with respect to the identity of members of that community by providing implicit tests of community membership.[37] Thus while doctrines may be used to express beliefs or symbolize experiences, their central function is to act as rules that regulate the beliefs and practices of a community. They undertake this function by defining what beliefs should be expressed or denied, and what practices are to be pursued or avoided if a person is to be a member of the community in good standing. Lindbeck argues that doctrines emerge and develop out of the type of internal and external conflict that MacIntyre sees as driving the development of a tradition.[38] There are therefore, clear analogies between Lindbeck's account of the origin of doctrine and MacIntyre's account of the evolution of a tradition. Indeed, some of the similarities between their positions can be seen as arising out of the common influence of Newman's work on the development of doctrine on both authors.[39]

MacIntyre's use of the term "fundamental agreements" suggests a parallel between his account of tradition and Lindbeck's account of doctrine. An agreement may go beyond the acceptance of some particular propositions by two or more parties; it may also point to the acceptance of a contract which requires the parties to act in certain ways. Such a contract may be formal or informal, but in either case it will serve to regulate the future conduct of the parties to the agreement. To breach the terms of such an agreement is to do more than change one's mind about a belief or set of beliefs. It is to open oneself to legitimate censure for a failure to conform to expected standards of conduct. Agreements can perform a regulative function which is analogous to the regulative functions of doctrine highlighted by Lindbeck. This analogy suggests that it may be fruitful to use Lindbeck's account of doctrine as a model for the fundamental agreements that constitute a MacIntyrean tradition.

However, such a model needs to have regard to the significant differences in their accounts. Traditions as defined by MacIntyre appear to be evolving patterns of social interaction and debate that do not have a formal

---

37. ND, 74.

38. ND, 75.

39. Lindbeck makes scattered reference to Newman's work on doctrine and assent in ND (13, 36, 75–76, 105 and 138), while MacIntyre specifically cites Newman's work on doctrine as a major source of his theory of tradition. See WJWR, 353–34 and Prologue to the 3rd edition of *After Virtue*, xii.

authority structure, while the doctrines of religious bodies are characteristically formal statements of belief and practice that are authoritative within the believing community. A tradition of enquiry is a far less formally organized social structure than a Church or a religious community, and will not necessarily have the type of authority embedded into its structure that would enable the tradition to construct, and to sustain as authoritative, formal statements of belief. How, then, can we apply Lindbeck's concept of doctrine to MacIntyre's account of a tradition?

Lindbeck makes an important distinction between formal and operative doctrines.[40] The construction of formal statements of doctrine is a process triggered by some pressing controversy or dilemma, and therefore the most important beliefs of a community may never become formalized in statements of doctrine.[41] The most central Christian beliefs, that God is love for example, may not be formalized precisely because they remain fundamentally unchallenged, at least in the process of internal debate.[42] Indeed, Lindbeck acknowledges that religious groups that define themselves as having no creed do not, thereby, escape from having some fundamental beliefs that serve to define communal identity and membership of the group.[43] Within those communities that are characterized by formal statements of doctrine, doctrines promulgated at one time, in response to some pressing issue for example, may no longer be accepted as binding by that community at a later time, even if these statements have not been formally rescinded. As a result, such formal statements of doctrine may no longer reflect the beliefs of a community. If the denial of a formal doctrine does not exclude someone from membership of a religious community

> it is evident that the belief has ceased to be communally formative, and it is therefore no longer an operative doctrine even though it may continue to be a formal or official one. In any case, operative doctrines, even if not official ones, are necessary to communal identity. A religious body cannot exist as a recognizably distinctive collectivity unless it has some beliefs and/or practices by which it can be identified.[44]

It is the operative rather than the formal doctrines of the community, then, that are most important in determining the identity of the group and

---

40. ND, 74.

41. ND, 75.

42. ND, 75.

43. Lindbeck refers to "many Quakers and the Disciples of Christ" as groups that would describe themselves as creedless: ND, 74.

44. ND, 74.

of its individual members, and it is necessary to examine the informal beliefs which are held to be non-negotiable if one is to comprehend the way in which a community understands its identity and the identity of its members. Informal operative doctrines are therefore central to defining identity and group membership, both in those communities which possess formal doctrines, and in those groups which do not have such formal mechanisms. There is therefore no theoretical barrier to extending Lindbeck's account of operative doctrines to social groups who do not have a formal body of doctrine but which share a set of beliefs that define both their purpose and what it is to be a member of the group.

An analogy with operative doctrines can, therefore, provide a basis for the characterization of the "fundamental agreements" that partially define the identity of a MacIntyrean tradition. Such agreements can be interpreted as regulative principles that define those conceptual categories and practices that are central to community identity. These operative doctrines will require members of the tradition to assert certain beliefs in appropriate circumstances, and will promote the adherence of members to those practices which contribute to the well-being of the community. Such regulative principles will also enable the tradition to manage and control processes of internal debate which have emerged as responses to internal disagreements and external challenges, and which are seen as enabling the tradition to pursue its telos.

Applying the notion of "operative doctrines" to MacIntyre's account of tradition is valuable in three ways. Lindbeck's regulative account of doctrine provides a means by which those beliefs that are fundamental to the identity of a tradition and its members can be distinguished from more peripheral beliefs. Secondly, the notion of operative doctrines can provide more specificity to the notions of epistemological crisis and the rationality of a tradition, as we shall see below. Thirdly, drawing an analogy between the fundamental agreements that constitute a tradition and Lindbeck's notion of operative doctrines also points to the way in which such agreements can act as rules that govern legitimate assertion and rules of conduct. As a result of this function such rules will shape the distinctive standards of justification and argument that characterize the tradition, that is, the nature of its tradition-constituted rationality.

A particular strength of the concept of operative doctrines is that it acts as a counterbalance to the over-intellectualization of traditions that characterizes MacIntyre's account in WJWR and TRV. Members of a tradition or interpretative medium will understand themselves as having particular beliefs and responsibilities imposed by the regulative functions of the operative doctrines of the tradition, even if for the most part this understanding is implicit and only brought to consciousness by a reaction to some perceived challenge to these beliefs or practices. Conceptualizing membership of a tradition in terms of the adherence to the operative doctrines that regulate what can be asserted, and therefore how one must act if one is to be a continuing member, explains why even the least theoretically inclined member of a tradition has a stake in the continued coherence of the rules defined by its operative doctrines: a challenge to these rules threatens core components of the member's identity.

4.4 Applying the Notion of a Hermeneutic Framework

The emergence of concepts, rules of assertion and tradition-constituted standards of rationality in a tradition which are incommensurable with those that emerge in alternative traditions can be explained if the fundamental agreements that constitute the identity of a tradition act as regulative principles. Regulative principles create the capacity of a tradition to act as a hermeneutic framework by defining the non-negotiable elements that constitute the core presuppositions of the tradition. Recalling my previous definition of a tradition, these rules define the "conceptual categories. . .whose abandonment would constitute a rejection of the tradition's fundamental presuppositions"[45] and therefore define what it is necessary to assert or do if one is to be a member of the tradition in good standing. They also limit what can be asserted without contradicting the requirements of belief; and in doing this they set limits to the way in which phenomena external to the tradition can be legitimately interpreted, and through this generate rules of assertion and processes of interpretation.

Such regulative principles will also shape the set of concepts that are unique to the tradition. As a result of their relationship to these tradition-based rules of assertion, these concepts may be incommensurable with the concepts formed in some alternative tradition, even though both traditions may use the same words in similar contexts. Thus both Trinitarian Christians and Jehovah's Witnesses (JW) would describe Jesus Christ as the "Son of God," but this description conveys a different meaning to the latter because JWs deny the divinity of Christ.[46] The rules as to what it is legitimate to assert of Christ in different contexts will therefore vary between the different groups, and will also shape what can be inferred from the use of the description "Son of God." For the JWs such a description does not indicate

---

45. See section 4.2 above.
46. See JW.Org http://www.jw.org/en/bible-teachings/questions/is-jesus-almighty/.

that he is God, but that he is the first created being,[47] and they would thus deny the divinity accorded to him by Trinitarian Christians.

The beliefs of Jehovah's Witnesses can also help to illustrate more general characteristics of a hermeneutic framework, and its relationship to the interpretation of rational belief and practical reasoning. JW's hold that to take blood into the body as either food or as a form of medical treatment is explicitly against the will of God as expressed in Scripture.[48] It has been asserted that around 1000 members of the sect die each year as a result of this prohibition.[49] A member of the sect who accepts transfusion and is not repentant will be "disfellowshipped"—in effect excommunicated from the sect.[50] The prohibition on blood transfusion therefore acts as an operative doctrine of the community. It is a belief whose abandonment would represent a rejection of one of the fundamental agreements which are required for membership of the church. Such agreements also embody "rules of assertion," which limit what propositions can be held to be true while maintaining intellectual consistency with the operative doctrines of the sect. For example, it would not be consistent with the belief system for someone to assert that it is legitimate for members to accept blood transfusion on the basis of the promptings of their private conscience.

The question of the rationality of JW decisions on transfusion has been debated within the medical ethics literature. Julian Savulescu and Richard Momeyer argue that the prohibition is not rationally based, although they do not suggest that the wishes of JW should simply be overruled. Rather they suggest that Medical Practitioners should act as educators in order to encourage people to recognize when the beliefs on which they are basing their decisions are not rationally held.[51] But the judgment that such beliefs are not rationally held presupposes not only that there may be stronger evidence for some alternative set of underpinning beliefs, but also that what *counts* as evidence for or against a set of beliefs can be identified independently of the presuppositions of the individuals concerned. They dismiss the scriptural basis on which JW reject transfusion as based on a selective and unjustified reading,[52] but their critique of the foundations of these beliefs

---

47. See JW.Org http://www.jw.org/en/bible-teachings/questions/jesus-gods-son/.

48. See Bock, "Jehovah's Witnesses and Autonomy."

49. See Wilson, "Jehovah's Witness Children," 35. This is also cited by Bock, "Jehovah's Witnesses and Autonomy," 652.

50. Bock, "Jehovah's Witnesses and Autonomy," 653.

51. Savulescu and Momeyer, "Should Informed Consent be Based on Rational Beliefs?" 287–88.

52. The beliefs Savulescu and Momeyer criticize are summarized (provocatively) by them as "God forbids eating blood.... Accepting a blood transfusion is no different

has been criticized in turn by Bock.[53] Bock's arguments indicate that the sect would not be without some of the resources needed to repudiate such external criticism. Where Savulescu and Momeyer accuse them of inconsistency, for example in allowing consumption of wine in communion as the blood of Christ, a more careful examination of their underlying beliefs demonstrates that their practice is consistent with the prohibition, as they do not believe in transubstantiation or any notion of the real presence.[54]

The prohibition on transfusion is justified by the community's interpretation of a number of Biblical texts, including the belief that the sect is the "'faithful and discreet slave' referred to in Jesus' parable at Matthew 24:45." This belief is used in turn to underpin the claim that only the JW can appropriately interpret the Bible, and enables the sect to resist claims that its interpretation of the bible is arbitrary and selective. The priority that the sect gives to conformity with the rule concerning blood transfusion also reflects the priority given to other beliefs held by the sect. For example, the sect holds that the time of judgment is near at hand and that salvation depends on how well individuals follow the rules that define appropriate conduct for JW, including the prohibition on blood transfusion.[55]

The sect's teachings around blood transfusion provide a basis for practical reasoning because they are connected to a range of other commitments that together shape the identity of the sect and of its members. These beliefs render both the prohibition and also the behavior of members of the tradition intelligible and show how a member may rationally choose a course of action which they recognize may end their life (by refusing transfusion) on the basis of a set of beliefs that are not shared by their critic. From the perspective of the committed believer their action in refusing a lifesaving transfusion could be seen to be based on a version of Pascal's wager, in that they are choosing to pursue an infinite good (eternal life) at the cost of a more limited good (extending one's life on earth).[56] If the tenets on which they have based their decision are correct, their decision is arguably rationally founded.

The process of describing the relationship between the practical decisions and the underlying network of commitments renders the member's

---

from eating blood. . . . If one eats blood when alive, one turns to dust upon death. . . . We know (the above) to be true based on faith that a (selectively) literal interpretation of the Bible reveals God's will." Ibid., 286.

53. Bock, "Jehovah's Witnesses and Autonomy," 653.

54. Ibid.

55. Ibid., 652.

56. This interpretation is suggested by Savulescu and Momeyer, "Should Informed Consent be Based on Rational Beliefs?" Footnote 17, 288.

behavior intelligible, illustrates the nature of practical reasoning and sheds light on the distinctive rationality of the sect. In this process of elucidation, we may move from a perception of the sect as having a set of concepts of well-being (for example) that are incoherent and incommensurable with our own understanding of well-being, to an understanding of those concepts as intelligible and rationally based, although we may still reject the fundamental presuppositions that are used to justify them. But in this process the debate has shifted from a critique of the rationality of their behavior (or, alternatively, from a conflict between incommensurable concepts of well-being), to a dispute about the truth of the beliefs and the processes of reasoning that are used to justify different moral judgments. This example therefore illustrates the process described by Stout (see section 2.6), in which traditions divided by incommensurable concepts may come to establish an understanding of the judgments made by each community through processes of thick description, but remain in dispute over the legitimacy of these judgments, and the strength and relevance of the evidence used to justify them.

If we consider the example of JW beliefs in terms of MacIntyre's account of a tradition of enquiry, then MacIntyre's theory of tradition-constituted rationality suggests that the rules, practices and concepts which together define the identity of the JW sect will interact with its history of debate to shape the distinctive rationality of that tradition. However, for MacIntyre the test of the rationality of any tradition is its epistemological openness: for, he argues, only a degenerate tradition will construct defenses that will ensure that it cannot be brought into question.[57] But the JW (and other groups of religious believers) are unlikely to accept that counter-examples to elements of their faith have undermined the coherence of their belief system. They are much more likely to modify one or other elements of their belief system in order to remove the inconsistency between belief and experience. For example, the JW originally held to the view that the last days would occur while some of those people who were living in 1914 were still alive. The passage of time has rendered such a specific millenarian belief less plausible, and the sect has now revised its doctrine, a process mapped by David Weddle.[58]

Weddle points out that the JWs have had to reconsider their position because the passage of time has naturally led to a decline in the numbers of people alive who were born in the early part of the twentieth century. As a result an apparently identity defining doctrine faces falsification rather than

---

57. ECS, 12.
58. Weddle, "New Generation of Jehovah's Witnesses," 351–52.

confirmation. Weddle notes that "as the twentieth century draws to a close the only predictive text that has so far been confirmed is the actuarial table charting the dwindling numbers of the generation of 1914."[59] He sensitively describes the evolution of JW eschatology in response to this challenge. This has involved an implicit acceptance that the original doctrine has been falsified by history. In order to retain the integrity of the belief system the sect has reinterpreted the term "generation" so that it has come to symbolize the sinful but unrepentant people who are present in every age, rather than referring to a specific cohort living at a particular period.[60] This has the benefit of protecting the sect from the challenge that its beliefs have been falsified, as the revised doctrine is consistent with virtually any timescale for the occurrence of Armageddon. But while this protective reconstruction of the doctrine renders the belief system less vulnerable to falsification, it also raises questions as to the extent to which such religious groups can be interpreted as engaged in pursuit of a tradition of enquiry whose object is truth.

And this also reveals a more general challenge to MacIntyre's position. The strategy of tolerating anomalies or seeking a limited change to beliefs and principles so that the overall position is protected from challenge is not only a form of defense employed by religious sects. It is also a characteristic of the perspective Kuhn describes as normal science, in which inconsistencies are not treated as counter-examples but as puzzles to be resolved within the framework specified by the dominant paradigm.[61] Indeed, the ability to recognize challenges and adapt one's beliefs to the demands of evidence is in itself a sign of a rational response to experience. To abandon the full range of one's beliefs and adopt a new set at the first sign of inconsistency would result in such frequent changes of belief system as to render the individual's behavior inconsistent and apparently irrational. But if any system is able to defend itself by modifying one or more tenets in order to avoid falsification then we would appear to have no basis on which to choose between different belief-systems, and the problems which led to MacIntyre's epistemological crisis at the end of the 1960s will remain unresolved. The challenge for MacIntyre's theory lies in whether it is able to clearly specify the circumstances in which an epistemological crisis may arise which will, if unresolved, result in the dissolution of the tradition so that there is a clear basis for identifying a failed system of belief.

---

59. Ibid., 354.
60. Ibid., 351.
61. Kuhn, *Structure of Scientific Revolutions*, section iv.

Identity and Epistemological Crisis

In section 2.5 I described MacIntyre's account of the development of a personal epistemological crisis in terms of the subversion of the conceptual scheme or "schemata" through which an individual interprets the world, and holds their beliefs about the world to be justified.[62] The notion of operative doctrines as the identity-forming elements of a tradition of enquiry suggests that such doctrines may be interpreted as embodying the rules which underpin these processes of interpretation and criteria of justification and which therefore contribute to the distinctive rationality of the tradition. If this model is accepted, one way to explain the nature of epistemological crisis might be to suggest that such crises will arise when the viability of the fundamental agreements/operative doctrines of a tradition are challenged by contradictory events or internal inconsistencies, and the tradition lacks the resources to respond. In order to give this account precision one would have to be able to identify those beliefs that are intrinsic to the identity of the tradition.

Lindbeck attempted to address this problem by constructing a taxonomy of doctrines, in which he distinguishes between those doctrines that are "unconditionally necessary" because "they are part of the indispensable grammar or logic of the faith,"[63] and other doctrines that may simply be conditionally necessary, such as the doctrine of the immortality of the soul. Lindbeck suggests that the latter may be abandoned without compromising the integrity of the faith when the conceptual resources available to the community have changed.[64] Unconditionally necessary doctrines, however, cannot be abandoned without undermining the coherence of the belief system. It might be argued, therefore, that an epistemological crisis will arise when there are unresolved challenges to some of these unconditionally necessary doctrines. Does this solve the problem of specifying the circumstances under which an epistemological crisis may arise?

If the concepts of "schemata" or "unconditionally necessary doctrines" are to explain the genesis of epistemological crises they would have to be identifiable independently of their involvement in an epistemological crisis. But whether a doctrine comes to count as indispensable and identity-forming for a tradition will reflect the history of that tradition, rather than being determined by some particular content of the doctrine. Beliefs that might in other circumstances be considered peripheral to the identity of the

---

62. See ECS, 4.
63. ND, 85.
64. ND, 86.

faith may become identity-defining when subject to challenge, as Lindbeck himself points out, citing Luther and Newman in support of this contention.[65] Moreover a limited readjustment of presuppositions will always be a possible response to an unresolved challenge, as the example of the JWs has indicated. If this strategy is employed a belief or practice that apparently constituted an unconditionally necessary doctrine will be redefined in terms which mean that it can be dispensed with without undermining the coherence of the belief system.

The possibility of employing such strategies to redefine challenged beliefs means that it is not possible to specify *a priori* criteria to identify the beliefs or rules that are unconditionally necessary elements of a belief system. Moreover, the evolution of a tradition may generate changes in the set of doctrines that are considered to be necessary at different times, although one would anticipate that there would be identifiable "family resemblances" (in Wittgensteinian terms) between the network of beliefs and practices that characterize the tradition at one time and those that characterize it at a later time. If this is the case the question as to whether a particular belief-statement or principle of action acts as an unconditionally necessary operative doctrine of a particular religious group or tradition of enquiry will have to be determined by examining what doctrines the group members hold to be the indispensable tenets of group membership at that particular point in time.

Determining whether a particular belief acts as an operative doctrine would therefore require a process of Geertzian "thick description"[66] to explore how particular beliefs govern the way members of a religion or tradition conceptualize the identity of that belief system—and therefore how members of that system also conceptualize their own identity. One way forward for research in this area would be the detailed analysis of the accounts of members of traditions (religious and secular) in order to identify their understanding of the non-negotiable elements of community membership, perhaps drawing on the techniques of discourse analysis that have been developed in social psychology.[67] Once the repertoire of rules, practices, and beliefs that are considered to be identity-forming have been identified it will be possible to identify the way in which challenges to these beliefs may or may not precipitate epistemological crises.

There may, however, be other elements of a tradition which can provide a complementary basis for an understanding of the grounds of an

---

65. ND, 75.
66. ND, 115.
67. See (for example) Potter and Wetherall, *Discourse and Social Psychology*.

epistemological crisis, over and above the existence of some doctrines that are considered necessary. The continuity of a tradition of enquiry may not depend on the existence of some unchanging doctrines but on the extent to which the evolution of its doctrines in response to challenge can be seen by participants to represent progress in the pursuit of the goal of that enquiry. This progress will strengthen the claims of the community to knowledge, by enabling it to explain the reasons why the unmodified tradition was originally unable to resolve the challenges which it has now resolved. In this process of modification and evolution it will have developed a deeper understanding of the nature of its object of enquiry and a deeper understanding of that process of enquiry itself. What acts as the center of identity of the tradition may not, therefore, be a set of fixed beliefs (although these may play an important role), but an ability to identify progress towards the achievement of its central purpose.

If we take MacIntyre's resuscitation of the Aristotelian tradition as an example, it is apparent that in his work the identity and continuity of the tradition is balanced with conceptual development. The aim of articulating the overall good for human beings has remained constant through the historical transmutations of that tradition, and that aim is also central to MacIntyre's account. According to MacIntyre, the decline of the Aristotelian tradition occurred when the growth of non-teleological forms of explanation (among other factors) eroded the credibility of the notion of a human telos.[68] MacIntyre's work in AV onwards represents an attempt to revive a version of Aristotelian ethics by reconstructing its central aim of constructing an account of the human good, without relying on the metaphysical presuppositions of its founder. Despite the significant conceptual changes he has introduced, MacIntyre's work remains an extension of the Aristotelian ethical tradition rather than a replacement for it, because development is balanced with continuity in three ways. Firstly, the overall goal of the enquiry has remained the same despite changes to the concepts in which that goal is expressed—particularly the notion of a telos and the virtues. Secondly, these concepts are reinterpreted by MacIntyre in ways that are consistent with contemporary metaphysical presuppositions in order to enhance their credibility, but despite these changes their function in his overall philosophy remains the same as the role of the equivalent concepts in Aristotle's ethics. Thirdly, MacIntyre is able to demonstrate progress as well as continuity in enquiry by explaining why the original concepts were found to be inadequate and by demonstrating how these modified concepts have overcome these inadequacies.

---

68. AV, 81–82.

MacIntyre's revival of Aristotelianism therefore provides an illustration of Lindbeck's claim that an interpretative medium is capable of retaining its identity through successive transformations of the concepts in which it is expressed. It is the commitment to the notion of telos itself, and to the value of the process of enquiry aimed at elucidating that telos, that defines one as an Aristotelian, rather than the acceptance or rejection of particular conceptualizations of telos. In the same way, the second order activities of theology are united by the shared purpose of articulating the meaning of the Christian faith, notwithstanding major differences in the way that that meaning has been expressed. The identity of a tradition will be maintained by a continued commitment to its purpose and to the coherence of its processes of enquiry. And this explains why epistemological openness is an important characteristic of a living tradition: strategies which protect a belief-system's identity-forming doctrines from challenge, such as defensive redefinition (as in the example of the Jehovah's Witnesses) will also tend to frustrate progress in the pursuit of its purpose and act to undermine its intellectual credibility, even among its adherents.

To summarize, I have argued in this section that the emergence of an epistemological crisis can be understood in terms of the interaction between two characteristics of a tradition of enquiry. Firstly, an epistemological crisis may arise when one or more doctrines that are held to be unconditionally necessary are challenged, unless the tradition is able to respond to this challenge in a way that maintains its overall coherence. Defensive redefinition of doctrines is always a potential strategy for dealing with such challenges to particular elements of the belief system. However, such responses risk undermining the coherence of the processes of enquiry which embody the rationality of the tradition and, as a result, may frustrate its progress in enquiry. This may undermine the credibility of the tradition as a rational belief system, frustrate progress towards the achievement of its purpose and lead to epistemological crisis in a second way, through the loss of its credibility as a form of enquiry amongst its own adherents. The development of these ideas would require empirical investigation aimed at examining the way in which adherents of different traditions conceptualize the identity forming characteristics of their tradition, the nature of the rational (and a-rational) processes of justification used within the tradition, and the consequences of unresolved challenges on the stability and coherence of that tradition.

4.5 Lindbeck on Inter-religious Superiority

The first part of this chapter has used Lindbeck's account of doctrine to provide a more precise account of the nature of a tradition, and in doing this it has shed some light on the conditions under which an epistemological crisis may arise. The second part of the chapter now shifts the focus to the identification of two unresolved issues in Lindbeck's work, and the relevance of MacIntyre's philosophy to their resolution. These issues are both related to the question of superiority in matters of religion. The first issue is the basis on which one religion might be considered superior to another religion, which is the focus of the current section. The second issue is the question of the basis on which one can distinguish between authentic and inauthentic interpretations of the faith in controversies within the Christian religion. This issue is addressed in the following section.

Inter-religious Superiority and Relativism

Different religions characteristically assert their superiority to others by claiming that they are true while their rivals are (at least partially) false. The question of inter-religious superiority is therefore intimately entwined with questions about the nature of religious truth, and how such truth can be recognized. The question of the nature of truth is problematic for Lindbeck because he holds that religions can be identified with interpretative mediums that set their own incommensurable standards of truth and justification.[69] A historical or anthropological perspective can describe the criteria that have evolved within these different traditions or religions, subject to the limits set by translatability and conceptual commensurability, but a repudiation of tradition-transcendent standards of justification appears to rule out the possibility of making universally cogent judgments as to which set of standards are superior to others. As Lindbeck acknowledges, the CL model of religion does not appear to be fertile ground for the interpretation of concepts of superiority, because it treats religions as cultural constructions and "one language or culture is not generally thought of as "truer" than another, much less unsurpassable, and yet that is what some religions profess to be."[70]

If the CL model cannot show how one religion (or secular philosophy) can be superior to another it would appear to legitimate a form of relativism or perspectivism, and this would be inconsistent with a believer's claim that their religion represents unique and unsurpassable truth. Lindbeck's

---

69. ND, 49.
70. ND, 46.

discussion is, therefore, shaped by the desire to show that the CL model allows for a coherent account of the meaning of claims of superiority, without claiming ultimate and unsurpassable truth for one particular religion or sect. In ND Lindbeck therefore pursues a "nontheological" analysis of the implications of the cultural-linguistic model, which is restricted to elucidating the *meaning* of claims to superiority:

> It is not the business of a nontheological theory of religion to argue for or against the superiority of any one faith; but it does have the job, if it is to be religiously useful, of allowing the possibility of such superiority. It must not, in other words, exclude the claims religions make about themselves, and it must supply an interpretation of what these claims mean.[71]

Lindbeck develops his CL account of superiority by contrasting it with CP and EE accounts of superiority. He suggests that the CP model identifies superiority with the possession of propositional truth as opposed to propositional falsity, and would identify as superior to all others the religion that asserts the greatest number of significant propositional truths about ultimate reality. It would hold a religion to be unsurpassably true if it only asserted true propositions about the object of ultimate concern and was "exempt from error."[72] In contrast, experiential-expressive models presuppose that, while there may be diverse routes to religious experiences, all such experiences arise from an experience of the divine that is common to everyone.[73] One religion therefore cannot claim to be superior to others on the basis that it uniquely provides access to an experience of the divine, although it might claim to provide a greater intensity of religious experience than others, and this might act as a measure of superiority.[74]

In contrast to CP and EE models, the CL model explains the capacity of religions to assert propositional truths and to mediate religious experience as flowing from their creation of a set of interpretative resources that can be used to understand reality and experience, in accordance with culturally-approved norms of usage. Lindbeck terms these resources "categories," and argues that only those categories which can be used to make reference to what is *real* can underpin the expression of religious truth and the appropriate characterization of religious experience, and thereby underpin judgments of superiority or inferiority.

71. ND, 46.
72. ND, 49.
73. ND, 47.
74. ND, 49–50.

> In a cultural-linguistic outlook, religions are thought of primarily as different idioms for construing reality, expressing experience, and ordering life. Attention, when considering the question of truth, focuses on the categories (or "grammar" or "rules of the game") in terms of which truth claims are made and expressive symbolisms are employed. Thus the questions raised in comparing religions have to do first of all with the adequacy of their categories. Adequate categories are those which can be made to apply to what is taken to be real and which therefore make possible, though they do not guarantee propositional, practical and symbolic truth. A religion that is thought of as having such categories can be said to be categorially true.[75]

The CL model therefore identifies the overall criterion of superiority in religion with the possession of categorial truth, defined as the capacity of the semiotic categories to be used (in principle) to interpret reality and human experience correctly. This capacity is a precondition of the religion's power to formulate assertoric propositions that are (potentially) true and to categorize experience in a meaningful way. Categorial truth therefore underpins those functions of religions which CP and EE models mistakenly privilege.[76] Lindbeck's account of inter-religious superiority can, therefore, be summarized as follows:

A religion is categorially adequate if it has created semiotic resources (categories) which can correspond to aspects of ontological and experiential reality. Categorial adequacy will make possible the expression of truth about such aspects of reality by those versed in the semiotic system. A religion which possesses such categories is superior to one that does not.

Participation in a categorially adequate religion provides the capacity to construct meaningful propositions about ultimate reality, but does not guarantee their truth. It also provides a capacity to characterize spiritual experience, but does not guarantee that such characterizations correctly represent the nature of that experience. However, Lindbeck suggests that religions which are categorially false would never be capable of either propositional truth or falsity or symbolic efficacy: "they would be religiously meaningless."[77] Lindbeck suggests that if there is only one religion that has constructed the unique set of categories that can be used to refer to the ultimate reality then such a religion would be the only one with resources capable of expressing propositional and expressive truth and would

---

75. ND, 47–48.
76. ND, 48.
77. ND, 50.

therefore be unsurpassably true.[78] However, Lindbeck does not exclude the possibility that several different religions may possess some categories that are adequate, and which allow those religions to address aspects of the ultimate "that are not within the direct purview of the peoples of Messianic witness, but that are nevertheless God-willed and God-approved aspects of the coming kingdom."[79] If this is the case, several religions (and indeed some secular philosophies) may have created categories that are categorially true, and which can underpin the construction of true (and false) propositions about ultimate reality and appropriate characterizations of spiritual experience.

However, unless there is some criterion by which one can distinguish between those categories that are adequate and those that are empty of significance Lindbeck's account of inter-religious superiority will be devoid of any practical application. Specifying such a criterion is problematic for Lindbeck because he claims that the notions of categorial adequacy and truth constructed in one religion may be incommensurable with those constructed in another religion. As a result there will be "no common framework . . . within which to compare religions."[80] If there is no such common framework for evaluation, it would appear that Lindbeck's non-theological account of religion does not provide a practical basis for judgments of superiority/inferiority which transcend the conflicting standards formulated within different religions. The superior religion may be that religion which is true rather than false—but how do we tell which religion is true?

Categorial and Performative Truth

The question of identifying religious truth is made more complicated by the fact that Lindbeck identifies several different varieties of truth in ND, including categorial, intrasystematic, and ontological forms of truth. Categorial truth was defined in the previous section in terms of a religion's possession of semiotic categories which can be made to apply to what is real, but the possession of such categories is a necessary rather than sufficient condition for "propositional, practical, and symbolic truth."[81] Lindbeck defines intrasystematic truth in terms of the coherence of an utterance or action with the total context defined by the discourse and practices of a religion:

78. ND, 50–51.
79. ND, 54–55.
80. ND, 49.
81. ND, 47–48.

> Utterances are intrasystematically true when they cohere with the total relevant context, which, in the case of a religion when viewed as a cultural-linguistic terms, is not only other utterances but also the correlative forms of life. Thus for a Christian, "God is Three and One," or "Christ is Lord" are true only as part of a total pattern of speaking, thinking, feeling and acting. They are false when their use in any given instance is inconsistent with what the pattern as a whole affirms of God's being and will.[82]

For an utterance to be intrasystematically true, therefore, it must be expressed in categories which can be made to apply to that which is real (as otherwise it will be meaningless[83]), and cohere with the overall form of life that constitutes the religion. The combination of categorial and intrasystematic truth makes possible the expression of ontological truth, but such truth is not to be identified with a conventional correspondence theory of truth in which sentences or propositions are true by virtue of their relationship to what is real. In Lindbeck's account, religious ontological truth is created through the correspondence of the whole person and community to aspects of the divine.[84] The creation of ontological truth requires the use of the religion's categories in a more complex range of human activities than in the construction of grammatically correct sentences. Such sentences have to "be made to apply to what is taken to be real,"[85] through their employment within a set of religious practices.[86] Ontological religious truth therefore has to be expressed in a pattern of life, rather than through the assertion of a set of abstract propositions. According to Lindbeck:

> A religion thought of as comparable to a cultural system, as a set of language games correlated with a form of life, may as a whole correspond or not correspond to what a theist calls God's being and will. As actually lived, a religion may be pictured as a single gigantic proposition. It is a true proposition to the extent that its objectivities are interiorized and exercised by groups and

---

82. ND, 64.
83. See ND, 50.
84. ND, 65.
85. ND, 48: emphasis added.
86. Lindbeck makes this point very clearly in the "Excursus on truth." He notes that "religious sentences . . . acquire enough specificity to have first-order or ontological truth or falsity only in determinate settings." He continues by suggesting that the sentence "Christ is Lord" "only becomes a first order proposition capable (so non-idealists would say) of making ontological truth claims only as it is used in the activities of adoration, proclamation, obedience, promise-hearing and promise-keeping which shape individuals and communities into conformity to the mind of Christ" (ND, 68).

individuals in such a way as to conform them in some measure in the various dimensions of their existence to the ultimate reality and goodness that lies at the heart of things. It is a false proposition to the extent that this does not happen.[87]

The truth (and therefore the superiority) of a religion cannot be divorced from its ability to shape the life of an individual and her community, by "guiding thought, passions and action in a way that corresponds to ultimate reality, and of thus being ontologically (and "propositionally") true."[88] The truth of the Christian religion for Lindbeck is thus expressed in its capacity to foster the development of "Christic identities."[89] Lindbeck's account therefore emphasizes that ontological truth is about shaping human behavior in ways that correspond to the understanding of the divine embodied in a religion.

Lindbeck's account of religious truth has led some commentators to suggest that his position undermines ontological realism in religious belief. I have already noted Adonis Vidu's reservations in this respect in section 4.2 above,[90] and Father Colman O'Neill has also suggested that Lindbeck is committed to a "moral or pragmatic definition of truth" rather than to a realist position.[91] Such interpretations are entirely inconsistent with Lindbeck's intentions.[92] One of Lindbeck's most sympathetic commentators, Bruce Marshall, has argued that Lindbeck's account of multiple varieties of truth is misleading and should be reframed into a set of theories about meaning, warrant, and ontological truth to avoid such difficulties of interpretation. He suggests that

> [ontological truth] lines up directly with traditional notions of truth as correspondence to reality or adequatio mentis ad rem. But categorial "truth" has to do with . . . matters of meaning and reference, and intrasystematic "truth" has to do with warrant or justification . . . It is therefore misleading for Lindbeck to speak as though there were three different kinds of truth; it would have been clearer to speak of meaning, warrant and truth. That Lindbeck insists on an unusually intimate connection between practice and belief when it comes to meaning and warrant

---

87. ND, 51.
88. ND, 52.
89. Lindbeck, "Infallibility," 125.
90. Vidu, *Postliberal Theological Method*, 241–45.
91. O'Neill, "The Rule Theory of Doctrine and Propositional Truth," 429.
92. See ND, 63–64, in which Lindbeck emphasizes the importance of ensuring that the CL model preserves the possibility of propositional truth.

(categorial and intrasystematic "truth") has served to heighten the provocation [to his critics].[93]

In his paper "Aquinas as Postliberal Theologian," Marshall distinguishes between Lindbeck's understanding of ontological realism, and his *justification* of that realism in terms of categorial and intrasystematic coherence. Marshall responds to Father O'Neill's criticisms and argues that O'Neill had wrongly assumed that Lindbeck's account of justification cannot underpin a robustly realist account of religious truth.[94] As Marshall points out in his paper, Lindbeck's account of ontological truth is *defined* in terms of the conformity of a person to a religious reality that exists independently of human institutions and conceptualizations.[95] Lindbeck's account therefore presupposes the truth of ontological realism. The notions of Intrasystematic and categorial truth specify the necessary conditions under which a claim to ontological truth can be held to be justified,[96] they do not replace the notion of ontological truth. Lindbeck himself has endorsed Marshall's interpretation (or development) of his position.[97]

Marshall identifies two challenges to Lindbeck's account of ontological truth in his paper. Firstly, he asserts that for Lindbeck "adequate categories and intrasystematic coherence are not only necessary but sufficient conditions for the truth of religious utterances in this [ontological] sense." Marshall suggests that this is a position that needs further development in order to show how it was possible for these two criteria to act as guarantors of ontological truth.[98] An analogous task has been addressed in Marshall's subsequent work on the nature of Christian truth.[99] In that work he has sought to develop an account of religious truth which is comparable to Lindbeck's account and which illuminates the way in which the nature of Christ can underpin that conformity of the mind (and the whole person) to the divine.[100] Marshall's account assumes and does not seek to justify the truth of the central beliefs of Christianity and makes these religious beliefs

---

93. Marshall, "Introduction" to ND 25th Anniversary Edition, xvii.
94. Marshall, "Aquinas as Postliberal Theologian," 355–56.
95. Ibid., 358.
96. Ibid., 367.
97. Lindbeck, "Response to Bruce Marshall," 403–4.
98. Marshall, "Aquinas as Postliberal Theologian," 367 footnote 28.
99. Marshall, "'We Shall Bear the Image of the Man of Heaven': Theology and the Concept of Truth"; Marshall, *Trinity and Truth*.
100. Marshall, "Aquinas as a Postliberal Theologian," 367; see also Marshall, *Trinity and Truth*, 256.

Lindbeck and MacIntyre as Complementary Thinkers

control what can be taken to be epistemologically legitimate.[101] However, assuming the categorial and intrasystematic truth of one religion will appear to be question begging to someone who is not already committed to the truth of Christianity.

Marshall's second challenge to Lindbeck's account of ontological truth is, therefore, concerned with the question of the justification of the claim that Christianity (or any other religion) possesses such categorial and intrasystematic truth. As a Christian, Lindbeck holds that Christianity meets these requirements, and is, therefore, capable of achieving ontological truth. But on what basis can such a claim be made? Marshall comments that

> Lindbeck's account of the justification . . . of Christian beliefs is bound to seem like a flagrant evasion [to his critics]. To say that we are justified in holding a given proposition to be (ontologically) true because it coheres with the norms of Christian belief and practice is, so the objection goes, to beg the decisive question: how can these norms themselves be justified? . . . The problem can be seen as explicating how the whole internally normed scheme of belief and practice called "Christianity" can be justified. . . [At this point some critics claim that] Lindbeck's account of justification seems to degenerate into fideism and relativism.[102]

To respond to this demand for a general justification of the validity of the Christian faith (or any other faith that claims ontological truth) in a way that would be convincing to the challenger would apparently require an appeal to publicly accepted standards to adjudicate between the claims to justification of such "comprehensive systems of belief."[103] But as Marshall has pointed out, this assumption is inconsistent with Lindbeck's view that there is no "neutral, framework-independent language" in which such standards can be formulated.[104] The criteria for the truth of the system must, therefore, be internal to it.[105] As a result, each religion will justify itself in its own terms and will not need (or be able) to justify itself in terms of the standards evinced by other religions or by secular philosophies.[106] But every belief system considered as a cultural-linguistic form of life would also appear to be able to justify its claims to truth in the same way. Lindbeck's posi-

101. Marshall, *Trinity and Truth*, 4–5.
102. Marshall, "Aquinas as Postliberal Theologian" 368.
103. Ibid., 369.
104. Ibid., 369.
105. Ibid., 368.
106. ND, 49; ND, 55.

tion does not, therefore, appear to provide any criteria that could be used to identify one religion as superior to another in a way which might transcend the limits of a particular cultural perspective. Can Lindbeck's account be modified in order to address this point?

A pessimistic answer to this question would ignore the fact that religions are not only patterns of life and worship: they are also self-conscious and reflexive forms of life which seek to articulate and develop their own understanding of truth in their engagement with their cultural and intellectual contexts. They are driven to construct the type of warranted assertions that Lindbeck and Marshall identify with "intrasystematic truth" by self-consciously articulating the meaning of the doctrines, practices, and experiences that arise within the life of the community in ways that are both internally consistent and reconcile conflicts with external perspectives and events. While ontological truth may not be embodied in these second-order reflections on the meaning of the religious faith, the coherence and rationality of this developing self-conceptualization will be under test both internally, from rival interpretations of the meaning of beliefs and practices, and externally through the religion's engagement with incompatible ideas in its wider environment. In section 4.6 I will consider Rowan Williams' criticisms of Lindbeck and argue that the progressive development of such statements of the meaning of the faith echoes MacIntyre's description of the evolution of a tradition of enquiry. In Williams' terms such attempts to formulate and articulate the meaning of the religion interact with and judge the world—but are themselves judged by the world in this process of engagement.[107]

Through these processes of mutual judgment Christian theologies can come to embody, in MacIntyre's phrase, traditions of enquiry into the nature of the good. Such a theology will seek to articulate the community's interpretation of that good, and seek to clarify and systematize the community's understanding of reality by elucidating beliefs and reconciling inconsistencies. It will seek to expound the meaning of practices and provide a focus for debate and for the reconciliation of divided opinions. It will help the community to respond to the challenge of external events by articulating new concepts which may be incorporated into the community's self-understanding. These processes may result in the development and revision of informal and formal doctrines. If these theological reflections are successful in overcoming the problems and inconsistencies that have emerged from challenge they will strengthen the hermeneutic framework embodied

---

107. Williams, "Postmodern Theology and the Judgement of the World," 330.

in the religion. This capacity to evolve may provide a test of that framework's superiority or inferiority to other hermeneutic frameworks.

MacIntyre's account of tradition-constituted rationality provides a way of exploring this notion of superiority. But before I turn to the relevance of MacIntyre's philosophy to this question, I want to examine a related issue discussed by Lindbeck, which is the question of how one can adjudicate between conflicting theological perspectives *within* the same religion. Lindbeck uses the notion of "intratextuality" as a way of conceptualizing the basis on which such judgments can be made. This discussion, and the identification of the limitations of Lindbeck's account of intratextuality, will further clarify the resemblance between Lindbeck's account of a religion as an interpretative medium and MacIntyre's account of a tradition of enquiry.

4.6 Intratextuality and Superiority

When controversies arise within a tradition or religion, judgments have to be made as to whether one position is superior to another. Such controversies might relate to the question of which of two formulations of doctrine is correct, or which of several interpretations of scripture are valid, and the conflict generated by these debates may threaten the identity and stability of the religious community. Failure to resolve such disputes has the potential to create crises which may result in schism and the creation of two or more separate sects from what was initially a single community. The question of which of two competing interpretations is faithful to the religion may, therefore, become central to the stability of the religious community. As a result, such disputes may act as a driving force for the formulation of doctrinal statements which are intended to resolve conflict by constructing a fixed authoritative position on the matter in question. Such a position however has to be capable of being seen as faithful to the underlying identity of the religion. A critical question, therefore, is the question of how interpretations and developments within a religion can be identified as faithful to the religion as a whole.

Experiential-expressive and cognitive-propositional models seek to ground theological meaning on some reality that is external to the religion (religious experience or propositional correspondence). However such external validation would be inconsistent with the CL model, and the metaphor of a system that can "absorb the universe." The cultural-linguistic model focuses attention on the way in which religious practices and beliefs acquire their significance and justification from their function within the semiotic system of a religious community. Events which are external to this framework have to be interpreted within the parameters defined by that framework, and therefore cannot act as external tests of validity. There is nothing "outside" the system and as a result the meaning of terms used within the system, such as "God," has to be articulated *intratextually*, by showing how these terms are used within the semiotic system embodied in the culture, narratives, practices, and canonical scriptures of the religion. Such accounts of the meaning of terms can be accurate or inaccurate, and the test of authenticity is faithfulness to the other elements of the system. Lindbeck therefore puts forward the concept of "intratextuality" as the criterion of faithfulness in theological argument and interpretation.[108]

The reference to the interpretation of religious practices and canonical scriptures points towards two different senses of the term "intratextual." In the first sense an intratextual explication involves a process of Geertzian "thick description": that is, the very detailed analysis of the minutiae of religious life to articulate the cultural context which render religious words and practices intelligible. In this sense intratextuality is a term which can be applied to any cultural linguistic interpretation of any religion or religious practice.[109] However, religions such as Christianity also have a core canon of texts which provide that religion with an important source of stability and identity, and intratextuality in this less extended sense relates to the faithful explication of the meaning of these sacred texts, and the application of that meaning to the understanding of the external environment.[110] Lindbeck suggests that the criterion of superiority with respect to competing theological interpretations therefore has to be the degree to which such interpretations faithfully reflect the paradigmatic semiotic system encoded in these texts. He points out that "all [the world's major faiths] have relatively fixed canons of writings that they treat as exemplary or normative exemplifications of their semiotic codes. One test of faithfulness for all of them is the degree to which descriptions correspond to the semiotic universe paradigmatically encoded in holy writ."[111]

The second sense of "intratextual" therefore relates to the explication and application of these canonical texts in Christian discourse and practice, and at a second-order level, to the explication of their meaning in normative theological analysis. This concept therefore provides a programmatic perspective in terms of the way in which theology should be pursued in future: it should engage in the explication of this original framework of

108. ND, 114.
109. ND, 115.
110. ND, 116.
111. ND, 116.

Lindbeck and MacIntyre as Complementary Thinkers 209

meaning. The legitimacy of such interpretations is determined by some "intratextual norm of faithfulness."[112] Such a norm would specify what counts as a legitimate interpretation or theological development and what should be rejected, and therefore provides a criterion of intrasystematic truth or warranted assertion.

Lindbeck is aware of some limitations to the idea of intratextuality as a "norm of faithfulness." While there may be agreement that conformity to such a norm would be "to describe life and reality in ways conformable to what these [scriptural] stories indicate about God,"[113] different theologies may emphasise different aspects of those stories, depending on the cultural and philosophical environment, and therefore construct radically different interpretations. Lindbeck also acknowledges that there may be disagreement about the norm itself, perhaps reflecting disagreement as to the overall content of the canon or in terms of the relative priority given to different texts. The canon can be extended by debates within the tradition, but these potential extensions may be challenged, leading to different views as to what might count as the basis for interpretation. There may also be fundamental disagreements about how to interpret the genre of scripture and therefore disagreement as to what counts as an accurate reading.[114]

Disputes such as these cannot be resolved by appeals to intratextuality, because the choice one makes with respect to these positions determines what will count as an accurate intratextual reading. This observation provides support for Paul DeHart's criticisms of Lindbeck. DeHart argues that it is unclear how the scriptural foundations of intratextuality can give clear and unambiguous frameworks for interpretation.[115] DeHart asserts that in order to justify his position Lindbeck needs to be able to identify the archetypal semiotic system which can act as the basis for his norm of faithfulness, and DeHart questions whether such a system can be identified.[116] He suggests that without the possibility of such identification there is no criterion available to distinguish legitimate from illegitimate theological developments: "when intratextuality becomes a theological criterion of faithfulness demands are placed on semiotic networks informing Christian practice which they cannot bear."[117] The difficulty here is determining how one would resolve disputes around the legitimacy and authority of such a

112. ND, 122.
113. ND, 121–22.
114. ND, 122–23.
115. DeHart, *Trial of the Witnesses*, 173.
116. Ibid., 185–86.
117. Ibid., 189.

system—by a further appeal to a criterion of intratextuality? If so, an infinite regress of appeals to intratextuality beckons. In isolation the notion of intratextuality fails to provide a clear criterion by which one could distinguish correct from incorrect theological interpretations, because it presupposes a prior consensus on the legitimacy and authority of the system of interpretation. I will return to this issue in the following section.

The central defect of Lindbeck's account of intratextuality is that it appears to disregard the influence that external events can have on the interpretative system, because of the power of his metaphor of such a system absorbing the universe. Absorption is a unidirectional process. But a religion is not insulated from challenges and threats from its environment; it both acts upon and is influenced by that environment. DeHart claims that Lindbeck's position presupposes that the world is interpreted in terms of the frame of reference provided by scripture, while that frame of reference remains unchanged through this interaction. This is implausible, and DeHart[118] draws on work by theologians such as Rowan Williams[119] and Terrence Tilley, who emphasise the importance of the dialogue between the Christian semiotic universe and the secular culture. They both depict the relationship between Christianity's semiotic practices and those of the wider environment as a matter of mutual interaction and influence, and their essays are instructive.

Tilley challenges the coherence of the idea that religions can form independent semiotic systems. His argument turns on a point that I discussed in section 4.3, which is the question of what constitutes an independent tradition. Tilley asks, "Do St. Augustine, St. Thomas, Luther, and Lindbeck live in the *same* cultural-linguistic framework?"[120] Tilley argues that they do not, because the semiotic system which they and each of us occupies and instantiates in our behavior is shaped by both temporal and geographical factors. Different times and places will shape different semiotic systems, but if this is the case then there will not be a single Christian semiotic system that continues through history that can be used as a basis for interpretation of texts and as a basis for conflict resolution. Moreover, if the non-religious concepts which characterize these varying geographical and historical settings have to be invoked to interpret the meaning of the Christian semiotic

---

118. Ibid., see 180–83.

119. Williams, "Postmodern Theology and the Judgement of the World."

120. Tilley, "Incommensurability, Intratextuality, and Fideism," 96; emphasis original.

system, that system will be partly constituted by these concepts and cannot be conceptualized as existing entirely independently of its environment.[121]

Tilley points out that the depiction of a semiotic system in texts can only ever be an abstraction from the form of life embedded in the community, and therefore Lindbeck's attempt to identify the paradigmatic semiotic system with something that is embedded in canonical texts must be mistaken.[122] Tilley argues persuasively that Lindbeck's notion of the Christian text absorbing the world in some unidirectional way is incoherent, because the concepts that constitute the world that is being interpreted have to be reinterpreted and expressed within that Christian framework. In this process the resources of the original Christian framework will not be sufficient for this task in themselves, because if genuinely alien concepts have to be absorbed, the existing semiotic resources of the system will have to be extended. New concepts will have to be incorporated into the Christian semiotic system and as a result that system will be extended through its engagement with the external culture, and will no longer be identical with the original semiotic system.[123]

Tilley argues that there is a second reason why the idea of a semiotic system embedded in texts is incoherent. The meaning of a text is not something fixed and given, but something which is constructed in the interaction between text and audience. If the Christian semiotic system is to be communicated to a non-Christian audience (and that is something that the mission of the Church requires) it will have to be put into terms that are comprehensible to the target audience. If that audience lives in another semiotic world (as will be the case if the audience is non-Christian) the communication of that text will initially need to begin by translating Christian ideas into a form that is intelligible within the alien semiotic framework.[124] Both semiotic systems will be extended in this process and this interaction will open up the possibility of transformation on both sides.[125]

It is this possibility of mutual transformation that is at the heart of Rowan Williams' paper. Williams challenges the image of a static hermeneutic framework that underpins the unidirectional language of "absorbing

---

121. Ibid., 96–97.
122. Ibid., 102.
123. Ibid., 98.
124. Ibid., 98–100.
125. It might be claimed that Tilley is ignoring the issue of incommensurability here. However, he deals effectively with this type of challenge earlier in his paper, when he argues that incommensurability does not imply incomparability or incommunicability (89–93). His position is comparable to Stout's viewpoint which was described earlier in section 2.6.

the universe": "the church may be committed to interpreting the world in terms of its own foundational narratives; but the very act of interpreting affects the narratives as well as the world for good and ill."[126] Williams argues that the application of scriptural narratives to the new contexts that emerge in the world reshapes the meaning of those stories, at the same time as those stories reshape the interpretation of world events. Thus the meaning of the Abraham and Isaac story has been redefined by Wilfred Owen's reconstruction of the sacrifices of the First World War within its imagery. Owen's account "of how the old man refused to hear the angel 'and slew his son. And half the seed of Europe, one by one' . . . points up what we might miss in Genesis: the final drawing back from slaughter is an act of obedience as great as or greater than the first decision to sacrifice Isaac."[127]

The discovery of the meanings of scriptural narratives is generated through the encounter with new contexts, cultures and events, and through the interpretation of these alien contexts within the framework of the narrative. This in turn can change the interpretation of the original narratives. As a result, interpretation is bi- rather than uni-directional,[128] and in this process of mutual interpretation the church re-identifies and reconstructs its own identity. Its engagement with external cultures is necessary because it is the vehicle that brings the message of Christ to the world. The church is "essentially missionary in its nature"[129] and as such must have something to contribute to all cultures at all times and places. This essential openness to the world is a contribution to the "construction of meanings"[130] through interaction between church and culture, and through this process the church both judges and is judged by the world.[131]

The underlying complacency of the image of a religion as a community that is capable of absorbing and interpreting the world within its own semiotic framework is replaced in Williams' paper by the image of a Christian community whose grasp of a transforming truth is always tentative

126. Williams, "Postmodern Theology," 322.

127. Ibid., 322–23.

128. In Gadamer's terms interpretation involves a "fusion of horizons." The text interprets us to ourselves as we interpret the text (using the word "text" in the broadest sense of any interpretable concatenation of circumstances), and a precondition of such a process of mutual reinterpretation is a recognition of the extent to which our consciousness is limited and defined by our historical situation (see Gadamer, *Truth and Method*, 300–305). It therefore requires recognition of the limitations of our capacity for knowledge and truth which Lindbeck's notion of intratextuality as a definitive mode of interpretation tends to subvert.

129. Williams, "Postmodern Theology," 323.

130. Ibid.

131. Ibid., 324.

and provisional. The ability of that community to apply that truth to the events with which it engages in its history is equally provisional, and its understanding of that truth will be challenged and ultimately deepened in its interaction with what is alien and new. And this implies that the understanding of Christian truth is itself continually changing in response to changing environments. As Rowan Williams says:

> The Christian engaged at the frontier with politics, art or science will frequently find that he or she *will not know what to say*. There can be a real sense of loss in respect to traditional formulae—not because they are being translated, but because they are being tested: we are discovering whether there is any sense in which the other languages we are working with can be at home in our theology.[132]

What is put to the question in these engagements is the identity of the truth, the identity of the church and the identity of the participants in this process of missionary engagement. But if this is the case the problematic issue of the nature of Christian identity (and the identity of any hermeneutic framework) cannot be resolved by establishing some definitive criterion of identity or justification. The identity and legitimacy of the hermeneutic framework is an achievement negotiated in the process of interpretation. Dissonant events and information will challenge that legitimacy and force the creation of new meanings. Through this process the framework will change and develop in pursuit of an ultimately unachievable final stability.

> The Christian claim, then, is bound *always* to be something evolving and acquiring definition in the conversations of history; it offers a direction for the historical construction of human meaning, but it does not offer to end history . . . it envisages a "long revolution," at best an asymptotic approach to a condition that history is itself (by definition) incapable of realizing—a perfect communality of language and action . . .[133]

What is encoded in the semiotic systems of the Christian religion is a developing but never fully realized image of the good for humanity. The history of Christianity is the progressive elaboration of the meaning of that good as it is embodied and expressed in the life, death and resurrection of Christ. This is a continuing history which will unfold and develop in response to the church's engagement with the boundary between the religious and the secular, in ways that remain unpredictable That development,

---

132. Ibid., 329 (emphasis original).
133. Ibid., 327 (emphasis original).

however, must demonstrate consistency and coherence with the underlying principles of the faith at the same time as it helps to elaborate these principles and deepen the understanding of the church and its nature and role. The importance of faithfulness to the scriptural cannon is not that it provides an answer to a criteriological problem but that it expresses a set of underlying beliefs and values whose meaning is constantly being explored, modified and elaborated through the process of engagement with new contexts and challenges.

The criticisms of DeHart, Tilley and Williams have considerable validity if Lindbeck's image of a unidirectional process of interpretation from scripture to the world is accepted as defining his position. But Lindbeck is a victim of his own rhetoric. There is textual evidence in ND to support the view that his position is more complex and balanced than these criticisms would suggest. DeHart and the other critics overemphasize the extent to which Lindbeck sees the absorption of the world by a religion as a straightforwardly unidirectional process. Lindbeck points out that the interpretation of the canon, and, indeed, what *counts* as the canon will be variable and subject to debate. Lindbeck also acknowledges that there will be mutual influence between the environment and the Christian hermeneutic framework:

> as current debates over feminism vividly remind us, past tradition or present consensus can serve as extensions of the canon and deeply influence the interpretation of the whole. These extensions can on occasion go beyond the specifically Christian or religious realm. The philosophical tradition from Plato to Heidegger operates as the canonical corpus for much Western reflection on God or the human condition; and when this reflection is recognized as operating with a peculiarly Western rather than transculturally available idiom, it begins to acquire some of the features of intratextuality. In short intratextuality may be a condition for the faithful description and development of a religion or tradition, but the material or doctrinal consequences of this self-evidently depend in part on what canon is appealed to.[134]

And, one should add, the outcome of this appeal will be determined not only by the part of the canon appealed to but the specific principles of interpretation that are applied. As Lindbeck points out, different theological perspectives imply that different elements of the canon should be given

---

134. ND, 122.

greater priority than others.[135] Together with his acknowledgment of development in the canon in interaction with the environment, this is sufficient to repudiate the suggestion that he is conceptualizing the Christian semiotic framework as a rigid template that can be applied to external events without being changed in this process. DeHart is correct, however, in arguing that intratextuality does not provide a criterion for the resolution of internal disputes about the nature of that Christian framework, nor will it resolve disputes in relation to the significance and interpretation of the different elements of that canon. An intratextual understanding has to be *constructed* through engagement in such debates.

Intratextuality does not, therefore, provide a criterion for distinguishing between superior and inferior perspectives within theology, any more than the concept of categorial adequacy provides a solution to the question of choosing between the conflicting claims to superiority of different religions. The inability to specify a robust tradition transcendent criterion of categorial adequacy and truth and the inability to specify a robust intratextual criterion to resolve internal disputes leaves Lindbeck open to the challenge that his position endorses fideism or relativism.[136] Lindbeck acknowledges this challenge, even though such broad epistemological issues are not central to his concerns. He raises the question as to

> whether postliberal theologies would help make religions more intelligible and credible. This is a practical as well as a theoretical question, and it can be formulated in terms of two closely related problems. First, intratextuality seems wholly relativistic: it turns religions, so one can argue, into self-enclosed and incommensurable ghettoes. Associated with this is the fideistic dilemma: it appears that choice between religions is purely arbitrary, a matter of blind faith.[137]

Lindbeck argues that the assumption that his position must lead to relativism and fideism depends on a false foundationalist model of reason. He points out that the repudiation of foundationalism should not be equated with irrationalism. Reason, he argues, is more subtle than this.[138] What this observation points towards is the need for an alternative account of the nature of rationality to the foundationalist model of reason if Lindbeck's

---

135. ND, 122.

136. This is a point which Terrence Tilley makes well. See "Incommensurability, Intratextuality, and Fideism," 105. I will return to this issue in the penultimate section of this chapter.

137. ND, 128.

138. ND, 130.

account is to avoid relativism. For such an alternative account we can turn to Alasdair MacIntyre and his account of tradition-constituted rationality. The notion of intratextuality points towards the processes through which such tradition-constituted rationality and its associated standards emerge and develop, and I will argue that the function of doctrines as regulative principles is to embody, express, and enforce elements of this emergent rationality. In the next section I will seek to strengthen Lindbeck's account of superiority by uniting his account with MacIntyre's account of the superiority of a tradition. In the final section I will then turn to the question of whether this account of superiority enables Lindbeck and Macintyre to repudiate accusations of relativism.

4.7 Superiority and the Rationality of a Tradition

Criteria, Consensus, and Tradition-Constituted Rationality

Lindbeck's concept of categorial adequacy represents an attempt to specify the conditions that have to be met if a religion is to possess a capacity to construct ontological truths, while intratextuality represents an attempt to formulate a general criterion of authentic theological development. But the application of a concept of categorial adequacy would require an ability to distinguish between those categories that can genuinely correspond to aspects of reality and those that cannot, and Lindbeck does not specify how such a distinction could be made in practice. Equally, the concept of intratextuality appears to rely on the assumption that there is an original and fixed semiotic core to Christianity which defines the abiding identity of the religion and which can provide the basis for judgments of authenticity. But for intratextuality to be a practicable mechanism for resolving theological debate there would need to be consensus around the nature of that original interpretative system, and agreement with respect to the criteria for its application. Paradoxically it is the *lack* of such consensus that the concept of intratextuality is intended to address. As a result of these limitations I argued in the two preceding sections that neither concept is able to provide a robust basis for judgments of superiority.

Moreover, these attempts to define invariable criteria of authenticity and ontological truth conflict with other aspects of Lindbeck's account. For example, the idea of categorial adequacy does not sit easily with the notion of correspondence to ultimate reality as embodied in performative truths that are only tentatively and transiently created through the practice of worship within a Christian community. Equally, the notion of the existence

Lindbeck and MacIntyre as Complementary Thinkers 217

of an original semiotic core to Christianity sits uneasily with Lindbeck's contention that the operative and formal doctrines that are identified with the rules that define the religious semiotic system are themselves subject to change, development and abandonment as cultural and conceptual contexts change over time. If doctrines change and develop contemporary divisions and disagreements cannot be resolved by reference to some general criterion of legitimate interpretation and development of the Christian faith, if only because such a criterion will also be subject to challenge and modification. As Kathryn Tanner has pointed out, the image of a culture generated by Lindbeck fails to recognize the extent to which all aspects of that culture will be subject to continued contest between differing perspectives.[139] The outcome of such debates can neither be anticipated nor enforced by reference to an archetypal semiotic system embedded in scripture. judgments have to gain their authority from the accepted presuppositions of a community, from its established modes of argument, and from its culturally determined assumptions about warranted assertion. These beliefs and standards arise through victories and compromises between competing perspectives forged in an evolutionary process. If consensus is to be achieved, it has to be generated through debate underpinned by shared faith and mutual trust, and taken forward by the ad hoc application of logic, rhetoric and other means of persuasion.

Such historical processes drive cultural change and conflict and can result in the emergence of rival sects and churches. These processes are therefore the creators of religious diversity, but the historical relationships that can be traced between these divergent communities provide an underlying continuity that makes these separate communities different but related elements of a single religious movement, a movement which maintains its unity despite the differences in belief that can be identified at different times, in different places and in different cultures. The common history and shared devotion to Christ of Christian communities makes them part of the same religious movement, and creates networks of family resemblance and difference that shape their common and separate identities. But as a result of these processes, each community may have divergent beliefs, practices, and standards of authenticity. My argument is that these variant beliefs, practices, and standards shape the distinct (and continually contested and developing) tradition-constituted rationality (TCR) of each community. That rationality has two dimensions. The first is the implicit or unconscious rationality that guides the judgment of the community and is embodied in what Lindbeck refers to as the operative doctrines of the community. The

139. Tanner, *Theories of Culture*, 105.

second dimension relates to the community's attempt to formally articulate that rationality through the promulgation of formal doctrines and the pursuit of theological reflection and enquiry.

The rationale for applying the concept of TCR to a religion lies in the parallels between Lindbeck's and MacIntyre's accounts of religion and tradition. As we saw in section 3.6, Lindbeck's definition of a religion in ND is very broad and emphasizes its role in providing an integrative framework for all aspects of intellectual and moral life.[140] These functions are shared by what MacIntyre calls a tradition of enquiry. On Lindbeck's definition, therefore, those traditions that have sought to clarify the nature of the human telos could be considered to be religions, given that within these traditions the pursuit of the good acts as the organizing principle of human life. I will therefore use the term "tradition" to refer both to traditions of enquiry and to religions in this section, but I will also seek to identify significant differences between religions and traditions when this is appropriate.

Informal Rationality

In section 2.5 I briefly discussed MacIntyre's account of the emergence of the distinctive rationality of a tradition of enquiry. I now need to describe this aspect of his thought in greater detail in order to demonstrate the relevance of his account to Lindbeck's cultural linguistic model. For MacIntyre the origins of a tradition lie in the pre-theoretical utterances of figures whose statements shape the consciousness of their community in significant ways.

> Consider first those founders of traditions of rational enquiry who themselves may not even have engaged in something recognizable at the time at which they spoke or write as rational enquiry. They perhaps uttered aphorisms or recounted myths, they gave enigmatic advice, they were valued by their contemporaries as oracular sages or as poets . . . But it is only of course insofar as their aphorisms, myths and counsels turn out retrospectively, often through some later work of reinterpretation, to have contributed to systematic argument and questioning that they become figures in the history of enquiry, revealing to us, although without having done so to themselves, how aphorism and myth may contribute to enquiry. It is only insofar as this occurs that these primal cultural figures become the founders of traditions of rational enquiry.[141]

---

140. Lindbeck, "Afterword," ND 2nd Edition, 132.
141. MacIntyre, "Reply to Dahl, Baier and Schneewind," 175–76.

This creation myth need not be taken too literally, given that traditions of enquiry may have emerged from centuries of pre-theoretical debate whose origins are obscure. But MacIntyre's image emphasizes that the evolution of a tradition may develop initially from the inchoate assertion of beliefs or imperatives which become significant in shaping the moral behavior and theoretical understanding of a community, and which provide a conceptual framework for the interpretation of its environment. At first, the assumptions that underpin the emerging beliefs of a tradition may be unchallenged, but MacIntyre suggests that this initial unquestioning phase is inevitably followed by a second stage in which members of a tradition have become aware of inconsistencies and inadequacies in their initial beliefs, and will enter into debate in order to reformulate their beliefs in ways that address these inconsistencies.[142] Such questions of meaning and consistency will arise for the disciples of a nascent religion as well as for the adherents of a tradition, and both traditions and religions will evolve and change in response to challenges from their external environment and in response to processes of internal debate.[143] How communities respond to these challenges

> will depend not only on what stock of reasons and questioning and reasoning abilities they already possess but also upon their inventiveness. And these in turn will determine the possible range of outcomes in the rejection, the emendation, and reformulation of beliefs, the revaluation of authorities, the reinterpretation of texts, the emergence of new forms of authority, and the production of new texts. Since beliefs are expressed in and through rituals and ritual dramas, masks and modes of dress, the ways in which houses are structured and villages and towns laid out, and of course by actions in general, the reformulations of belief are not to be thought of only an intellectual terms; or rather the intellect is not to be thought of as either a Cartesian mind or a materialist brain, but as that through which thinking

---

142. WJWR, 354–55.

143. It might be argued that a religion can be characterized by some inviolable core narratives or beliefs which are seen as representing "normative instantiations of its semiotic code" (ND, 116), and that this semiotic core is not subject to the process of challenge and evolution that MacIntyre's account of tradition-constituted rationality demands. However, the fixed and abiding status of the canon is itself the outcome of debate and challenge, and the canon itself remains subject to controversy about content, interpretation, and authoritative status, as Lindbeck acknowledges (see ND, 122). The authoritative status of the canon is thus an outcome of the processes which underpin MacIntyre's model of tradition-constituted rationality.

individuals relate themselves to each other and to natural and social objects as these present themselves to them.[144]

The processes of debate, conceptual development, and social innovation that characterize the evolution of a tradition are embodied, therefore, not only in forms of argument but also in modes of life and social practices, and in power relationships and authority structures. The resolution of a dispute may be exemplified in the crystallization of definitive statements of belief, but it may also be exemplified in the formalization of rituals and other practices. This process of conceptual innovation and social evolution shapes the development of the distinctive form of rationality that characterizes the particular tradition, by defining what activities, arguments and patterns of inference are counted as legitimate and consistent with the founding assumptions of the tradition—and, indeed, in determining what will count as *legitimate* assumptions in the first place. One way of conceptualizing this emergent rationality is through the notion of the regulative function of operative doctrines. The informal rules that emerge through debate crystallize the developing grammar of the religion, and determine what can count as legitimate forms of speech, inference, and practice for those who are expert in the semiotic system. If we integrate MacIntyre's notion of the rationality of a tradition with Lindbeck's regulative view of doctrine, formal doctrines can be seen as embodying the rationality of the tradition by acting as "exemplary instantiations or paradigms of the application of rules"[145] and by specifying what are held to be legitimate patterns of argument or inference at a particular point in time.

The role of operative and formal doctrines in addressing conflicting beliefs and in constituting forms of rationality can be illustrated by Lindbeck's account of the development of the creeds. Lindbeck argues that the Nicene formulation of doctrine reconciles three principles that were already evident in the earliest apostolic traditions of the church. These are: the monotheist principle—that there is only one God; the principle of historical specificity—that Jesus was a real person who lived through real events; and the principle of "Christological maximalism . . . that every possible importance is to be ascribed to Jesus that is not inconsistent with the first two rules."[146] For Lindbeck, the Nicene Creed represents the reconciliation of these three principles in a way that was less dissonant than any of the rejected (heretical) alternatives.[147] This reconciliation is exemplified for

---

144. WJWR, 355.
145. ND, 81.
146. ND, 94.
147. ND, 95.

Lindbeck in the type of rule enunciated by Athanasius for the interpretation of consubstantiality: that "whatever is said of the Father is said of the Son, except that the Son is not the Father."[148]

While the extent to which Athanasius treated consubstantiality as a semiotic rather than an ontological issue is disputed,[149] the creed illustrates the way in which the evolution of the distinctive rationality of a tradition or religion can be interpreted as a response to internal tensions created by the dissonance of important but potentially conflicting beliefs. Indeed, John Henry Newman graphically described the way in which the formalization of the Athanasian Creed reflected the strongly held commitments of the faithful, and their successful resistance to alternative formulations which were promulgated by the Ecclesiastical authorities of the time, but which were subsequently deemed heretical. Ultimately the operative doctrines of the community determined the outcome of debate and shaped the endorsement of the Nicene interpretation of the Trinity, an interpretation that had seemed unlikely to triumph for much of the fourth century.[150]

The reconciliation of these tensions in the Athanasian Creed is not, of course, primarily a way of ordering argument. It is an expression of faith in the divinity of Christ. The evolution of doctrines can therefore be seen as driven both by the desire to better articulate the underlying beliefs that constitute the religion, and to resolve tensions and inconsistencies within and between different formulations of these beliefs. The rules that emerge from this process may formalize elements of the distinctive rationality of the community which are already embodied in its informal patterns of assertion, argument, and practice. The operation of this rationality provides a communally approved basis for determining the appropriate response to questions that arise within the tradition, acts as a limit to the kind of statements that can be legitimately made when speaking of Christ and God (for example), and expresses the operative doctrines that underpin the practices of the community and form core elements of its identity at that point in time.

Rationality and Formal Doctrines

It is important to make a distinction between a form of life and the implicit rules that constitute the rationale for its practices, and the articulation of

---

148. ND, 94.

149. See, for example, O'Neill, "The Rule Theory of Doctrine and Propositional Truth," 438–9; McGrath *The Genesis of Doctrine*, 33.

150. Newman, "On Consulting the Faithful in Matters of Doctrine."

that rationale in philosophical or theological reflection. The explicit expression of the operative rules that underpin assertion, argument and practice will help to render that form of life intelligible, but this process bears the same relationship to the form of life as anthropological description bears to participation in a culture, and the construction of a formal code of ethics bears to the moral practices it seeks to make intelligible. Indeed, it was the underlying difference between characterizing the nature of participation in a tradition and making explicit the rules that articulate the rationality of such a tradition that led to the apparent differences between MacIntyre's account of a tradition in AV, TRV, and WJWR as identified by Jean Porter (see section 4.3). In this process of self-articulation, a tradition may progress from the implicit acceptance of certain rules of interpretation, to the explicit formulation and justification of those rules. At this stage the second order articulation of the rationality that underpins the form of life may come to play a central role in shaping the development of the tradition, and the tradition may generate formal processes of theological and philosophical enquiry, whose origins and justification lie in their attempt to articulate the rationale of a particular form of life.

According to MacIntyre, the transition to a form of enquiry takes place once a tradition has succeeded in reconciling the initial inconsistencies that emerge from the early formulations of its founding stories and beliefs. As a result of this reformulation it will recognize that these initial formulations of belief were incomplete or unsatisfactory in some respects. As a result, these formulations will have been replaced by constructions that are perceived as being superior to their predecessors in specific ways. Through this process of debate the tradition will develop methods of analysis, and standards for judging the success of different arguments, which will characterize the nature of rational investigation within the tradition (or religion). This does not mean that controversy is at an end. Multiple answers to questions may compete with each other, and each attempt at resolution will initiate new questions and directions for investigation. The tradition (and the religion in its intellectual or theological dimensions) will have become a form of enquiry.[151] Once this stage is reached

> Standard forms of argument will be developed, and requirements for successful dialectical questioning established. The weakest form of argument, but none the less that which will prevail in the absence of any other, will be the appeal to the authority of established belief, merely as established. The identification of incoherence within established belief will always provide a

---

151. WJWR, 358.

reason for enquiring further, but not in itself a conclusive reason for rejecting established belief, until something more adequate because less incoherent has been discovered. At every stage beliefs and judgements will be justified by reference to the beliefs and judgements of the previous stage, and insofar as the tradition has constituted itself as a successful form of enquiry, the claims to truth made within a tradition will always be in some specifiable way less vulnerable to dialectical questioning and objection than were their predecessors.[152]

Thus the concept of justification that emerges within a tradition is not absolute in the sense that the claim to truth is unassailable. It is progressive and dependent on the preceding history of the tradition. Claims to justification will rely on reference to the preceding stages of the argument, and the superiority of a formulation will be related to the very specific challenges that previous formulations have faced. Each formulation will be justified by reference to those related formulations that have survived dialectical examination to date, but this does not guarantee that these statements will not be found wanting in future. All that can be known is that the formulation is superior to other beliefs that have not survived the process of dialectical challenge and examination. The process of development in the tradition is therefore intratextual (in Lindbeck's term) rather than extratextual. What counts as successful development will be determined by the nature of the specific challenges to which the reformulation is a response, rather than by success in demonstrating some unassailable truths. This account of theoretical progress avoids the Enlightenment problem of identifying some set of indubitable foundations of knowledge, and is not therefore subject to the difficulties that were identified in the earlier discussion of Lindbeck's account of categorial adequacy. It does not, however, rule out the possibility of identifying the underlying meaning of a religion with ultimate truth, although the articulation of that truth through theological enquiry will always be tentative and subject to revision.

Progress and Knowledge

MacIntyre's account of the rational development of a tradition allows one to make a distinction between the gradual development and realization of the ultimate telos of a tradition, and the attempt to express that telos in language. The latter represents the self-conscious articulation of the goals of the tradition and in what follows I will be focusing on this process of

---

152. WJWR, 359.

reflexive formulation of a rational account of that goal and associated theses. Any and all attempts to construct such descriptions may be found to be inadequate. Both MacIntyre and Lindbeck hold that humanity does not have the power to construct statements that fully express transcendent truths, and any formulation will be provisional and subject to development. As we have seen, propositions which seek to articulate ontological truths are, for Lindbeck, generated by the re-interpretation of different world pictures within the framework provided by the Christian religion. As a result, as the conceptual resources of the societies in which Christian communities are embedded change so the form in which such truth claims are expressed will change. "The first-order truth claims of a religion change insofar as these arise from the application of the interpretive scheme to the shifting worlds that human beings inhabit."[153]

One limitation of Lindbeck's account is that it does not appear to provide any basis on which one might seek to distinguish between superior and inferior attempts to articulate such truths, and this is a feature of his account that leaves him open to the accusation of relativism. In contrast, MacIntyre argues that, while absolute truth cannot be fully expressed in propositional terms, rational progress within a tradition reflects the ability of the mind to recognize the limitations of each of its successive attempt to formulate such truths, and to recognize that some elements of what it had previously believed are now demonstrably false. This ability reflects the capacity of participants in a developing tradition to acknowledge that

> between those older beliefs and the world as they now understand it there is a radical discrepancy to be perceived. It is this lack of correspondence, between what the mind then judged and believed and reality as now perceived, classified, and understood, which is described when those earlier judgements and beliefs are called false. The original and most elementary version of the correspondence theory of truth is one in which it is applied retrospectively in the form of a correspondence theory of falsity.[154]

It is the reflexive ability of a person or community to recognize that their previous formulations of beliefs were in error that represents progress towards an understanding of truth. In recognizing this, the person also recognizes that the falsehood did not rest primarily in some inaccurately formulated proposition but in the constitution of their own mind. Truth on this model is not primarily conceived as a question of the correspondence of

---

153. ND, 82.
154. WJWR, 356.

propositions to some metaphysical realm of facts but in Thomistic terms as a matter of the correspondence of the mind to reality.[155] This correspondence is manifested through the active and effective engagement of the whole person with their environment, and the use of their beliefs to form expectations which may or may not be met: "the mind is adequate to its objects insofar as the expectations which it frames on the basis of these activities are not liable to disappointment and the remembering which it engages in enables it to return to and recover what it had encountered previously."[156]

The mind is constantly reaching out to incorporate aspects of that world into its understanding, and through this process it will build and test expectations of order and consistency. As these expectations of order are confirmed through successful engagement with activities they may become more generalized, and the confidence of the person that they have grasped some aspect of truth will grow. However, it is always possible that the expectations of order that have led to the belief that one has grasped some truth will be frustrated by some further event. What one can come to know definitively is that one's expectations have been disappointed. It is this process of provisional confirmation and absolute falsification that underlies the evolution of the distinctive form of rationality within a tradition. What can be claimed to be true within the tradition is that which has sufficiently withstood the process of dialectical questioning to secure confidence at that point in time. The criteria that are used to determine whether something has survived dialectical testing will also have been developed within the tradition and will form part of its rationality.[157]

In this process of development, the initial presuppositions of the tradition will have been subjected to such dialectical testing and will no longer be held as mere assumptions. However, although adherents of the tradition will come to see their fundamental precepts as rationally justified, their confidence may not be communicable to an outsider, because that person will lack the requisite understanding of the semiotic system and its history. As a result the outsider will not be able to understand the role played by its presuppositions and founding principles, nor grasp the methodology by which these assumptions and principles have been tested, and are held to be rationally justified by the adherents of the tradition: " . . . such first principles are not self-sufficient, self-justifying epistemological first principles. They may indeed be regarded as both necessary and evident, but their necessity and their evidentness will be characterisable as such only to and by those

---

155. WJWR, 357.
156. WJWR, 356.
157. WJWR, 358.

whose thought is framed by the kind of conceptual scheme from which they emerge..."[158]

The language of conceptual schemes suggests that engagement with a tradition involves abstract philosophical enquiry, and indeed engagement in a tradition of enquiry may include such reflection. However, both Lindbeck and MacIntyre emphasise that (provisional) truth can only be achieved by human beings through their active engagement in the world, and through the shaping of their minds towards conformity with that truth in a range of practices which extend beyond intellectual reflection. Knowledge within the tradition may be largely implicit and exhibited through the whole person's engagement with the world, through their activity and practical rationality rather than through the construction of propositions. How can this account of the development of rationality be linked to Lindbeck's CL model?

Lindbeck's account of performative truth conceives of correspondence to the divine as transiently exemplified in the lives of members of a religious community. However, it would appear to be impossible to specify strict criteria by which one could identify the achievement of such correspondence, if only because the formulation of such criteria would require a notion of the divine that is independent of, and prior to, such performative expressions of divine reality. Canonical texts, religious practices, theological reflection, tales of martyrs, acts of charity and love (among other elements of religious life) will provide some conceptual resources in which one can express an understanding of the divine. But the interpretations of these resources will also be illuminated, shaped and extended by acts which are seen by the community to be inspired by God's grace and embody moments of performative correspondence to the divine. Such acts will extend the communities understanding of God and reshape to a (more or less) limited extent the hermeneutic framework in which it seeks to understand and imitate the divine nature. I would suggest that a way of conceiving of such performative truth would be as a progressive movement towards the expression of the *telos* of the life of the religious community. This telos might be conceptualized in terms of progress towards a complete correspondence with Christ (the formation of "Christic identities" as Lindbeck puts it),[159] a telos which will never be finally realized prior to the eschaton. Such performative truth might be understood in terms of the achievement of a total consistency between thought and action in the lives of the faithful, as their lives are shaped by their religion's institutions and practices towards "a perfect communality

---

158. WJWR, 360.
159. Lindbeck, "Infallibility," 125.

of language and action," in the words that Rowan Williams uses to describe the ultimate and unachievable telos of history.[160]

The pursuit of such conformity of thought and action also entails the pursuit of a deeper understanding of the nature of the divine. Such deepening understanding will shape the development of the operative doctrines that govern practices, conduct and assertion in such a community. As controversies arise debates will address inconsistencies in the formulation of belief and dissonances between practices, and these debates will be informed by, and add to the rationality of, the religious tradition. This process will ensure that some formulations and practices are abandoned while others will be held to be justified—although this justification will always be provisional (in MacIntyre's sense). Such processes of discernment are intratextual in the sense that they do not rely on resources that are external to the tradition for the validation of judgment, but neither do they depend on the re-creation of an archetypal semiotic system. Rather, they depend on the renewal and continued development of the contemporary semiotic system whose faithfulness reflects its historical evolution from the events that established the Christian faith. It is this evolving system that embodies the developing rationality of the tradition.

Superiority

As we have seen, MacIntyre and Lindbeck share similar assumptions with respect to the contingency of standards of justification, and endorse similar notions with respect to the nature of truth and belief. I have suggested that Lindbeck's regulative account of doctrine can be used as a way of identifying the emergent rationality of a tradition. Given these similarities, it is not surprising that in his "Afterword" to ND Lindbeck turns to MacIntyre in order to clarify his account of how one religion may demonstrate its superiority to another.[161] In the "Afterword," Lindbeck is concerned that his characterization of religion as a comprehensive world-absorbing interpretative framework might legitimate religious imperialism or isolationism, because each religion will consider itself superior to other religions in accordance with its own frame of reference. However, neither imperialism nor isolationism is consistent with a religion's need to demonstrate its superior ability to en-

---

160. Williams, "Postmodern Theology," 327. See section 4.6 above for a fuller discussion of Williams' position. There are similarities between Williams' account of the provisional nature of Christian knowledge and MacIntyre's early position in MI: see MI, 20 and section 1.2 above.

161. Lindbeck, "Afterword," ND 2nd Edition, 138.

compass and interpret the whole of reality: "their very universalism impels them to seek for measuring rods, for public criteria of reasonableness, by means of which they can argue their respective cases for greater comprehensiveness to outsiders."[162]

The drive to universalism in Lindbeck's account pays a similar role to the principle of epistemological openness in MacIntyre's account of tradition. It impels a religion to seek to resolve and incorporate within its framework apparently dissonant elements of experience and belief. On this basis, Lindbeck argues that the superiority of one religion to another rests on the extent to which it can incorporate and explain the insights of another religion within its own conceptual framework, without compromising its identity.[163] Lindbeck himself compares this to MacIntyre's account of the interaction between conflicting traditions of enquiry. He suggests that arguments in inter-religious debates

> illustrate a pattern similar to the interaction of conflicting traditions of enquiry as described by Alisdair McIntyre (sic). To put it crassly, the religion that can better incorporate strengths from the other without losing its own is the one that wins. Conclusive victories will rarely if ever conclude such competitions before the eschaton.[164]

Lindbeck asserts that this argument is implicit in his comments in the first edition of ND, in which he suggests that "the reasonableness of a religion is largely a function of its assimilative powers; of its ability to provide an intelligible interpretation in its own terms of the varied realities and situations its adherents encounter."[165] The ability to accommodate the strengths of another religion is one example of this assimilative power. MacIntyre observes that the successful resolution of an epistemological crisis requires a tradition to formulate a new account of its history which explains and overcomes the difficulties which had led to the crisis emerging.[166] Lindbeck's observation suggests that one might extend this requirement to the possession of a more general capacity to explain, absorb and render intelligible both external events and the insights of rival traditions, thus demonstrating a superior interpretative ability. There needs to be sufficient conceptual overlap between religions to allow such debate to take place and in the "Afterword" Lindbeck see this as reflecting the universal dimension

162. Ibid., 136.
163. Ibid., 137–38.
164. Ibid., 138.
165. ND, 131.
166. WJWR, 363.

Lindbeck and MacIntyre as Complementary Thinkers

of the "particularistic universalism" that characterizes all religion. Religions have shared universalistic characteristics because they share an identity as interpretative mediums which provide a basis for dialogue and communication, if not agreement. But religions are also defined by their unique texts and belief systems, and in this sense they are also "particularistic."[167]

The argument in ND is developed further to anticipate the possibility of religions being subject to processes of testing akin to falsification, albeit a process which is unlikely to be conclusive:

> although a religion is not subject to decisive disproof, it is subject . . . to rational testing procedures not wholly unlike those which apply to general scientific theories or paradigms . . . Confirmation or disconfirmation occurs through an accumulation of successes and failures in making practically and cognitively coherent sense of relevant data, and the process does not conclude, in the case of religions, until the disappearance of the last communities of believers or, if the faith survives, until the end of history.[168]

Lindbeck's revised account of the superiority of religions in the *Afterword* places additional emphasis on two elements of his position in ND. The identity of a religion as an interpretative medium drives its search for universality, coherence, and standards through which it can demonstrate its (distinctive and tradition-constituted) rationality.[169] However, this engagement with alien perspectives will also lead to the recognition of inconsistencies between its own perspectives and other elements in the external environment. In this process of interaction religions must face challenges to their interpretative capacity, and it is these challenges that act as rational tests of their coherence. Religions are not, therefore, the isolated self-justifying systems that the rhetoric of absorbing the universe might seem to imply.

Similarly, MacIntyre also argues that traditions are not isolated self-justifying systems. MacIntyre points out that some traditions overlap each other in terms of their "beliefs, images and texts,"[170] and this provides a basis for their interaction. He argues that members of one tradition may ignore the arguments and contentions of another tradition only at the risk of ignor-

167. Lindbeck, "Afterword," ND 2nd Edition, 126.

168. ND, 131.

169. Lindbeck, "Afterword," ND 2nd Edition, 136; see also Lindbeck's discussion of applicability. Lindbeck points out that when it comes to the prediction of future events "all-embracing systems of interpretation possess their own internal criteria of applicability: they can be judged by their own standards" (ND, 124).

170. WJWR, 350.

ing substantive grounds for re-evaluating their own conclusions and beliefs, relative to the internal standards established within their own tradition.[171] MacIntyre contends that the need to develop and consolidate the underlying rationality of a tradition drives forward the search for consistency and coherence. Progress in rationality is demonstrated by a capacity to reconcile underlying inconsistencies.

The response to such challenges lies in conceptual innovation and the reformulation of certain beliefs (see WJWR 355), but there is a limit to the extent to which the fundamental telos of a tradition can be redefined if that tradition is to maintain its identity. As we saw in section 3.5, MacIntyre introduces the concept of "epistemological crisis" to mark the point at which such inconsistencies threaten the coherence of a tradition. As we have seen, "the solution to a genuine epistemological crisis requires the invention or discovery of new concepts and the framing of some new type or types of theory."[172]

Lindbeck also emphasizes the importance of conceptual innovation in responding to dissonance between a religion and its environment. "Prophetic figures apprehend, often with dramatic vividness, how the inherited patterns of belief, practice, and ritual need to be (and can be) reminted. They discover concepts that remove the anomalies."[173] Both Lindbeck and MacIntyre therefore argue that religions or traditions will seek to overcome dissonance through introducing new ways of thinking about the problematic which has given rise to the crisis: "Imaginative conceptual innovation will have had to occur"[174]. These innovations will extend the resources of the tradition in unanticipated ways, but they must also be consistent with and creatively derivable from the elements that define its identity. Such innovation will provide the resources for a retrospective account of why the difficulties had arisen, and how they have been resolved, as Einstein's Theory of Relativity explained why the motion of the earth through the ether could not be detected by the Michelson-Morley experiment. As MacIntyre argues:

> To have passed through an epistemological crisis successfully enables the adherents of a tradition of enquiry to rewrite its history in a more insightful way. And such a history of a particular tradition provides not only a way of identifying continuities in virtue of which that tradition of enquiry has survived and flourished as one and the same tradition, but also of identifying

---

171. WJWR, 350.
172. WJWR, 362.
173. ND, 39.
174. WJWR, 362.

more accurately that structure of justification which underpins whatever claims to truth are made within it.[175]

When an epistemological crisis is neither resolved nor resolvable, it may reveal that the interpretative medium lacks the resources and capacity to respond to internal and external challenges As a result of this failure the interpretative medium may lose its coherence and decay. In this fact lies the basis for judgments of inferiority and superiority, and these are, as MacIntyre indicates, judgments passed by history. Such a crisis may not initiate a sudden collapse, but may result in the gradual loss of adherents and the slow decline of the tradition.

To what extent can we see these concepts of epistemological crisis and superiority as relevant to the understanding of change and development in religion and theology? The example that is closest to hand is Lindbeck himself. Lindbeck's ecumenical work had shown that notwithstanding a perception of doctrinal differences as church-dividing disputes about spiritual truth, doctrinal reconciliation was possible in many circumstances. Lindbeck recognized that contemporary theories of religion and doctrine were unable to explain such ecumenical progress without presupposing doctrinal capitulation. As he puts it in the "Afterword" to ND: "How is it possible not to surrender or relativise historically church-dividing doctrines and yet maintain that these doctrines are no longer divisive? . . . Most starkly stated, the problem is how doctrines that contradicted each other in one historical context can cease to be contradictory in another and remain unchanged?"[176]

The dissonance between theological interpretations of doctrine on the one hand and ecumenical reality on the other represents an epistemological crisis for theology which could not be resolved within the conceptual frameworks of the dominant CP and EE models of religion.[177] Lindbeck's CL model attempts to provide a solution to this crisis through conceptual innovation aimed at reframing the understanding of religion, theology and doctrine. His approach embodies the features that MacIntyre argues are required for an effective response to such a crisis. These are that the solution:

1. Must resolve the problems which have proved intractable in a systematic and coherent way

2. Explain what it was that previously rendered the tradition incapable of solving these problems

---

175. WJWR, 363.
176. Lindbeck, "Afterword," ND 2nd Edition, 126–27.
177. ND, 15–16.

3. Complete the first two tasks in a way which demonstrates continuity with the previous elements of the tradition.[178]

Lindbeck's approach in ND matches these requirements by showing that the intractability of the issues lies in conceptual confusion about the nature of religion embodied in the CP and EE models of religion. The cultural-linguistic model provides the type of conceptual innovation that is required to resolve the dissonance between the understanding of doctrine and the reality of ecumenicism, and does so coherently and systematically. Lindbeck also shows how continuity with the tradition can be maintained by demonstrating that ecumenical progress can be made without doctrinal capitulation. The text of *The Nature of Doctrine* is, therefore, a demonstration of the relevance of MacIntyre's account of tradition to understanding the way in which religions may respond to internal and external challenges to their coherence, and through this continue to develop their own tradition-constituted forms of rationality.

Religions and their adherents are confident of the truth of their beliefs, and confident of their ability to withstand challenges. This confidence gives religious communities a resilience to challenge that is not possessed by most secular philosophies. Nonetheless, religious belief may crumble in the face of interaction with external challenges, as evidenced by the fate of the Polynesian belief system in the early nineteenth century.[179] These challenges cannot be avoided by religions, because their intrinsic drive towards universality requires that they engage with and make sense of this environment. In the early twenty-first century much of that environment is antagonistic to Christianity and to other religions. Christians must engage in debate with these hostile forces, not for apologetic reasons, but to demonstrate the coherence and resilience of their religion to themselves, and, to borrow a phrase from Rowan Williams once again, to shape the judgment of the world.

4.8 Overall Conclusions: MacIntyre, Lindbeck, and Relativism

The Contribution of This Book

My discussion to date has made a contribution in three main areas. Firstly, it has traced the relationship between MacIntyre's early philosophical

---

178. WJWR, 362.
179. AV, 111–2.

development and his mature philosophy, and shows that his work can be understood as exhibiting an overall historical coherence notwithstanding his changing epistemological, political and religious commitments. It has argued that the underlying continuity of his position rests on his continuing struggle to articulate the basis on which belief in a comprehensive metaphysical perspective can be held to be justified.

My discussion of the development of his mature philosophy led me to argue that his attempt to formulate an Aristotelian ethic that was relevant to the modern world had been enhanced by his biological account of human telos in *Dependent Rational Animals*, and that the significance of that work to MacIntyre's philosophy ought to be more widely acknowledged. My exposition of MacIntyre's mature position led me to identify some unresolved issues in his account. This book has focused particularly on the vagueness of the concept of a tradition and the associated lack of clarity as to the conditions under which an epistemological crisis might arise. This was an important deficit given that MacIntyre's account of rationality and justification is framed in terms of the concepts of tradition and epistemological crisis.

The book introduced the voice of George Lindbeck and his regulative account of the nature of doctrine as a way of providing greater specificity to MacIntyre's account. The book explored the similarities between the epistemological positions of MacIntyre and Lindbeck, and introduced the idea of a "hermeneutic framework" as a way of characterizing their shared assumptions about the culturally specific nature of knowledge claims, and the relation of such claims to rules of assertion, interpretation and practical rationality. MacIntyre argues that traditions are identified and differentiated by a set of "fundamental agreements," and I drew an analogy between such agreements and Lindbeck's regulative account of doctrine. I argued that understanding the agreements that constitute a tradition in these terms both illuminates the process through which tradition-constituted rationality develops and gives greater precision to the idea of epistemological crisis as well as to other elements of MacIntyre's theory. Incorporating elements of Lindbeck's work into Macintyre's philosophy therefore strengthens his account of tradition and tradition-constituted rationality.

The book then reviewed Lindbeck's account of inter-religious superiority in terms of categorial adequacy and his account of intra-religious or theological superiority in terms of the notion of intratextuality. It concluded that neither account provided a basis for judgments of superiority in practice. It argued that Lindbeck's position could be strengthened if MacIntyre's account of tradition-constituted rationality was incorporated into his account, a point that Lindbeck himself has acknowledged. Rowan Williams' criticism of Lindbeck helped to give this recommendation theological edge by providing an account of Christianity in which Christians are always at the boundary between the world and their religion, both judging and being judged. This boundary situation is precisely the circumstance in which standards of truth and justification and judgments of validity are brought into question, as MacIntyre pointed out in his presidential address to the American Philosophical Association in 1985.[180] It is in these circumstances that the rules which govern justification within a conceptual scheme are tested and renewed—or found wanting. Judgments of superiority and inferiority are therefore provisional, and subject to the test of further challenges, both to the adequacy of the evaluations made, and to the standards that are used to justify these evaluations. Through this testing process they develop the distinctive rationality of the tradition. This rationality is internal to the tradition in the sense that it formulates the standards that are applied in judgment (and it is therefore intratextual in Lindbeck's sense). But it is also engaged with the world that it interprets, and through this engagement it can be tested by its capacity to render the events that occur in that world intelligible within its framework.

There is a fourth question that has motivated this book. This is the question of the extent to which the epistemological perspectives adopted by MacIntyre and Lindbeck commit either or both to a form of relativism. This issue has been addressed implicitly throughout the book, but the conclusions of this element of the book now need to be made explicit.

Is MacIntyre a Relativist?

This book has argued that an underlying theme of MacIntyre's work is the question of the rational justification of belief in a comprehensive metaphysical framework. His initial attempts to address this question are illustrated by his engagement with Christianity and Marxism in his early work. What counts as an appropriate answer to the question of justification is dependent on the interpretation given to the associated notions of rationality, knowledge and truth. MacIntyre's response to this question in his mature philosophy involves a fundamental reconstruction of these concepts, and this book has provided an exposition of these revised accounts. The claim that MacIntyre's position is relativist reflects a failure to appreciate the extent of this reconstruction. This criticism assumes that there is no middle ground between Enlightenment epistemological standards, and a version of relativism which is based on the view that, without such standards, one is unable to rationally assess the merits of different traditions.

180. MacIntyre, "Relativism, Power and Philosophy," 7.

Richard Bernstein argues that this Enlightenment concept of relativism is parasitic on the concept of what he calls "objectivism." He defines objectivism as the view that there "is or must be some permanent ahistorical matrix or framework to which we can ultimately appeal in determining the nature of rationality, knowledge, truth, reality, goodness or rightness."[181] Let us call this the objectivist claim. Relativism, on the other hand he describes as the claim that "when we turn to the examination of those concepts that philosophers have taken to be the most fundamental [rationality, truth, reality, the good or norms] . . . all such concepts must be understood as relative to a particular conceptual scheme, theoretical paradigm, form of life, society or culture."[182] Let us call this the relativist thesis. If the relativist thesis is true, then the objectivist's claim that there is a framework which transcends these different and potentially incompatible culturally determined accounts of truth and so on must be false. Assertions of truth will be relative to such culturally determined frameworks, and there will be no rational basis on which one can choose between the evaluations of truth or justification that emanate from these frameworks. There is nothing beyond warranted assertability that can act as a test of truth, and it is only the ethical presuppositions of a particular culture that can justify moral evaluations. If this argument is correct then MacIntyre's position would be relativist, because he argues that "there is no standing ground , no place for enquiry, no way to engage in the practices of advancing, evaluating and rejecting reasoned argument apart from that which is provided by some tradition or another."[183]

If the truth of the objectivist thesis is a necessary condition of the repudiation of relativism, MacIntyre's repudiation of this thesis must lead to relativism. However, one flaw in this argument is the implicit assumption that it is *only* an objectivist meta-framework that could provide the basis for rationally founded judgments that transcend the limitations of a specific cultural perspective. If it is possible for something other than such a meta-framework to provide the basis for framework-transcendent judgments, there would be no contradiction involved in holding both that the objectivist's claim is false, and that one can be justified in claiming that the judgments made in one tradition may be shown to be demonstrably superior to those made in another. This is MacIntyre's position.

The tests of rational justification for MacIntyre can be ranked in series. The first is the consistency of a judgment with the standards established within a tradition at a particular point in time—warranted assertability.

---

181. Bernstein, *Beyond Objectivism and Relativism*, 8.
182. Ibid., 8.
183. WJWR, 350.

The second is the ability of that position to withstand subsequent challenge and critique as the theoretical resources of the tradition develop, both in response to internal debates and through its interaction with other traditions and external events. The third type of test arises when the tradition fails to render events or arguments intelligible within its framework of presuppositions and standards of justification. This may bring the internal standards of justification and ontological presuppositions of the tradition into question, and as a result an epistemological crisis may arise. In extreme cases the fundamental presuppositions and/or standards of justification of the tradition may be modified, or the tradition may lapse into incoherence and fail. This account does not require reference to a tradition transcendent meta-framework, but nor does it provide some absolute standard of justification. Rather it acknowledges that positions will be treated as justified until that assessment is shown to be inadequate with respect to the standards that have emerged within that tradition.

MacIntyre's position therefore undermines a second relativist thesis. This is the claim that the warranted judgments made in one tradition can always be justified by reference to the assumptions of that tradition. Justification is conditional, not only on the assumptions and rules of inference of the tradition, but also on whether that judgment can be sustained in the face of incompatible external events and arguments which are inconsistent with the rules that are held to endorse it. The potential mismatch between conceptual framework and experience drives MacIntyre's modification of the notion of truth. Correspondence theories of truth conceptualize the objectivist meta-framework as being provided by the relationship between propositions and states of affairs or facts which constitute what is ultimately real. However, this conceptualization of truth as correspondence to the real cannot be sustained if there is no theory-independent way of characterizing what is real. If this is the case, there will be no tradition-independent access to the states of affairs that allegedly validate truth-claims. MacIntyre therefore sketches an alternative Thomistic theory of truth in which it is the correspondence of mind to reality that is the goal of enquiry.[184]

This MacIntyrean mind is embodied in the active engagement of the whole person (and indeed the community of which that person is a part) with his or her environment. What can be discovered in this engagement is not primarily what is true, but what may come to be known to be false and unjustified. The original aim of such engagement is to secure a relationship between the individual or community and the environment which is coherent so that action is effective in meeting human need. The relationship

---

184. WJWR, 356–57.

between individual and environment will involve interpretation of what is the case and this interpretation will underpin practical reasoning and action. Learning to interpret and to act appropriately involves the socialization of the individual into the tradition and the assimilation of what I described earlier as a hermeneutic framework. However, there is no guarantee that the interpretations of reality which emerge from the application of this hermeneutic framework represent some ultimate truth, or indeed that the framework itself will remain adequate. Justification and claims of truth are always provisional rather than absolute.

One can therefore draw a legitimate distinction between what is believed to be true and what is actually the case on MacIntyre's account. Moreover, his position retains a notion of absolute truth as the comprehensive correspondence of mind to reality—but it is impossible for anyone to know whether they have acquired such truth, although progress in enquiry will be characterized by a series of attempts to shape the mind to embody such truths. However, every attempt to express such truths may be undermined by future events, and may need to be revised or abandoned. The question of the justification of a comprehensive metaphysical system is therefore a question of whether a system has sustained itself against challenge rather than whether the truth of its claims can be demonstrated. As a consequence, MacIntyre's account of superiority is pragmatic and empirical—what is credible are those beliefs and traditions that survive in practice. This notion of superiority acknowledges the limits of human knowledge, and its underlying humility is consonant with apophaticism, and with the recognition that human knowledge is (in Pecknold's happy phrase) always penultimate.[185]

At the heart of this account of superiority lies the principle of epistemological openness (PEO) which I identified as one of the four elements of MacIntyre's account of tradition-constituted rationality in section 2.6. If traditions can legitimately construct defenses that can fully insulate their presuppositions from challenge, then each could remain a self-justifying island of belief. It is unclear how they would achieve such isolation but let us concede this possibility for the sake of argument. If such traditions existed then it would not be possible to show that any of them were false, and acceptance of a form of relativism would appear to be legitimate. MacIntyre dismisses such self-justifying traditions on the basis that they are "degenerate." There appear to be three reasons for his judgment. The first is pragmatic. A tradition which insulates itself from openness may be vulnerable to overwhelming epistemological crisis when, through changes to its cultural context, it finds itself exposed to new concepts for which it is not prepared

---

185. Pecknold, *Transforming Postliberal Theology*, 101.

and which contradict its fundamental assumptions. MacIntyre illustrates this process by outlining the collapse of Polynesian ethics when exposed to Western cultural influences in the late eighteenth and early nineteenth centuries.[186] Openness is therefore a way of strengthening traditions by developing forms of rationality that are tested through challenge and provide the resources required to repudiate other challenges. The second reason is that the PEO is supported by observation and history: traditions, communities and individuals recognize that human knowledge is limited and fallible and accept that beliefs will develop in response to change. And this process can be observed in the history of the emergence, development and decline of different traditions of enquiry.

The third reason for accepting the PEO is more fundamental. If traditions are able to insulate themselves from any challenge there would be no progress in the discovery of falsehood and no movement in the direction of knowledge. MacIntyre is committed to a quasi-Aristotelian view of humanity as creatures whose defining characteristics lie in their mutual dependence, their animal nature and their rationality. Openness to challenge is a condition of rational belief. Without such openness we cannot fully realize our potentiality. The principle of epistemological openness is therefore required by our nature and is a condition of achieving our telos as rational animals.

Is Lindbeck a Relativist?

Pecknold argues in his recent book that Lindbeck's pragmatism does not entail relativism, as other critics have argued. He claims that Lindbeck's position is non-relativist because Lindbeck holds that there is an ultimate truth, even though it may not be possible to adequately articulate what constitutes that truth at any point in history.[187] Pecknold interprets Lindbeck's account of truth as pragmatic and empirical in orientation: it is what happens in the long term that determines what can be held to be true[188] and in this respect Lindbeck shares MacIntyre's historicism. Pecknold argues that Lindbeck's pragmatism enables him to balance the danger of relativism associated with the CL model with the recognition that God is the ultimate reality.[189] He suggests that postliberal theology does not exclude metaphysical or ontological commitments but encourages "a certain pragmatic tentative-

---

186. AV, 111–12.
187. Pecknold, *Transforming Postliberal Theology*, 100–101.
188. Ibid., 32.
189. Ibid., 101.

Lindbeck and MacIntyre as Complementary Thinkers

ness" towards them.[190] Lindbeck's position does not exclude the legitimacy of affirming a particular ontology but nor does his CL model require this commitment. The rule theory of doctrine relegates the discussion "of the possible correspondence of Trinitarian patterns of Christian language to the metaphysical structure of the Godhead" to something that is neither doctrinally necessary nor binding.[191] Whether the Trinitarian language of the Creeds embodies ontological truths is unknowable in this life. As Pecknold indicates, "Lindbeck locates ontological reference in the eschaton, in the future"[192]—as indeed does MacIntyre theory of justification.

Pecknold argues that those critics who accuse Lindbeck of relativism have misunderstood his intention in ND, which is not to offer a theory of truth but to offer scripturally founded guidance on the pragmatic exploration of the truth embodied in the scriptures. This aim does not require a treatise on truth, according to Pecknold:

> In sum, one of the strengths of Lindbeck's book, in response to his critics, is that he does not offer a definition of truth. His interest in the truth is always practically guided by that which is accessible within the mediating semiotic system in use. This does not mean that there is no truth "beyond" that semiotic system, only that truth is identified with God in such a way as to prevent the mind from grasping it as such without the mediation of signs. This is why Lindbeck is happier with likening Christianity to a whole gigantic proposition (a whole semiotic universe), rather than reducing it to a set of propositions. Communal engagement with the scriptures is itself a journey into truth for Lindbeck, but a journey of intensification, of searching out the truth of the Scriptures, discovering and performing the faith that is inscribed there.[193]

Pecknold's interpretation of Lindbeck's position on truth is only partially plausible. His interpretation is legitimate with respect to Lindbeck's exploration of his religious and theological concerns. In the latter part of ND Lindbeck is writing as a committed Christian theologian, and he is concerned to explore the implications of his theory for a postliberal approach to theology, rather than to justify the fundamentals of religious faith. However, Lindbeck's theological position in ND is built upon his philosophical or non-theological (in Lindbeck's term) account of the nature of religion as

190. Ibid., 8.
191. ND, 106.
192. Pecknold, *Transforming Postliberal Theology*, 30.
193. Ibid., 104.

a CL system, and on his prior attempt to formulate an account of the nature of truth and superiority that is consistent with this model. It is misleading to claim that Lindbeck does not offer a definition of truth, because as we have seen, Lindbeck explores several different characterizations of truth in *The Nature of Doctrine* and places great importance on his exposition of the nature of truth in the "Excursus" attached to ND chapter 3. These points indicate that Lindbeck recognized that he had to address the implications of his general model of religion for an account of truth. Pecknold's defense of Lindbeck's position as non-relativist depends on his interpretation of relativism as equivalent to the claim that there is no ultimate truth,[194] but as it stands this is not an adequate characterization of the concept of relativism. In the light of Bernstein's definition quoted above, it is more legitimate to see relativism as the claim that there is no basis on which one can choose between the competing claims to truth of different traditions or theories. Lindbeck's difficulties with relativism arise because he is unable to construct an account of the nature of truth and justification which can be applied *in practice* to distinguish between inferior and superior truth-claims. For that reason I argued that Lindbeck's position needs to be supplemented by MacIntyre's account of rationality and by Rowan Williams' account of the negotiation of Christian identity in interaction with the world, in order to develop a more adequate notion of superiority.

MacIntyre's notion of superiority and Williams' image of judgment can be applied to Lindbeck's position because Lindbeck himself acknowledges a logical gap between the human capacity to formulate an understanding of what is true, and the nature of reality as it is in itself. Such a logical gap means that any human formulation will be an inadequate attempt to assert a religious truth whose nature lies far beyond human powers of conceptualization. Error and revision will characterize the progress of human knowledge towards the asymptotic point of conformity of human understanding and practice with the nature of that reality. This is a point that Pecknold recognizes when he comments that "Lindbeck underlines the science-like reasonableness of religion and theology...as a "long-run" antidote to the relativistic and fideistic implications of his argument...And what he proposes is the constant testing that comes in the process of critical learning over a long period of time."[195] The "science-like reasonableness" of Lindbeck's theory provides the potential for a repudiation of relativism, but his account needed to be supplemented by an account of rational justification for that potential to be realized. The relativistic consequences of the absence

---

194. Ibid., 100–101.
195. Ibid., 32; the relevant passages in Lindbeck are in ND, 130–31.

of such an account can be illustrated by a quotation from a paper Lindbeck published in 1989:

> physics and poetry are not differentiated ontologically or epistemologically: it is not that they refer to distinct types of reality or arise in distinct ways of knowing which makes them different. Rather they are seen as products of social practices which, though diverse in structure and purpose, have overlapping features . . . The epistemological grounding of quarks and Homeric Gods is basically the same. It is rhetorical force rooted in communal practice which gives them their cognitive status, and when rhetoric and practice change, so does that status. Homeric Gods were real and quarks non-existent for ancient Greeks, their status is reversed for us, and there are no definitively formulatable context-free criteria for determining who is right and who is wrong (though there may be unformulated implicit ones).[196]

This seems to express a thoroughly relativist position—until one reads the final clause which refers to the existence of "unformulated implicit" criteria for distinguishing between the legitimacy of a belief in Greek mythology and a belief in the findings of particle physics. Lindbeck goes on to argue in another paper that there are criteria that can be used to justify different beliefs, although these vary from age to age.[197] These implicit criteria can be illuminated, I have suggested, by reference to MacIntyre's notion of tradition-constituted rationality. MacIntyre's work helps to conceptualize the way in which criteria for distinguishing between superior and inferior beliefs are formulated and tested in the development of a tradition. There is a basis on which the adequacy of explanation in terms of particle physics can be assessed relative to explanation in terms of Homeric Gods, although those standards are not universal standards, and could not have been understood or applied by the ancient Greeks. They are internal to our Western scientific tradition.

This is not to claim that the findings of particle physics are correct and represent some formulation of ultimate ontological truth. Propositions about quarks and Higgs bosons form provisional truth claims at best and may be shown to be inadequate by future events and come to be replaced by new theories that explain these events in a more comprehensive and consistent fashion. It is possible to acquire a more adequate understanding of the nature of reality. But claims to knowledge always remain provisional

---

196. Lindbeck, "Scripture, Consensus and Community," 218; Lindbeck makes a similar point with similar words in "The Search for Habitable Texts," 154.

197. Ibid., 154.

and subject to revision. The most important virtue in seeking knowledge is the virtue of humility; that is, the recognition that what one can achieve is only a provisional and tentative approximation to truth. This recognition provides the basis for an account of the rational superiority or inferiority of any intellectual position which incorporates the openness to challenge embodied in MacIntyre's PEO. Each response to challenge that successfully retains and elaborates the fundamental agreements that constitute the identity of a tradition will strengthen its claims to justification, and resist and shape the judgment of the world.

The Relevance of MacIntyre's Philosophy

As we have seen, Pecknold argues that Lindbeck should not be considered a relativist because he holds that there is indeed some ultimate truth, albeit a truth which cannot be fully comprehended prior to the eschaton. While this might mean that Lindbeck's position avoids an extreme relativist denial of the existence of any universal truth, his failure to provide a practicable criterion of superiority renders his position epistemologically relativist in practice, as it provides no basis for choosing between conflicting positions. But does MacIntyre's account fare any better? There are two elements that need to be considered in relation to this question. Firstly, has he been successful in setting out a coherent account of the justification of a tradition? Secondly, does that account provide any help to the individual who is struggling to determine which of several traditions might be worthy of commitment?

In the final chapter of WJWR MacIntyre notes that his enquiry into

> justice and practical rationality was ... informed by a conviction that each particular conception of justice requires as its counterpart some particular conception of practical rationality and vice versa ... it has become evident [in the process of enquiry] that conceptions of justice and of practical rationality generally and characteristically confront us as closely related aspects of some larger ... overall view of human life and its place in nature. Such overall views, insofar as they make claims upon our rational allegiance, give expression to traditions of enquiry which are at one and the same time traditions embodied in particular types of social relationship.[198]

I called such overall views of human life and its place in nature "comprehensive metaphysical systems" (CMS) in section 1.1, and defined such

---

198. WJWR, 389.

systems as "a set of ontological and ethical presuppositions which are taken to encompass and explain the nature of the universe of which our species is a part, and which also provide a framework for human practical reasoning and action." The attempt to ensure that such systems are coherent and comprehensive accounts of human life and its place in nature, and to apply them to the interpretations of events and experience, gives rise to what MacIntyre calls a tradition of enquiry. As we have seen MacIntyre argues that while the tradition of enquiry is able to make progress and to resolve the challenges that emerge from its engagement with external events and from internal and external criticism, it can consider itself and its parent tradition to be provisionally justified. A failure to resolve such challenges may result in a tradition falling into crisis and into decline. Ultimately, the judgment of success or failure is based on the historical trajectory of a tradition, rather than on universal criteria of adequacy or truth.

I have argued that MacIntyre's account is successful in avoiding relativism because it provides a clear criterion with respect to the superiority of one tradition to another. Through historical study it is possible to identify those traditions and their associated forms of enquiry which are provisionally justified,[199] and those which can be considered to have failed, although, as I pointed out in section 2.6, apparently moribund traditions may be revived. This observation suggests that caution should be exercised in passing judgment on the failure of particular traditions. Despite this caveat, MacIntyre's account of superiority can be applied in practice to underpin retrospective judgments of superiority and inferiority, and in that respect it avoids the deficits of Lindbeck's account. It meets the objective of providing a measure of the success or failure of a comprehensive metaphysical system by providing a historical assessment of its capacity to deal with challenges to its coherence. But is it of any practical value in the here-and-now? This is a question MacIntyre considers briefly at the end of *Whose Justice? Which Rationality?*[200]

In considering this second question it is important to recognize that MacIntyre's account may be more or less relevant to different people in different situations.[201] I will consider three examples. Firstly, a person who is a committed adherent to a tradition whose enquiry is proceeding smoothly and which appears to be making progress in response to its current challenges. Secondly, a person who is a committed adherent of a tradition which is at a point of epistemological crisis; and, thirdly, a person who is con-

---

199. MacIntyre would cite Thomism as such a tradition: WJWR, 402–3.
200. WJWR, 393–8
201. WJWR, 393.

sidering the respective claims of different traditions of enquiry from the perspective of an uncommitted but earnest enquirer after truth.

An awareness of MacIntyre's account of justification will be of intellectual interest to the first type of person and may promote a degree of humility with respect to the ability of their tradition to sustain progress in future. It may also help to illuminate the tradition's history by providing a conceptual framework within which to understand its historic difficulties and the developments which helped to resolve them. The individual is, however, entirely justified in their adherence to the tradition at that stage because it has demonstrated that it is capable of overcoming the challenges that it has faced to date. She may recognize that this progress may not continue, and may be cautious in describing the assertions enunciated by the tradition as unconditionally demonstrated, but has no reason to abandon her confidence in the tradition—unless it falls into an irresolvable epistemological crisis.

MacIntyre's theory is relevant to the adherent of a tradition in epistemological crisis in two ways. Firstly, it explains the nature of that crisis and describes what the tradition as a whole must do in order to resolve that crisis, provided it is able to acquire the resources needed for that resolution. In this book, this process of resolution has been illustrated by Lindbeck's construction of a cultural-linguistic account of the nature of religion and rule theory of doctrine in order to resolve a theological impasse engendered by CP and EE accounts. Lindbeck did not conceptualize his work in terms of MacIntyre's theory, but that theory potentially provides a way in which participants of a tradition in crisis can understand the challenges it faces, and enable them to address these challenges in a way which recognizes the nature of progress and justification in a tradition. MacIntyre's philosophy can, therefore, play a role in guiding tradition-constituted enquiry which is similar to the role played by Kuhn's account of the nature of scientific revolutions in shaping the contemporary understanding of progress in scientific enquiry. Macintyre's work can encourage an awareness of the limitations of tradition-constituted enquiry; an awareness of the possibility of epistemological crisis, and an awareness of the need to engage with alternative traditions as a means of conceptual cross-fertilization.

Secondly, MacIntyre's philosophy may also be of value to the individual engaged in a tradition in crisis by enabling that person to understand the nature of the challenge to their personal beliefs, and by encouraging them to engage in debate and evaluation in order to test and develop their noetic coherence. The opportunity to respond to the "judgement of the world" is an opportunity to witness to their beliefs and to test and strengthen their personal belief system through engaging with external challenges. The success experienced by individuals in addressing such challenges will also help to build the conceptual resources available to the whole tradition to address underlying inconsistencies.

Finally, is MacIntyre's account relevant to the individual who is not an adherent of any tradition, but who is considering which, if any, should gain her commitment? MacIntyre argues that the answer to this question depends on the type of person you are.[202] The most extreme example is the individual who applies the impossible standards of justification promoted by the Enlightenment as a condition of their commitment to any position. As such standards cannot be met, they will find that they are unable to commit themselves to any tradition, and as a result they will be excluded from processes of communal enquiry.[203] MacIntyre asks: "how, if at all, could such a person as a result of an encounter with some particular tradition of enquiry come instead to inhabit that tradition as a rational agent? What kind of transformation would be required?"[204]

The first stage in resolving their intellectual isolation is for the individual to recognize that their adherence to Enlightenment standards of justification is a commitment to the problematic standards of rational justification that have developed in one challenged tradition.[205] Her adoption of these standards is, therefore, not an expression of tradition independence, but an unreflective commitment to one such tradition, a commitment which excludes her from engagement with an alternative tradition which might enable her to progress towards (provisional) knowledge. A precondition of progress is therefore for her to reassess these Enlightenment standards, and to consider the alternative standards that are embedded in rival traditions of enquiry. Addressing the question "which of these rival traditions is superior?" requires an understanding of the basic concepts and modes of enquiry of the different traditions, which can only be acquired through at least partial socialization into more than one of these traditions, and, ultimately, by making a commitment to the rational standards of evaluation that characterize one of those traditions. This is the second step required to overcome their intellectual isolation.[206]

202. WJWR, 393
203. See WJWR, 395.
204. WJWR, 396.
205. WJWR, 395–96.

206. Rorty makes the point that it is first necessary to be educated in a prevalent epistemological scheme before one can legitimately innovate and challenge the presuppositions of such a scheme and subject them to hermeneutical critique (Rorty *Philosophy and the Mirror of Nature*, 365–6). If this is the case, then the individual who resists education into a tradition will prevent themselves from making intellectual progress.

The knowledge of rival traditions that such a process presupposes is perhaps not as problematic as it might appear. As MacIntyre points out, our diverse liberal culture is characterized by a lack of awareness of the extent to which our knowledge claims and patterns of argument are in fact derived from multiple traditions of enquiry,[207] whether those traditions of enquiry are founded in natural science, philosophy, political thought, literature, art or religion (among others). Paradoxically, assumptions about universal standards of rational justification are so engrained in our culture that their foundations in tradition have become invisible. To recognize this is to recognize that any claim to rational justification is always the provisional claim of some particular cultural group at a particular point in its historical development. Such claims may prove to be valid but they may also ultimately prove to be invalid. Our task is to determine the community to which we should commit ourselves, but this cannot be done from a tradition-independent perspective.

The individual who seeks to stand outside all traditions in order to judge their merits lacks awareness of the extent to which some of these traditions will have shaped their identity through their upbringing and education. Such a person needs to develop the self-knowledge that will enable them to recognize the elements of their noetic structure that are derived from different traditions and consider which of these elements is of greatest significance to them. Like MacIntyre in his early development, they will become aware of inconsistencies in the different elements of their belief system; they will engage with that tradition that speaks to them most clearly, and will have the opportunity to address those inconsistencies. In this process of re-evaluation and reconstruction they may ultimately come to identify themselves with one tradition and commit themselves to its process of enquiry, as MacIntyre came to identify with Thomist Catholicism.

MacIntyre's journey is unusual only because it has been expressed through the development of an innovative account of rationality and tradition. We may not be faced with the conflict between the tales of Iain Lom and Brian Boru on the one hand and an inchoate liberalism on the other that had characterized MacIntyre's childhood, but each of us will have been exposed to multiple tradition based influences as we developed, because of the diversity of our society—some of them secular, some religious. Each of us, therefore, may arrive at a point in which we have to decide where our commitments lie. At that stage we may be called upon to recognize and address inconsistencies in our beliefs, and seek to identify our most important spiritual, ethical, and political commitments. MacIntyre's philosophy and

---

207. WJWR, 397–38.

personal history can help us to understand the nature of that process of intellectual and moral development, and enable us to recognize that we need to seek for the support of a tradition and its communities if we are to be able to continue our journey.

BIBLIOGRAPHY

Achtenberg, Deborah. "On the Metaphysical Presuppositions of Aristotle's Nichomachean Ethics." *Journal of Value Enquiry* 26 (1992) 317–40.
Adam, Matthias. "Two Notions of Scientific Justification." *Synthese* 158 (2007) 93–108.
Adams, Nicholas. "Reparative Reasoning." *Modern Theology* 24 (2008) 447–57.
Adiprasetya, Joas. "George A. Lindbeck and Postliberal Theology." (2005). In *The Boston Collaborative Encyclopedia of Modern Western Theology*. No pages. Online: http://people.bu.edu/wwildman/WeirdWildWeb/courses/mwt/dictionary/mwt_themes_862_lindbeck.htm.
Aiken, C. "Apologetics" (1907). In *Catholic Encyclopedia*. No pages. Online: http://www.newadvent.org/cathen/01618a.htm.
Allen, A. "MacIntyre's Traditionalism." *Journal of Value Inquiry* 31 (1997) 511–525.
Allen, Richard C. "When Narrative Fails." *Journal of Religious Ethics* 21 (1993) 27–67.
Alston, W. P. *Perceiving God: The Epistemology of Religious Experience*. Ithaca: Cornell University Press, 1991.
Annas, Julia. "MacIntyre on Traditions." *Philosophy and Public Affairs* 18 (1989) 388–404.
Anscombe, G. E. M. "Modern Moral Philosophy." *Philosophy* 33 (1958) 1–19.
Appel, Fredrick. Review of *Whose Justice? Which Rationality?* by Alasdair MacIntyre. *Philosophy of the Social Sciences* 20 (1990) 135–138.
Aquinas, Thomas. *Summa Theologica*. 2nd ed., 1920; translated by Fathers of the English Dominican Province. No pages. Online: http://home.newadvent.org/summa/.
Aristotle. *The Nichomachean Ethics*. Translated by David Ross; revised by J. L. Ackrill and J. O. Urmson. Oxford: Oxford University Press, 1998.
Ayer, A. J. *Language, Truth and Logic*. London: Gollancz, 1967.
Badham, Roger A., and Ola Sigurdson. "The De-centered Post-Constantinian Church: An Exchange." *Cross Currents* 47 (1997) 154–65.
Baier, Annette A. "MacIntyre on Hume." *Philosophy and Phenomenological Research* 50 (1991) 159–63.
Baker, Deane-Peter. *Tayloring Reformed Epistemology: Charles Taylor, Alvin Plantinga and the de jure Challenge to Christian Belief*. London: SCM, 2007.
Barrett, Lee C. "Theology as Grammar: Regulative Principles or Paradigms and Practices." *Modern Theology* 4 (1988) 155–72.
Battaglia, Anthony. "'Sect' or 'Denomination'? The Place of Religious Ethics in a Post-Churchly Culture." *Journal of Religious Ethics* 16 (1988) 128–42.

Baxter, Michael J. "Catholicism and Liberalism: Kudos and Questions for Communio Ecclesiology." *Review of Politics* 60 (1998) 743–64.

Benn, S. I. "Persons and Values: Reasons in Conflict and Moral Disagreement." *Ethics* 95 (1984) 20–37.

Bernstein, Richard J. *Beyond Objectivism and Relativism: Science, Hermeneutics and Praxis.* Philadelphia: University of Pennsylvania Press, 1983.

Bettenhausen, Elizabeth. Review of *Three Rival Versions of Moral Enquiry: Encyclopaedia, Genealogy, and Tradition*, by Alasdair MacIntyre. *Theology Today* 48 (1991) 74–76.

Blackledge, Paul, and Neil Davidson, eds. *Alasdair MacIntyre's Engagement with Marxism: Selected Writings, 1953–1974.* Chicago: Haymarket, 2009.

Bock, G. W. "Jehovah's Witnesses and Autonomy: Honouring the Refusal of Blood Transfusions." *Journal of Medical Ethics* 38 (2012) 652–56. Online: http://jme.bmj.com/content/early/2012/07/11/medethics-2012-100802.short?rss=1.

Bradley, M. C. "A Note on Mr. MacIntyre's 'Determinism.'" *Mind* 68 (1959) 324–26.

Brown, Sally A. "Exploring the Text-Practice Interface: Acquiring the Virtue of Hermeneutical Modesty." *Theology Today* 66 (2009) 279–94.

Buckley, James. "Introduction." In George A. Lindbeck, *The Church in a Postliberal Age*, edited by James Buckley, vii–xviii. London: SCM, 2002.

Butler, Christopher. *Postmodernism: A Very Short Introduction.* Oxford: Oxford University Press, 2002.

Calhoun, Craig. "Charles Taylor." In *Routledge Encyclopedia of Philosophy*, edited by E. Craig. London: Routledge. No pages. Online: http://www.rep.routledge.com/article/DD089SECT5.

Caputo, John D. *On Religion.* London: Routledge, 2001.

Carroll, Lewis. "What the Tortoise Said to Achilles." *Mind* 4 (1895) 278–80.

Chapman, Mark D. "Why the Enlightenment Project Doesn't have to Fail." *Heythrop Journal* 39 (1998) 379–93.

Christian, William A., Jr. *Doctrines of Religious Communities: A Philosophical Study.* New Haven: Yale University Press, 1987.

Clark, Thomas W. "Relativism and the Limits of Rationality." *Humanist* 52 (1992) 25–32. Online: http://www.naturalism.org/relativi.htm.

Clayton, Philip. "On Holisms: Insular, Inclusivism, and Postmodern."*Zygon* 33 (1998) 467–74.

Cochran, Clarke E. "The Thin Theory of Community: The Communitarians and their Critics." *Political Studies* 32 (1989) 422–35.

Cohen, Andrew Jason. "Does Communitarianism Require Individual Independence?" *Journal of Ethics* 4 (2000) 283–305.

———. "In Defense of Nietzschean Genealogy." *Philosophical Forum* 30 (1999) 269–88.

Comstock, Gary L. "Two Types of Narrative Theology." *Journal of the American Academy of Religion* 55 (1987) 687–71.

Coulson, John. *Newman and the Common Tradition.* Oxford: Oxford University Press, 1970.

Cowling, Maurice. "Alasdair MacIntyre, Religion and the University." *New Criterion* 12 (1994) 32–42.

Crisp, Roger. *Reasons and the Good.* Oxford: Clarendon, 2006.

Critchley, Simon. *Continental Philosophy: A Very Short Introduction.* Oxford: Oxford University Press, 2001.

Curran, Mary Bernard. Review of *Edith Stein: A Philosophical Prologue*, by Alasdair MacIntyre. *Heythrop Journal* 48 (2007) 829–30.

Curthoys, Jean. "Thomas Hobbes, the Taylor thesis and Alasdair MacIntyre." *British Journal for the History of Philosophy* 6 (1998) 1–24.

Dahl, Norman O. "Justice and Aristotelian Practical Reason." *Philosophy and Phenomenological Research* 50 (1991) 153–57.

Dancy, Jonathan, ed. *Normativity*. Oxford: Blackwell, 2000.

Davidson, Donald. "On the Very Idea of a Conceptual Scheme." *Proceedings and Addresses of the American Philosophical Association* 47 (1973–74) 5–20.

Davydova, Irina, and Wes Sharrock. "The Rise and Fall of the Fact/Value Distinction." *Sociological Review* 51 (2003) 357–75.

DeHart, Paul J. *The Trial of the Witnesses*. Oxford: Blackwell, 2006.

Descartes, Rene. *Discourse on Method and the Meditations*. Translated by F. E. Sutcliffe. Harmondsworth: Penguin 1968.

DeVille, Adam. "Alasdair MacIntyre and Edith Stein: Apophatic Theologians?" *Logos* 11 (2008) 77–90.

Diamond, Cora. "Losing Your Concepts." *Ethics* 98 (1988) 255–77.

Dorrien, Gary. "Truth Claims." *Christian Century* 118 (2001) 22–29.

Doyle, Dennis M. "The Contribution of a Lifetime: George Lindbeck's *The Church in a Postliberal Age*." *Modern Theology* 21 (2005) 157–62.

Dueck, Al, and Thomas D. Parsons. "Integration Discourse: Modern and Postmodern." *Journal of Psychology and Theology* 32 (2004) 232–47.

Dunne, Joseph. "Ethics Revised: Flourishing as Vulnerable and Dependent." *International Journal of Philosophical Studies* 10 (2002) 339–63.

Early, Christian E. "Beyond Faith and Reason: The Consequences of Alasdair Macintyre's Conception of Tradition-Constituted Rationality for Philosophy of Religion." PhD diss., University of Wales, 2001.

———. "MacIntyre, Narrative Rationality and Faith." *New Blackfriars* 82 (2001) 35–43

Eger, Martin. "A Tale of Two Controversies: Dissonance in the Theory and Practice of Rationality." *Zygon* 23 (1988) 291–324.

Eriksson, Stefan. "Refining the Distinction between Modern and Postmodern Theologies: The Case of Lindbeck." *Studia Theologica* 56 (2002) 156–63.

Fergusson, David. *Community, Liberalism and Christian Ethics*. Cambridge: Cambridge University Press, 1998.

Fleischacker, Samuel. "Enlightenment and Tradition: The Clash within Civilizations." *Journal of Ecumenical Studies* 42 (2007) 351–54.

Fletcher, Jeannine Hill. "As Long as We Wonder: Possibilities in the Impossibility of Interreligious Dialogue." *Theological Studies* 68 (2007) 531–54.

Flew, Antony. "Theology and Falsification: Section A." In *New Essays in Philosophical Theology*, edited by Antony Flew, and Alasdair C. MacIntyre, 96–98. London: SCM, 1955.

Flew, Antony, and Alasdair C. MacIntyre, eds. *New Essays in Philosophical Theology*. London: SCM, 1955.

Fowl, Stephen. "Could Horace Talk with The Hebrews? Translatability and Moral Disagreement in MacIntyre and Stout." *Journal of Religious Ethics* 19 (1991) 1–20.

Fredericks, James L. "Interreligious Friendship: A New Theological Virtue." *Journal of Ecumenical Studies* 35 (1998) 159–74.

Fuller, Michael B. *Making Sense of MacIntyre*. Aldershot: Ashgate, 1998.

Gadamer, Hans-Georg. *Truth and Method*. 2nd ed. Translation revised by Joel Weinsheimer and Donald G. Marshall. London: Continuum, 2004.

Gardiner, Patrick. *Kierkegaard: A Very Short Introduction*. Oxford: Oxford University Press, 2002.

Geertz, Clifford. *The Interpretation of Culture*. New York: Basic, 2000.

———. "Religion as a Cultural System." In *The Interpretation of Culture*, 87–125. New York: Basic Books, 2000.

———. "Thick Description: Toward an Interpretative Theory of Culture." In *The Interpretation of Culture*, 3–30. New York: Basic Books, 2000.

George, Robert P. "Moral Particularism, Thomism and Traditions." *Review of Metaphysics* 42 (1989) 593–605.

Gettier, Edmund L. "Is Justified True Belief Knowledge?" In *Knowledge and Belief*, edited by A. P. Griffiths, 144–46. Oxford: Oxford University Press, 1967.

Gill, Emily R. "MacIntyre, Rationality, and the Liberal Tradition." *Polity* 24 (1992) 433–57.

Glanzberg, Michael. "Truth." In *The Stanford Encyclopedia of Philosophy*, edited by Edward N. Zalta. Summer 2006 ed. No pages. Online: http://plato.stanford.edu/archives/sum2006/entries/truth/.

Grassie, William. "Postmodernism: What One Needs to Know." *Zygon* 32 (1997) 83–94.

Grayling, A. C. "Wittgenstein on Scepticism and Certainty." No date. No pages. Online: http://acgrayling.com/wittgenstein-on-scepticism-and-certainty.

Green, Ronald M. "Recovering Moral Philosophy." *Journal of Religious Ethics* 23 (1995) 367–85.

Gregory-Jones, L. "Alasdair MacIntyre on Narrative, Community, and the Moral Life." *Modern Theology* 4 (1987) 53–69.

Griffiths, Paul J., and Reinhard Hütter, eds. *Reason and the Reasons of Faith*. New York: T. & T. Clark, 2005.

Haldane, John. Review of *Dependent Rational Animals*, by Alasdair MacIntyre. *Mind* 110 (2001) 225–28.

Hampson, Norman. *The Enlightenment*. Harmondsworth: Penguin, 1968.

Harrison, Victoria S. "Narrative, Postmodernity and the Problem of 'Religious Illiteracy.'" *New Blackfriars* 89 (2008) 591–605.

Hauerwas, Stanley. *A Better Hope: Resources for a Church Confronting Capitalism, Democracy and Post-Modernity*. Grand Rapids: Brazos, 2000.

———. "The Virtues of Alasdair MacIntyre." *First Things*, October 2007. No Pages. Online: http://www.firstthings.com/article/2007/09/004-the-virtues-of-alasdair-macintyre.

Healy, Nicholas M. "Practices and the New Ecclesiology: Misplaced Concreteness?" *International Journal of Systematic Theology* 5 (2003) 287–398.

Hedley, Douglas. "Should Divinity Overcome Metaphysics? Reflections on John Milbank's *Theology beyond Secular Reason* and *Confessions of a Cambridge Platonist*." *Journal of Religion* 80 (2000) 271–98.

Herdt, Jennifer. "Alasdair MacIntyre's 'Rationality of Traditions' and Tradition-Transcendental Standards of Justification." *Journal of Religion* 78 (1988) 524–46.

———. "Religious Ethics, History and the Rise of Modern Moral Philosophy." *Journal of Religious Ethics* 22 (2000) 167–88.

Heyer, K. E. "How Does Theology Go Public? Rethinking the Debate between David Tracy and George Lindbeck." *Political Theory* 5 (2004) 307–27.

Bibliography

Hinchman, Lewis P. "Virtue or Autonomy: Alasdair MacIntyre's Critique of Liberal Individualism." *Polity* 21 (1989) 635–54.

Hookway, C. "Epistemic Norms and Theoretical Deliberations." In *Normativity*, edited by Jonathan Dancy, 60–77. Oxford: Blackwell, 2000.

Horton, John, and Susan Mendus, eds. *After MacIntyre: Critical Perspectives on the Work of Alasdair MacIntyre*. Cambridge: Polity, 1994.

———. "Alasdair MacIntyre: *After Virtue* and After." In *After MacIntyre: Critical Perspectives on the Work of Alasdair* MacIntyre, edited by John Horton and Susan Mendus, 1–15. Cambridge: Polity, 1994.

Hovey, Craig. "Putting Truth to Practice: MacIntyre's Unexpected Rule." *Studies in Christian Ethics* 19 (2006) 169–86.

Hume, David. *A Treatise of Human Nature*. Online: http://www.gutenberg.org/files/4705/4705-h/4705-h.htm#link2H_4_0043.

Hunsinger, George. "Postliberal Theology." In *The Cambridge Companion to Postmodern Theology*, edited by Kevin Vanhoozer, 42–57. Cambridge: Cambridge University Press, 2003.

Hyman, Gavin. "The Study of Religion and the Return of Theology." *Journal of the American Academy of Religion* 72 (2004) 195–219.

Jantzen, Grace. *Becoming Divine*. Manchester: Manchester University Press, 1998.

John Paul II. *Fides et Ratio*. 14 September 1998. No pages. Online: http://www.vatican.va/holy_father/john_paul_ii/encyclicals/documents/hf_jp-ii_enc_15101998_fides-et-ratio_en.html.

Johnson, R. P. "MacIntyre, Kierkegaard and the Post-Metaphysical Critique of Rational Theology." PhD diss., Bristol University, 2000.

Jones, L. Gregory. "Alasdair MacIntyre on Narrative, Community, and the Moral Life." *Modern Theology* 14 (1987) 53–56.

JW.Org. "Is Jesus Almighty?" No pages. Online: http://www.jw.org/en/bible-teachings/questions/is-jesus-almighty/.

———. "Why Is Jesus Called God's Son?" No pages. Online: http://www.jw.org/en/bible-teachings/questions/jesus-gods-son/.

Kant, Immanuel. *The Critique of Practical Reason*. Translated by T. K. Abbott. Online: http://philosophy.eserver.org/kant/critique-of-practical-reaso.txt.

———. *The Critique of Pure Reason*. Translated by Norman Kemp Smith. London: Macmillan: 1968.

———. *Religion within the Limits of Reason Alone*. Translated by T. M. Greene and H. H. Hudson. New York: Harper & Row, 1960.

———. "What Is Enlightenment?" Translated by Paul Halsall. Online: http://www.fordham.edu/halsall/mod/kant-whatis.html.

Kenny, Anthony. *The God of the Philosophers*. Oxford: Clarendon, 1979.

———. *The Unknown God*. London: Continuum, 2004.

———. *What Is Faith?* Oxford: Oxford University Press, 1992.

Kerr, Fergus: *Theology after Wittgenstein*. 2nd ed. London: SPCK, 1997.

Kierkegaard, Søren. *Concluding Unscientific Postscript*. Vol. 1. Translated by H. V. Hong and E. H. Hong. Princeton: Princeton University Press, 1992.

———. *Either/Or, A Fragment of Life*. In *The Essential Kierkegaard*, translated and edited by H. V. Hong and E. V. Hong, 37–83. Princeton: Princeton University Press, 2000.

———. *Fear and Trembling*. In *The Essential Kierkegaard*, translated and edited by H. V. Hong and E. V. Hong, 93–101. Princeton, Princeton University Press, 2000.

———. *Philosophical Fragments, or a Fragment of Philosophy*. In *The Essential Kierkegaard*, translated and edited by H. V. Hong and E. V. Hong, 116–25. Princeton, Princeton University Press, 2000.

Kilby, Karen. *Karl Rahner*. London: HarperCollins, 1997.

———. *Karl Rahner: Theology and Philosophy*. London: Routledge, 2004.

Knight, Kelvin. "Aristotelianism versus Communitarianism." *Analyse & Kritik* 27 (2005) 259–73.

———. "Introduction." In *The MacIntyre Reader*, edited by Kelvin Knight, 1–27. Cambridge: Polity, 1991.

———. "MacIntyre's Progress." *Journal of Moral Philosophy* 6 (2009) 115–26.

Knight, Kelvin, ed. *The MacIntyre Reader*. Cambridge: Polity, 1991.

Kommers, Donald P. "Comment on MacIntyre." *The Review of Politics* 52 (1990) 362–68.

Kuhn, Thomas S. *The Structure of Scientific Revolutions*. 4th ed. Chicago: University of Chicago Press, 2012.

Kuna, M. "MacIntyre on Tradition, Rationality and Relativism." *Res Publica* 11 (2005) 251–73.

Lawson, James. "Secularisation and Human Identity in Christ." *New Blackfriars* 89 (2008) 418–30.

Lear, Jonathan. *Aristotle: The Desire to Understand*. Cambridge: Cambridge University Press, 1988.

Levy, Neil. "Stepping into the Present: MacIntyre's Modernity." *Social Theory and Practice* 25 (1999) 471–90.

Lewis Thomas A. "On the Limits of Narrative: Communities in Pluralistic Society." *Journal of Religion* 86 (2006) 55–80.

Lindbeck, George A. "Article IV and Lutheran/Roman Catholic Dialogue: The Limits of Diversity in the Understanding of Justification." In *The Church in a Postliberal Age*, edited by James J. Buckley, 39–52. London: SCM, 2002.

———. "An Assessment Reassessed: Paul Tillich on the Reformation." *Journal of Religion* 63 (1983) 376–93.

———. "Barth and Textuality." *Theology Today* 43 (1986) 361–76.

———. "The Church." In *The Church in a Postliberal Age*, edited by James J. Buckley, 145–65. London: SCM, 2002.

———. *The Church in a Postliberal Age*. Edited by James J. Buckley. London: SCM, 2002.

———. "Confession and Community: An Israel-like View of the Church." In *The Church in a Postliberal Age*, edited by James J. Buckley, 1–9. London: SCM, 2002.

———. "Ecumenical Imperatives for the Twenty-First Century." *Currents in Theology and Mission* 20 (1993) 360–66.

———. "Ecumenism and the Future of Belief." In *The Church in a Postliberal Age*, edited by James J. Buckley, 91–105. London: SCM, 2002.

———. "Foreword to the German Edition of *The Nature of Doctrine*." In *The Church in a Postliberal Age*, edited by James J. Buckley, 190–200. London: SCM, 2002.

———. "The Gospel's Uniqueness: Election and Untranslatability." In *The Church in a Postliberal Age*, edited by James J. Buckley, 223–52. London: SCM, 2002.

———. "A Great Scotist Study." *Review of Metaphysics* 7 (1954) 422–35.

———. "Hesychastic Prayer and the Christianizing of Platonism: Some Protestant Reflections." In *The Church in a Postliberal Age*, edited by James J. Buckley, 106–19. London: SCM, 2002.

———. "How a Lutheran Saw It." *Commonweal* 129 (2002) 15–17.

———. "Infallibility." In *The Church in a Postliberal Age*, edited by James J. Buckley, 120–42. London: SCM, 2002.

———. "An Interview with George Lindbeck: Performing the Faith." *Christian Century* 123 (2006) 28–35.

———. "Martin Luther and the Rabbinic Mind." In *The Church in a Postliberal Age*, edited by James J. Buckley, 21–37. London: SCM, 2002.

———. *The Nature of Doctrine: Religion and Theology in a Postliberal Age*. Philadelphia: Westminster, 1984.

———. *The Nature of Doctrine: Religion and Theology in a Postliberal Age: 25th Anniversary Edition*. Louisville: Westminster John Knox, 2009.

———. "Nominalism and the Problem of Meaning as Illustrated by Pierre D'Ailly on Predestination and Justification." *Harvard Theological Review* 52 (1959) 43–60.

———. "A Note on Aristotle's Discussion of God and the World." *Review of Metaphysics* 2 (1948) 99–106.

———. "Paris, Rome, Jerusalem: An Ecumenical Journey." *Journal of Ecumenical Studies* 41 (2004) 389–408.

———. "Philosophy and *Existenz* in Early Christianity." *Review of Metaphysics* 10 (1957) 428–40.

———. "Reflections on Trinitarian Language." *Pro Ecclesia* 4 (1995) 261–64.

———. "The Reformation Heritage and Christian Unity." In *The Church in a Postliberal Age*, edited by James J. Buckley, 53–76. London: SCM, 2002.

———. "Reminiscences of Vatican II." In *The Church in a Postliberal Age*, edited by James J. Buckley, 10–18. London: SCM, 2002.

———. "Response to Bruce Marshall." *Thomist* 53 (1989) 403–6.

———. "Response to Michael Wyschogrod's 'Letter to a Friend.'" *Modern Theology* 11 (1995) 205–10.

———. Review of *The Gospel in a Pluralist Society*, by Leslie Newbigin. *International Bulletin of Missionary Research* 14 (1990) 182–83.

———. Review of *The Myth of God Incarnate*, by John Hick. *Journal of Religion* 59 (1979) 248–50.

———. "The Search for Habitable Texts." *Daedalus* 117 (1988) 153–56.

———. "Scripture, Consensus and Community." In *The Church in a Postliberal Age*, edited by James J. Buckley, 201–22. London: SCM, 2002.

———. "Unbelievers and the 'Sola Christi.'" In *The Church in a Postliberal Age*, edited by James J. Buckley, 77–87. London: SCM, 2002.

———. "The Unity We Seek: Setting the Agenda for Ecumenism." *Christian Century* 122 (2005) 28–31.

Lints, Richard. "The Postpositivist Choice: Tracy or Lindbeck?" *Journal of the American Academy of Religion* 61 (1993) 655–77.

Locke, John. *An Essay Concerning Human Understanding*. London: Fontana, 1968.

Lott, Micah. "Reasonably Traditional: Self-Contradiction and Self-Reference in Alasdair MacIntyre's Account of Tradition-Based Rationality." *Journal of Religious Ethics* 30 (2002) 315–39.

Lutz, Christopher Stephen. *Tradition in the Ethics of Alasdair MacIntyre: Relativism, Thomism and Philosophy*. Lanham, MD: Lexington, 2009.

McCall, Tom. "Ronald Thiemann, Thomas Torrance, and Epistemological Doctrines of Revelation." *International Journal of Systematic Theology* 6 (2004) 148–68.

McGrath, Alister. *The Genesis of Doctrine: A Study in the Foundation of Doctrinal Criticism*. Oxford: Blackwell, 1990.

MacIntyre, Alasdair C. *After Virtue*. 2nd ed. London: Duckworth, 1985.

———. *After Virtue*. 3rd ed. Notre Dame: University of Notre Dame Press, 2007.

———. *Against the Self-Images of the Age: Essays on Ideology and Philosophy*. London: Duckworth, 1971.

———. "The Antecedents of Action." In *Against the Self-Images of the Age*, 191–210. London: Duckworth, 1971.

———. "Critical Remarks on '*Sources of the Self* by Charles Taylor." *Philosophy and Phenomenological Research* 54 (1994) 187–90.

———. *Dependent Rational Animals: Why Human Beings Need the Virtues*. London: Duckworth, 1999.

———. "Determinism." *Mind* 56 (1957) 28–41.

———. *Difficulties in Christian Belief*. London: SCM, 1959.

———. "Epistemological Crises, Dramatic Narrative and the Philosophy of Science." In *The Tasks of Philosophy*, 3–23. Cambridge: Cambridge University Press, 2006.

———. *Ethics and Politics: Selected Essays, Volume 2*. Cambridge: Cambridge University Press, 2006.

———. *God, Philosophy, Universities: A Selective History of the Catholic Philosophical Tradition*. Lanham, MD: Rowan and Littlefield, 2009.

———. "God and the Theologians" In *Against the Self-Images of the Age*, 12–26. London: Duckworth, 1971.

———. "Imperatives, Reasons for Action, and Morals." In *Against the Self-Images of the Age*, 125–35. London: Duckworth, 1971.

———. "An Interview for *Cogito*." In *The MacIntyre Reader*, edited by Kelvin Knight, 267–75. Cambridge: Polity, 1998.

———. "An Interview with Giovanna Borradori." In *The MacIntyre Reader*, edited by Kelvin Knight, 255–66. Cambridge: Polity, 1998.

———. "The Logical Status of Religious Belief." In *Metaphysical Beliefs*, edited by Alasdair C. MacIntyre, 167–221. London: SCM, 1957

———. *Marcuse*. London: Fontana, 1970.

———. *Marxism and Christianity*. London: Duckworth, 1968 (2nd ed. 1995).

———. *Marxism: An Interpretation*. London: SCM, 1953.

———, ed. *Metaphysical Beliefs*. London: SCM, 1957 (2nd ed. 1970).

———. "Moral Dilemmas." *Philosophy and Phenomenological Research* 50 (1990) (Supplement) 367–82.

———. "Notes from the Moral Wilderness 1 and 2." In *The MacIntyre Reader*, edited by Kelvin Knight, 32–49. Cambridge: Polity, 1998.

———. "A Partial Response to My Critics." In *After MacIntyre*, edited by John Horton and Susan Mendus, 283–304. Cambridge: Polity, 1994.

———. "Pascal and Marx: On Lucien Goldmann's Hidden God." In *Against the Self-Images of the Age*, 76–87. London: Duckworth, 1971.

———. "Philosophy: Past Conflict and Future Direction." *Proceedings and Addresses of the American Philosophical Association* 61 (1987) 81–87.

———. "Précis of *Whose Justice? Which Rationality?*" *Philosophy and Phenomenological Research* 50 (1991) 149–52.

———. "'The Privatization of Good: An Inaugural Lecture' with Comments by Donald P. Kommers and W. David Solomon and a Rejoinder to his Critics." *The Review of Politics* 52 (1990) 344–77.

———. Prologue to *After Virtue* (3rd ed.), ix–xvi. Notre Dame: University of Notre Dame Press, 2007.

———. "Psychoanalysis: The Future of an Illusion?" In *Against the Self-Images of the Age*, 27–37. London: Duckworth, 1971.

———. "Purpose and Intelligent Action." *Proceedings of the Aristotelian Society* Supplementary Volume 34 (1960) 79–96.

———. "Rejoinder to My Critics, Especially Solomon." *The Review of Politics* 52 (1990) 375–77.

———. "Relativism, Power and Philosophy." *Proceedings and Addresses of the American Philosophical Association* 59 (1985) 5–22.

———. "Reply to Dahl, Baier and Schneewind." *Philosophy and Phenomenological Research* 50 (1991) 169–78.

———. "Reply to Roque." *Philosophy and Phenomenological Research* 51 (1991) 619–20.

———. *Secularization and Moral Change*. London: Oxford University Press, 1967.

———. *A Short History of Ethics*. London: Routledge and Kegan Paul, 1967.

———. "Social Structures and Their Threats to Moral Agency." *Philosophy* 74 (1999) 311–29.

———. *The Tasks of Philosophy: Selected Essays, Volume 1*. Cambridge: Cambridge University Press, 2006.

———. *Three Rival Versions of Moral Enquiry*. London: Duckworth, 1990.

———. *The Unconscious: A Conceptual Analysis*. London: Routledge & Kegan Paul, 1958.

———. "Visions." In *New Essays in Philosophical Theology*, edited by Antony Flew and Alasdair Macintyre, 254–60.

———. "What Morality Is Not." *Philosophy* 32 (1957) 325–35.

———. *Whose Justice? Which Rationality?* London: Duckworth, 1988.

———. "Why Is the Search for the Foundations of Ethics So Frustrating?" *Hastings Center Report* 9 (1979) 16–22.

MacIntyre, Alasdair C., and Paul Ricoeur. *The Religious Significance of Atheism*. New York: Columbia University Press, 1969.

McMylor, Peter. *Alasdair MacIntyre: Critic of Modernity*. London: Routledge, 1993.

———. "Marxism and Christianity: Dependencies and Differences in Alasdair MacIntyre's Critical Social Thought." *Theoria* 55 (2008) 45–66.

Madigan, Patrick. Review of *Aristotelian Philosophy: Ethics and Politics from Aristotle to Macintyre*, by Kelvin Knight. *Heythrop Journal* 48 (2007) 1026–27

Marcuse, Herbert. "Repressive Tolerance." No pages. Online: http://www.marcuse.org/herbert/pubs/60spubs/65repressivetolerance.htm.

Marshall, Bruce D. "Aquinas as Postliberal Theologian." *Thomist* 53 (1989) 353–402.

———. Introduction to *The Nature of Doctrine* (25th anniv. ed.), vii–xxvii. Louisville: Westminster John Knox, 2009.

———. *Trinity and Truth*. New York: Cambridge University Press, 1999.

———. "'We Shall Bear the Image of the Man of Heaven': Theology and the Concept of Truth." *Modern Theology* 11 (1995) 93–117.

Milbank, John. *Theology and Social Theory*. Oxford: Blackwell, 1990.

Mill, John Stuart. "Utility of Religion" No pages. Online: http://oll.libertyfund.org/?option=com_staticxt&staticfile=show.php%3Ftitle=241&chapter=21522&layout=html&Itemid=27.

Mitchell, Mark T. "Michael Polanyi, Alasdair MacIntyre and the Role of Tradition." *Humanitas* 19 (2006) 97–125.

Moore, Geoff. "Churches as Organisations: Towards a Virtue Ecclesiology for Today." *International Journal for the Study of the Christian Church* 11 (2011) 45–65.

Mulhall, Stephen. "Theology and Narrative: The Self, the Novel the Bible." *International Journal for the Philosophy of Religion* 69 (2011) 29–43.

Murphy, Mark C. *Natural Law and Practical Rationality*. Cambridge: Cambridge University Press, 2001.

Murphy Mark C., ed. *Alasdair MacIntyre*. Cambridge: Cambridge University Press, 2001.

Murphy, Nancey. "Anglo-American Postmodernity: A Response to Clayton and Robbins." *Zygon* 33 (1998) 475–80.

———. "Is Altruism Good? Evolution, Ethics and the Hunger for Theology." *Zygon* 41 (2006) 985–94.

Murphy, Nancey, and James Wm. McClendon, Jr. "Distinguishing Modern and Postmodern Theologies." *Modern Theology* 5 (1989) 191–214.

Nathanson, Stephen. "In Defense of 'Moderate Patriotism.'" *Ethics* 99 (1989) 535–52.

Newman, John Henry. *The Arians of the Fourth Century*. Online: http://www.newmanreader.org/works/arians/index.html.

———. *An Essay in Aid of a Grammar of Assent*. 1870. Reprint, Notre Dame: University of Notre Dame Press, 1979.

———. *An Essay on the Development of Christian Doctrine*. Edited by J. M. Cameron. Harmondsworth: Penguin, 1974.

———. *The Idea of a University*. New York: Image, 1959.

———. "On Consulting the Faithful in Matters of Doctrine." No pages. Online: http://www.newmanreader.org/works/rambler/consulting.html.

———. "The Theory of Developments in Religious Doctrine." No pages. Online: http://www.newmanreader.org/works/oxford/sermon15.html.

Nicholson, Hugh. "Comparative Theology after Liberalism." *Modern Theology* 23 (2007) 229–51.

———. "The Political Nature of Doctrine: A Critique of Lindbeck in Light of Recent Scholarship." *Heythrop Journal* 48 (2007) 857–76.

Nicholson, Michael W. "Abusing Wittgenstein: The Misuse of the Concept of Language Games in Contemporary Theology." *Journal of the Evangelical Theological Society* 39 (1996) 617–29.

Nietzsche, Friedrich. *The Gay Science*. No pages. Online: http://www.lexido.com/EBOOK_TEXTS/THE_GAY_SCIENCE_FOURTH_BOOK_.aspx?S=335.

———. *Thus Spoke Zarathustra*. Translated by R. J. Hollingsworth. Harmondsworth: Penguin, 2003.

Nobis, Nathan. "Truth in Ethics and Epistemology: A Defense of Normative Realism." PhD diss., University of Rochester, 2004. Online: https://www.morehouse.edu/facstaff/nnobis/papers/dissertation/nathan-nobis-dissertation.pdf.

O'Neill, Colman E. "The Rule Theory of Doctrine and Propositional Truth." *Thomist* 49 (1985) 417–42.
Ormerod, Neil. "Faith and Reason: Perspectives from MacIntyre and Lonergan." *Heythrop Journal* 46 (2005) 11–22.
———. "Vatican II—Continuity or Discontinuity? Toward an Ontology of Meaning." *Theological Studies* 71 (2010) 609–36.
Outka, Gene. "Equality and the Fate of Theism in Modern Culture." *Journal of Religion* 67 (1987) 275–88.
Pak, Kenneth. "Affirming Rationality of Religious Traditions, Approximating the Ultimate Reality and Advancing Goodwill: a Proposal for Religious Dialogue." *International Journal of Religion and Spirituality in Society* 1 (2011) 25–31.
Pakaluk, Michael. "A Defence of Scottish Common-Sense." *Philosophical Quarterly* 52 (2002) 564–81.
Pecknold, Chad C. *Transforming Postliberal Theology: George Lindbeck, Pragmatism and Scripture*. London: T. & T. Clark, 2005.
Penelhum, Terence. "The Religious Ambiguity of the World." Online: http://www.ucalgary.ca/rels/files/rels/Penelhum.pdf.
———. "Reflections on Reformed Epistemology." No pages. Online: http://www.ucalgary.ca/~nurelweb/papers/other/penel.html.
Perry, John. "The Weight of Community: Alasdair MacIntyre, Abraham Kuyper, and the Problem of Public Theology in a Liberal Society." *Calvin Theological Journal* 39 (2004) 303–31.
Placher, William C. *Unapologetic Theology: A Christian Voice in a Pluralistic Conversation*. Louisville: Westminster John Knox, 1989.
Plantinga, Alvin. *God and Other Minds*. Ithaca: Cornell University Press, 1967.
———. "On 'Proper Basicality.'" *Philosophy and Phenomenological Research* 75 (2007) 612–21.
———. "Reason and Belief in God." In *Faith and Rationality: Reason and Belief in God*, edited by Alvin Plantinga and Nicholas Wolterstorff, 16–93. Notre Dame: University of Notre Dame Press, 1983.
———. *Warrant: The Current Debate*. New York: Oxford University Press, 1993.
———. *Warrant and Proper Function*. New York: Oxford University Press, 1993.
———. *Warranted Christian Belief*. New York: Oxford University Press, 2000.
Plantinga, Alvin, and Nicholas Wolterstorff, eds. *Faith and Rationality: Reason and Belief in God*. Notre Dame: University of Notre Dame Press, 1983.
Plato. *Phaedo*. In *The Problem of Universals*, edited by Andrew B. Schoedinger, 1–15. Atlantic Highlands, NJ: Humanities, 1992.
———. *Protagoras and Meno*. Translated by W. C. Guthrie. Harmondsworth: Penguin, 1970.
———. *The Republic*. Translated by F. M. Cornford. Oxford: Clarendon, 1966.
Pope John Paul II. *Fides et Ratio*. 14 September 1998. Online: http://www.vatican.va/holy_father/john_paul_ii/encyclicals/documents/hf_jp-ii_enc_15101998_fides-et-ratio_en.html.
Porter, Jean. "Openness and Constraint: Moral Reflection as Tradition-Guided Inquiry in Alasdair MacIntyre's Recent Works." *Journal of Religion* 73 (1993) 514–36.
———. "Tradition in the Recent Works of Alasdair MacIntyre." In *Alasdair MacIntyre*, edited by Mark C. Murphy, 38–67. Cambridge: Cambridge University Press, 2001.

Potter, Jonathan, and Margaret Wetherell. *Discourse and Social Psychology*. London: Sage, 1987.

Rahner, Karl. *Hearer of the Word*. Translated by J. Donceel. New York: Continuum, 1994.

———. *Spirit in the World*. Translated by W. Dych. New York: Continuum, 1994.

Railton, P. "Normative Force and Normative Freedom." In *Normativity*, edited by Jonathan Dancy, 1–33. Oxford: Blackwell, 2000.

Raz, Joseph. "Explaining Normativity: Rationality and the Justification of Reason." In *Normativity*, edited by Jonathan Dancy, 34–59. Oxford: Blackwell, 2000.

Rigby, Paul, et al. "The Nature of Doctrine and Scientific Progress." *Theological Studies* 52 (1991) 669–88.

Robinson, John. *Honest to God*. London: SCM, 1963.

Rogers, Eugene F., Jr. "How the Virtues of an Interpreter Presuppose and Perfect Hermeneutics: The Case of Thomas Aquinas." *Journal of Religion* 76 (1996) 64–81.

Roque, A. J. "Language Competence and Tradition-Constituted Rationality." *Philosophy and Phenomenological Research* 51 (1991) 611–17.

Rorty, Richard. *Philosophy and the Mirror of Nature*. Princeton: Princeton University Press, 1981.

Ryle, Gilbert. *The Concept of Mind*. Harmondsworth: Penguin, 1973.

———. "The Thinking of Thoughts: What Is 'Le Penseur' Doing?" No pages. Online: http://lucy.ukc.ac.uk/CSACSIA/Vol14/Papers/ryle_1.html.

Savulescu, Julian, and Richard W. Momeyer. "Should Informed Consent Be Based on Rational Beliefs?" *Journal of Medical Ethics* 23 (1997) 282–88.

Schneewind, J. B. "MacIntyre and the Indispensability of Tradition." *Philosophy and Phenomenological Research* 50 (1991) 165–68.

Schoedinger, Andrew B., ed. *The Problem of Universals*. Atlantic Highlands, NJ: Humanities, 1992.

Schueler, G. F. *Reasons and Purposes: Human Rationality and the Teleological Explanation of Action*. Oxford: Clarendon, 2003.

Scruton, Roger. *Kant: A Very Short Introduction*. Oxford: Oxford University Press, 2001.

Searle, John. *The Construction of Social Reality*. London: Allen Lane, 1995.

———. *Mind, Language and Society*. London: Weidenfield and Nicholson, 1999.

———. *Speech Acts*. Cambridge: Cambridge University Press, 1970.

Sherlock, Richard: "Must Ethics Be Theological? A Critique of the New Pragmatists." *Journal of Religious Ethics* 37 (2009) 631–49.

Singer, Peter. *Hegel: A Very Short Introduction*. Oxford: Oxford University Press, 2001.

Smith, Dean. "Are Liberals and Evangelicals Singing from the Same Song Sheet?" *Heythrop Journal* 51 (2010) 831–46.

Sockness, Brent W. "The Forgotten Moralist: Friedrich Schleiermacher and the Science of Spirit." *Harvard Theological Review* 96 (2003) 317–48.

Solomon, W. David. "Comment on MacIntyre." *Review of Politics* 52 (1990) 369–74.

Sommerville, C. J. "Is Religion a Language Game? A Real World Critique of the Cultural-Linguistic Theory." *Theology Today* 51 (1995) 594–99.

Soskice, Janet Martin. *Metaphor and Religious Language*. Oxford: Oxford University Press, 1985.

Stell, Stephen L. "Hermeneutics in Theology and the Theology of Hermeneutics: Beyond Lindbeck and Tracy." *Journal of the American Academy of Religion* 81 (1993) 679–702.

Stackhouse, Max L. "Alasdair MacIntyre: An Overview and Evaluation." *Religious Studies Review* 18 (1992) 203–8.
Strawson, Peter F. "Truth." In *Logico-Linguistic Papers*, 190–213. London: Methuen, 1971.
Swinburne, Richard. *Faith and Reason*. Oxford: Clarendon, 1981.
Stout, Jeffrey. "Commitments and Traditions in the Study of Religious Ethics." *Journal of Religious Ethics* 25, 25th Anniversary Supplement (1998) 23–56.
———. *Ethics after Babel*. Cambridge: James Clarke, 1988.
Tanner, Kathryn. *Theories of Culture: A New Agenda for Theology*. Minneapolis: Fortress, 1997.
Taylor, Charles. "Overcoming Epistemology." No pages. Online: http://www.marxists.org/reference/subject/philosophy/works/us/taylor.htm.
———. *Sources of the Self: The Making of the Modern Identity*. Cambridge: Cambridge University Press, 1989.
Thomas, Alan. "Alasdair MacIntyre." In *Routledge Encyclopedia of Philosophy*, edited by E. Craig. No pages. Online: http://www.rep.routledge.com/article/R045.
Thomas, Owen C. "Interiority and Christian Spirituality." *Journal of Religion* 80 (2000) 41–60.
Tilley, Terrence W. "Incommensurability, Intratextuality, and Fideism." *Modern Theology* 5 (1989) 87–111.
Trigg, Roger. *Rationality and Religious Belief*. Oxford: Blackwell, 1998.
Vanhoozer, Kevin, ed. *The Cambridge Companion to Postmodern Theology*. Cambridge: Cambridge University Press, 2003.
———. "Scripture and Tradition." In *The Cambridge Companion to Postmodern Theology*, edited by Kevin Vanhoozer, 149–69. Cambridge: Cambridge University Press, 2003.
Vatican. "Decree on Ecumenism *Unitatis Redintegratio*." No pages. Online: http://www.vatican.va/archive/hist_councils/ii_vatican_council/documents/vat-ii_decree_19641121_unitatis-redintegratio_en.html.
Vidu, Adonis. "Lindbeck's Scheme-Content Distinction: A Critique of the Dualism between Orders of Language." No pages. Online: http://www.jsri.ro/old/html%20version/index/no_9/adonisvidu-articol.htm.
———. *Postliberal Theological Method: A Critical Study*. Milton Keynes: Paternoster, 2005.
Volf, Miroslav. "Theology, Meaning and Power." In *The Future of Theology: Essays in Honor of Jürgen Moltmann*, edited by Miroslav Volf et al., 98–113. Grand Rapids: Eerdmans, 1996.
Volf, Miroslav, et al., eds. *The Future of Theology: Essays in Honor of Jürgen Moltmann*. Grand Rapids: Eerdmans, 1996.
Wachbroit, Robert. "A Genealogy of Virtues." *Yale Law Journal* 92 (1983) 564–76.
———. "Relativism and Virtue." *Yale Law Journal* 94 (1985) 1559–65.
Wallace, R. Jay. *Normativity and the Will: Selected Papers on Moral Psychology and Practical Reason*. Oxford: Oxford University Press, 2006.
———. "Practical Reason." In *The Stanford Encyclopedia of Philosophy*, edited by Edward N. Zalta. Winter 2003 ed. No pages. Online: http://plato.stanford.edu/archives/win2003/entries/practical-reason/.
Wang, Xinli. "On Davidson's Refutation of Conceptual Schemes and Conceptual Relativism." *Pacific Philosophical Quarterly* 90 (2009) 140–64.

Warnke, Georgia. "Communicative Rationality and Cultural Values." In *The Cambridge Companion to Habermas*, edited by S. K. White, 120–42. Cambridge: Cambridge University Press, 1995.

Weaver, Alain Epp. "After Politics: John Howard Yoder, Body Politics, and the Witnessing Church." *Review of Politics* 61 (1999) 637–73.

Webster, John. "The Human Person." In *The Cambridge Companion to Postmodern Theology*, edited by Kevin Vanhoozer, 219–34. Cambridge: Cambridge University Press, 2003.

Webster, John, and George P. Schner, eds. *Theology after Liberalism*. Oxford: Blackwell, 2000.

Weddle, David L. "New Generation of Jehovah's Witnesses." *Nova Religio: Journal of Alternative and Emergent Religions* 3 (2000) 350–67.

Weigel, George. "Re-viewing Vatican II." [Interview with George Lindbeck] *First Things*, December 1994. No pages. Online: http://www.firstthings.com/article/2007/01/re-viewing-vatican-iian-interview-with-george-a-lindbeck-2.

Werpehowski, William. "Ad Hoc Apologetics." *Journal of Religion* 66 (1986) 282–301.

Westphal, M. "Hegel." In *The Blackwell Companion to Modern Theology*, edited by Gareth Jones, 293–306. Oxford: Blackwell, 2004.

White, S. K., ed. *The Cambridge Companion to Habermas*. Cambridge: Cambridge University Press, 1995.

Williams, John R. Review of *Tradition, Rationality and Virtue: The Thought of Alasdair MacIntyre*, by Thomas D'Andrea. *Heythrop Journal* 49 (2008) 513–15.

Williams, Rowan. "Postmodern Theology and the Judgement of the World." In *Theology after Liberalism*, edited by John Webster and George P. Schner, 321–34. Blackwell: Oxford, 2000.

Wilson, Phil. "Jehovah's Witness Children: When Religion and the Law Collide." *Journal of Paediatric Nursing* 17 (2005) 34–37.

Wittgenstein, Ludwig. *On Certainty*. Edited by G. E. M. Anscombe and G. H. von Wright. Translated by Denis Paul and G. E. M. Anscombe. Oxford: Blackwell, 1969.

———. *Philosophical Investigation*. Translated by G. E. M. Anscombe. Oxford: Blackwell, 1968.

———. *Tractatus Logico-Philosophicus*. Translated by D. F. Pears and B. F. McGuinness. Oxford: Blackwell, 1961.

Wohler Robert. "Projecting the Enlightenment." In *After MacIntyre: Critical Perspectives on the Work of Alasdair MacIntyre*, edited by John Horton and Susan Mendus, 108–26. Cambridge: Polity, 1994.

Wolterstorff, Nicholas. "Can Belief in God Be Rational?" In *Faith and Rationality: Reason and Belief in God*, edited by Alvin Plantinga and NicholasWolterstorff, 135–85. Notre Dame: University of Notre Dame Press, 1983.

Wright, John, ed. *Postliberal Theology and the Church Catholic: Conversations with George Lindbeck, David Burrell and Stanley Hauerwas*. Grand Rapids: Baker Academic, 2012.

Young, Frances. *The Making of the Creeds*. London: SCM, 2002.

Ziegler, P. "Review of DeHart, Pecknold, Vidu." *European Journal of Theology* 17 (2008) 39–45.

Zoll, Patrick. "How to Proceed Philosophically? A Critique of Alasdair MacIntyre's Narrative-Historicist Conception of Progress." *Heythrop Journal* 52 (2011) 104–12.

Zorn, Hans. "Grammar, Doctrines and Practice." *Journal of Religion* 75 (1995) 509–20.

INDEX

Action: voluntary and involuntary, 1, 6, 7, 38, 63, 73–76, 81–82, 94–96, 100–103, 178, 180n25
After Virtue (AV), 4, 60–66, 69–92, 106, 186n39
Analytic philosophy, 60, 66
Anthropological perspective, 134, 155, 160, 163–64, 173, 179–80, 198, 222
Allen, A., 126, 127–29, 181, 185
Annas, Julia, 182
Anscombe, G. E. M. (Elizabeth), 62–63, 72, 76
Aquinas, Thomas, 124, 173, 182, 204–5, 243
Aristotle, 38, 53, 54, 63, 68, 75, 76, 80, 90, 98, 124, 178, 196
  account of the good, 83, 110
  account of human nature, 57, 59, 61–63, 73
  Aristotelianism, 5, 21–22, 36, 38, 62, 69–72, 103, 104, 122, 123–24, 176, 182, 196–97
  ethics, 11, 21, 36, 75, 76, 86, 87–88, 89, 106, 233
  metaphysical biology, 80, 89, 91–93, 104–5
Athanasian Creed, 221
Augustine, 182, 210

Bernstein, Richard, 235, 240

Categorial adequacy. *See* truth
Charity, principle of, (Davidson), 131–32

Christ. *See* Jesus Christ
Christianity, 1, 5, 7, 8–9, 29, 31–35, 45–48, 50, 57–58, 60, 69–71, 108, 129, 136, 140–46, 147, 152, 153, 156–60, 162, 165–66, 168, 172–73, 177, 182, 187, 189–90, 197, 198, 202–7, 208–17, 224, 227, 232, 234, 239–40
  Christic identity, 203, 206
  relationship to Marxism, 11–24, 48–50
Church, 8, 12, 14–16, 19, 57, 140–42, 144–45, 148, 155, 158, 172, 187, 190, 211–14, 217, 220, 231
Clark, Thomas, 125n222, 137
Class struggle, 20, 39
Community, 10–14, 40–41, 43–44, 57, 76–81, 83–89, 93–96, 98, 100–103, 108–12, 114, 117, 123, 125, 143–47, 149–56, 160, 162–66, 168, 172, 174–80, 186–88, 190–96, 202–3, 206–7, 211, 212–13, 216–19, 221, 224, 226, 227, 236, 241, 246
Communism, 8–9, 14–15, 35
Comprehensive metaphysical system, xi, 1–4, 6, 9, 10, 18–24, 59, 60, 138, 172, 173, 178, 233, 234, 237, 242–43, 130
Conceptual innovation, 116, 118, 124, 133–34, 149–52, 160, 220, 230–32
Conceptual schemes, 11, 16, 33, 42, 76, 84, 89, 105, 114–15, 119, 129–32, 175, 194, 226, 234, 235

Cognitive-propositional (CP) interpretations of religion, 146–48, 149, 151, 159, 168, 173, 199–200, 231–32, 244

Crisis of moral debate, 60, 62–65, 88, 123

Crisis of rational justification, 66–68, 88, 123

Criteriological problem in theology, 142–45, 168, 214

Culture and cultural change, 2, 6, 8, 10, 12, 15, 21, 41–51, 54–58, 60–65, 67, 75, 83, 90–93, 103–6, 115, 123–24, 125, 127, 134, 149, 151, 156, 161–66, 172, 174–75, 179, 198, 208, 210–12, 217, 222, 235, 246

Cultural-linguistic (CL) model of religion, 26n96, 139, 148–53, 160–68, 174–75, 198–205, 207–11, 231–32, 244,

Dahl, Norman, 135
Davidson, Donald, 131–34
DeHart, Paul J., 209–10, 214–15
Dependent Rational Animals (DRA), 3, 61, 87, 89–105, 233
Descartes, René, 23, 66, 115n189, 119, 219
Determinism, 7, 40–41, 163
Difficulties in Christian Belief (DCB), 25, 31–35, 177–78
Doctrine, 3, 10n33, 19–20, 26 n.98, 28, 30, 36, 44, 48–50, 109–10, 129, 138–39, 154 n.63, 206, 207, 239–40
   doctrine and Christian unity, 142–44, 231–32
   doctrine and epistemological crisis, 194–97, 231–32, 244
   doctrine and the identity of a religious community 189–93
   doctrines and the identity of a tradition, 181–89, 198, 233
   doctrines and the rationality of a tradition, 216–18, 219–23, 227
   Lindbeck's rule theory of doctrine, 145–61, 164, 166, 169–70, 171, 181, 206. *See also* cultural-linguistic (CL) model of religion, Lindbeck, *The Nature of Doctrine*
Doyle, Dennis, 172,

Early, Christian, 135
Ecumenism, 140–42, 145–48, 156, 160, 169, 231–32
Emotive theory of ethics, 52–53, 65
Empiricism, 66, 73
Encyclopedia, 66–68
Enlightenment, 148, 170, 173, 223, 234–35, 245
Epistemological crisis (EC), 3, 66, 114–18, 121, 128, 138, 149, 152, 160, 169, 176, 181, 188, 194–97, 228, 230–31, 233, 237, 243–44
   MacIntyre's personal epistemological crisis, 5, 23, 61, 119, 193
Epistemological foundationalism, 2, 33n130, 61n5, 144n20, 215–16
Epistemological openness, principle of, 119–20, 129–30, 138–39, 180–81, 192, 197, 228, 237–38, 242
Eschatology, 15–16, 141, 175, 193, 226, 226, 239, 242
Ethics. *See* moral theory
Experiential-expressive (EE) interpretations of religion, 26, 146–53, 168, 199–200, 207, 231–32, 244
Extratextual interpretation of religion, 168, 223

Falsificationism, 20–21, 29, 45–46, 58, 68, 108, 119–20, 122, 167, 178, 192–93, 225, 229
Fergusson, David, 175
Fideism, 5, 35, 46–47, 58–59, 68, 119, 135, 138–39, 169–70, 205, 215, 240–241
First principles, 32–33, 56, 66, 107, 110, 225
Flourishing, human, 61, 63, 69, 72, 92, 95–98, 100, 102–3
   care, dependency and human flourishing, 93, 96–99, 103–4
Flew, Antony, 24

Index

Foundationalism. *See* epistemological foundationalism
Fuller, Michael B., 135

Gadamer, Hans-Georg, 107n164, 212n128
Geertz, Clifford, 180
Gifford, Adam, Lord, 66–67
Gifford Lectures. *See Three Rival Versions of Moral Enquiry*
Good, human, *see* telos

Harrison, Victoria, 172
Healy, Nicholas, 172
Hegel, Georg, 13
Hermeneutic framework, 1–2, 165, 171–72, 176–81, 189–90, 206–7, 211, 213–14, 226
Hick, John, 143–44
Homer, 53, 77, 241
Human behaviour, explanation of, *see* action
Human happiness and morality, 34–35, 38, 43, 69
Human nature, 7, 10–11, 49–51, 54, 163, 242
   Aristotelian concept of, 57–63, 68–70, 76, 80
   in *Dependent Rational Animals*, 90–100, 102–5
   and Marxism, 13–16, 36–41
   and religious belief, 34–35, 41–44

Incommensurability, 3–4, 63, 64, 112–13, 125–27, 129, 130–34, 167, 171, 179–80
"Infallibility," 142–43,
Interview for *Cogito*, 6, 60
Interview with Giovanna Borradori (GB), 8
Interpretative medium (IM), 10, 18, 144, 148, 151, 161, 162, 166–67, 170, 174, 176, 178, 180, 197, 198, 207, 229, 231. *See also* cultural-linguistic model of religion, hermeneutic framework
Intratextuality, 168–69, 207–16, 233
Intuitionism, 53, 86

Jehovah's Witnesses (JW), 189–93, 197
Jesus Christ, 14, 20, 33–34, 143, 177, 189–91, 202, 204, 212–13, 217, 220–21, 226
Justice, 55, 63, 79, 85, 98–99, 242
Justification of belief, 2–6, 8–11
   and comprehensive metaphysical systems, 17–24, 172, 174–75, 178–81
   and the crisis of rational justification, 66–68
   and the cultural-linguistic model of religion, 167 –70, 198, 203–7 213–16, 239–42
   of moral judgements, 35–51, 54–59, 60–62, 64–65, 69–72, 88–90, 100–106
   and religious belief, 24–35
   and tradition 105–23, 125–30, 134–38, 188–93, 194–97, 216–32, 233–38, 242–47. *See also* epistemological crisis, rationality, relativism, superiority and truth

Kant, Immanuel, 8, 26, 34, 44, 66, 67, 133, 148, 150
Kierkegaard, Soren, 31, 67,
Knight, Kelvin, 5
Kuhn, Thomas, 67, 117–18, 193, 244

Lewis, David, 66
Liberalism, 6, 8, 9, 12–13, 21, 26, 37–38, 40, 44, 47, 57, 59, 83, 87, 106, 126, 136, 246
Lindbeck, George A., 2–4, 26, 29–30, 57, 126, 129, 138–39
   "Afterword" to *The Nature of Doctrine*, 2nd Edition, 138, 165, 227–31
   biographical sketch, 140–42
   the criteriological problem in religion 142–45
   doctrine, superiority and the rationality of a tradition, 216–32
   on inter-religious superiority, 180–81, 198–207
   on intra-religious superiority and intratextuality, 207–16

Lindbeck, George A. *(cont.)*
  Lindbeck's criticism of contemporary models of religion, 146–48
  The Nature of Doctrine (ND), 145–65
  permanence of belief, 157–61
  relationship between Lindbeck and MacIntyre's thought, 165–76
  and relativism, 238–42. *See also* cultural-linguistic model of religion; doctrine; epistemological crisis; hermeneutic frameworks, superiority.
"The logical status of religious belief." (LS), 18, 24, 26–31, 35, 68
Lutz, Christopher, 5, 91–92,

MacIntyre, Alasdair
  criticisms of MacIntyre's position, 124–26
  early philosophical development 6–9, 59
  personal epistemological crisis, 5, 23, 60–61, 119, 193
  relationship to the enlightenment, 126–35
  relevance of MacIntyre's philosophy to belief, 242–47. *See also passim.*
McMylor, Peter, 5, 12, 19,
Marshall, Bruce, 203–6
Marxism, 1–2, 6–9, 10–22, 35–38, 48–50, 57, 234
Marxism and Christianity (MC), 22–24, 48–50
Marxism: An Interpretation (MI), 10–22, 66
Materialism, 15, 20
Metaphysics, 18–21, 24, 36, 58, 76, 92, 153, 159, 196, 225, 238–39. *See also* comprehensive metaphysical system.
Metaphor, 18
  and Lindbeck's account of religion, 161–63, 207, 210
Milbank, John, 136–37, 175
Momeyer, Richard, 190–91
Moore, G.E., 52
moral theory, 7, 8, 10–13, 24, 29, 49–59
  60–62, 66, 71, 112, 123–24, 133–35
  Aristotelian moral theory, 21–22, 69–72
  76–77: and community, 83–84
  and the crisis of moral debate, 62–65
  in *Dependent Rational Animals*, 3, 61, 87, 89–105, 233
  and individualism, 51, 86–87
  and Marxism, 35–34
  and participation in a tradition, 84–85
  and practices, 76–81
  and relativism, 2, 61, 65, 88–92, 103–5
  and religious belief 33–35, 41–44
  and secularization, 44–48
  and telos, 81–83
  and theory of action, 73–76
  and the virtues in contemporary life, 85–87. *See also* practical reasoning, virtue
Myth, 8, 10, 17–21, 24, 28–29, 57, 116, 218–19, 241

Naturalistic fallacy, 38, 50, 62–63, 70, 73
Nazi Germany, 91, 104–5
Newman, John Henry, 186, 195
Nicaea, 158, 220–21
Nietzsche, Friedrich, 65, 67–68, 71, 86–87, 102
"Notes from the Moral Wilderness 1 and 2." (NMW), 35–41, 66

O'Neill, Colman, 203
Ontological presuppositions, 11, 24, 30, 59, 174, 236
Ormerod, Neil, 135

Paradigm change, 67, 117–18, 193, 229,
Particularistic universalism, 229
Pecknold, Chad C., 237–40, 242
Personal identity, 81–82, 125–26
Perspectivism, 4, 68, 118, 137, 198
Phronesis, 76, 82

Index

Placher, William, 160
Plato, 53–54, 111, 214
Porter, Jean, 185, 222
Postliberal theology, 166, 170, 175, 204, 215, 238–42
   and theological realism, 175. *See also* cultural-linguistic model of religion, doctrine, Lindbeck
Postmodernism, 2, 67, 143
Practical (moral) reasoning, 1, 2, 19, 75–76, 93, 94–100, 102, 103, 176, 178–79, 237, 243
   Aristotelian model, 75–76, 178
   and choice between different goods, 72, 76
   development of practical reasoning, 96–98
   and hermeneutic frameworks, 176, 178–79
   and Jehovah's Witnesses beliefs 190–92
   and justification, 101–4. *See also* moral theory, virtue, telos
Practices, social, 17, 22–23, 30, 54–56, 76–81, 84–85, 185, 186
   goods internal to practices, 22, 77–81, 178
   and moral relativism, 90–92, 103
   and postliberal theology, 145, 147–49, 151, 153–56, 207–8
   and tradition, 84–85, 235
   and tradition-constituted rationality, 217, 220, 221–23, 226–27
   and virtue, 76–81, 84, 87–89. *See also After Virtue*, tradition, tradition-constituted rationality, virtue
Pragmatism, 160, 169, 203, 237–39
Prayer, 17, 178
Prescriptivism, 52–53
Prophecy, 19–20, 230

Quine, Willard Van Orman, 73–75

Rationality
   and animality, 93–96, 103
   Enlightenment notion of, 59, 61, 67–68, 105–6

   and Marxism, 16–21 *See also* justification of belief, superiority, and tradition-constituted rationality.
Reflexivity, 38, 95–96, 206, 224
Relativism 2, 4, 11, 33, 53–59, 68, 88–89, 125–26, 135–39, 181, 234–38, 243
   epistemological relativism, 105–6, 118–23
   and Lindbeck, 169–70, 198–201, 205–6, 215–16, 224, 238–42
   moral relativism, 61, 65, 89–92, 103–5
Religious language, 17, 26–27, 147–49
Theism, 30, 41–44
The Religious Significance of Atheism (RSA), 5, 44–49, 51
Roque, Alicia .J. 126–27, 129
Rorty, Richard, 137
Rule theory of doctrine, *see* doctrine
Ryle, Gilbert, 28, 180,

Sartre, Jean Paul, 53, 59, 87, 106n161
Savulescu, Julian, 190–91
Scripture, 144, 151, 190, 207–10, 214, 217, 239
Secularization, 12–13, 41–48, 57, 165
Secularisation and Moral Change (SMC), 11, 45–49, 51,
Semiotic system, 151, 168, 174, 196, 200–201, 207–13, 215–17, 220–21, 225, 227, 239. *See also* intratextuality
A Short History of Ethics (SHE), 11, 36, 51–57
Smith, Dean, 173
Stalinism, 35–37, 40
Stout, Jeffrey, 133–34, 180, 192
Superiority
   of a comprehensive metaphysical system or tradition, 3–4, 21, 56, 62, 64, 66, 89–90, 105–6, 110, 122, 138, 166–70, 174–75, 180–81, 216–32
   Lindbeck and inter-religious superiority, 198–97
   Lindbeck on intratextuality and intra-religious superiority, 207–16

Tanner, Kathryn, 163–64, 217
Telos, 35, 40–41, 50, 58, 62, 196–97, 223, 226–27
   biologically based account of telos in *Dependent Rational Animals*, 89–102, 233, 238
   MacIntyre's account of telos in *After Virtue*, 69–72, 76–87
Three Rival Versions of Moral Enquiry (TRV), 5, 6, 61, 66–68, 128, 185, 188, 222
Thick description, 180, 192, 195, 208
Tilley, Terrence, 210–11, 214
Tradition of enquiry: evolution of a tradition, 108–16
   identity of a tradition, 116–18, 181–89
   participation in a tradition, 84–85, 222
   traditions and hermeneutic frameworks, 174–80. *See also* doctrine, justification of belief, Lindbeck, moral theory, practices, rationality, superiority, tradition-constituted rationality
Tradition-constituted rationality, 2–4, 31, 88–89, 106–23, 126–30, 135–39, 169–75, 181–82, 188–89, 192–93, 206–7, 215–32, 232–38, 240–42
Truth: as categorial adequacy, 166–68, 200–205, 215–16, 223, 233
   correspondence theory of truth, 137, 202–3, 207, 216, 236–37
   intrasystematic truth, 201–7
   MacIntyre's correspondence theory of falsity, 224–26
   ontological truth, 114, 120–21, 160, 175, 202–6, 216, 224, 239, 241
   performative truth, 168, 201–6, 216, 226. *See also* cognitive-propositional (CP) interpretations of religion, crisis of rational justification, epistemological crisis (EC), justification of belief, ontological presuppositions, rationality, superiority, tradition-constituted rationality, warranted assertability
Two-dimensional interpretations of religion, 146, 151

Vidu, Adonis, 175, 183, 203
Virtues, 12, 55, 57–58, 62
   and community, 83–84
   in contemporary life, 85–87
   and human telos, 94–96
   MacIntyre's definition of a virtue, 79–81
   and moral relativism, 89–92
   and practical reasoning, 96–100
   and practices, 76–82
   virtues of acknowledged dependence, 98–99
   virtue of integrity or constancy, 80
   virtue of just-generosity, 99–105. *See also* moral theory, practices
"Visions," 24–26

Wachbroit, Robert, 89–92
Warranted assertability, 111–14, 119–20, 206, 209, 217, 235
Weddle, David, 192–93
Western culture, 6–7, 11, 12–13, 15, 21, 41, 45, 48, 55, 62, 65, 91, 182, 214, 238, 241
Whose Justice? Which Rationality? (WJWR), 105–15, 118–21, 130–35, 137, 182–85, 218–20, 222–26, 235–38, 242–47
Williams, Rowan, 206, 210–14, 227, 232–33, 240
Wittgenstein, Ludwig, 17, 26, 33, 103, 130, 149–50, 173, 195

www.ingramcontent.com/pod-product-compliance
Lightning Source LLC
Chambersburg PA
CBHW070239230426
43664CB00014B/2355